COMMUNITY COLLEGE REFERENCE SERVICES

A Working Guide for and by Librarians

edited by
BILL KATZ

The Scarecrow Press, Inc.
Metuchen, N.J., & London
1992

The chapter "On-Line Search Services" by Wanda K. Johnson originally appeared as an article, "Online Search Services in the Community College," in *College & Research Libraries News* 50 (May 1989): 375-377 and is reprinted by permission of *College & Research Libraries News*.

The cartoons on pages 333 and 337 are reprinted courtesy of the artist, Eva Irrera.

British Cataloguing-in-Publication data available

Library of Congress Cataloging-in-Publication Data

Community college reference services : a working guide for and by librarians / edited by Bill Katz.
     p. cm.
     Includes bibliographical references.
     ISBN 0-8108-2615-1 (acid-free paper)
     1. Community college libraries—Reference services—United States.   2. Community college libraries—Reference services—Canada.   I. Katz, William A., 1924–
Z675.J8C67   1992
025.5′2777—dc20   92-39703

Copyright © 1992 by Bill Katz

Manufactured in the United States of America

Printed on acid-free paper

CONTENTS

PART IV   PERSONNEL

PART V   BIBLIOGRAPHIC INSTRUCTION

PART VI   COLLECTION DEVELOPMENT

PREFACE

This is a guide, written by working librarians, for the beginner or veteran in reference services. All of the contributions are original to this book. They represent current reference practices. The work seems necessary as there is nothing in print that is a text for librarians in this field. And, for that matter, few relative articles or reports deal specifically with the points discussed.

The particular focus is on the community college. As it may be argued that reference services are the same in every type and size of library, few of the discussions are solely the concern of the community college librarian.

The practical advice will interest and involve reference librarians in almost all situations. And for that reason, the book is planned to be of use to all toiling in the reference field.

Still, there are tangible diverse factors in what Richard Shaw describes as "lean and mean reference services in the small community college." Budgets are not what they might be, and the needs of students are an important shade different from that of some other academic settings.

All reference librarians follow a similar score. At the same time, each is concerned with a particular section of the orchestra, and that's what this guide is all about. The book, as the section, is tuned to the needs of the community college librarians.

Terminology can be a problem, at least for beginners with a memory. The labels "junior college" and "two-year college," as Roark and others explain, have given way to the now more common "community college." The name change is to emphasize the—yes—community nature of the institutions. The term "library," while still used, is replaced by "learning resource center" and "library resource center." A cursory search of ERIC and *Library Literature* indicates the descriptor "junior and community college libraries" is preferred.

The only journal devoted to these libraries reverses the phrase to "Community & Junior College Libraries." Ably edited by Peggy Holeman, the quarterly is published by The Haworth Press and has been reporting on the topic since the late 1970s. The journal is the only substantial one in an important area. A general overview is offered by *Community, Technical and Junior College Journal*. This discusses everything from administration and curriculum to libraries. See also, *Community College Review*. It is surprising how little is found in any issue of the otherwise substantial leader in the field, *College & Research Libraries*. Another publication of The Haworth Press, *The Reference Librarian* offers much of value, as does, of course, ALA's own, *RQ*.

There are about 1,500 community college libraries in the United States and Canada. A careful statistical examination will show many more qualify as community concerns. All, regardless of what they may call themselves, are deeply involved with reference services.

The experts who speak here are familiar with various types of institutions. Equally important are experienced reference hands who understand the challenge from the meaning of a question to the technology of the CD-ROM. Asked to write about their own answers to current problems, they offer practical, time-tested words of wisdom that will be of help to any reader.

To make this guide as useful as possible it is divided into six sections.

The first part is concerned with the history and the mission of the community college and the library or, if one prefers, the learning resource center. The contributors explain basics. The section concludes with a hard-hitting assessment of information needs in the community college.

Specific reference services are discussed next. Perhaps this part is summed up best by Mary Adams Loomba who offers a clear diagram of information literacy and the methods of achieving this major goal. Common problems, from what to do with the clerical staff to what to charge (if anything) for services, wind down the second part.

Enter the computer, and here is a clear account of what

V. Sue Hatfield calls the "electronic library's impact on reference services." Others elaborate.

When one turns to personnel, the professional librarian has the same joys and sorrows of any library. The real problem/question here is the place of the paraprofessional in reference services. This is addressed by the authors. Part-time faculty is another situation that is common to many academic libraries, but Pamela A. Price is among the first to consider just what this means for reference services.

This leads naturally enough to the use of computers in bibliographic instruction, as well as other paths to the goal of making the user independent and happy in the college. There are no more important areas than technology and instruction (which seem wed these days).

Finally, there is the direct and indirect implications of what is involved with collection development. Here the discussion moves from the general overall collection to the difficulties concerned with building the reference collection.

While the six parts seem neat enough, this is only to highlight the obvious. Reference services are a dependent, not an independent, part of the overall college library mission. It may be divided in this book, but in daily activity it is an important whole that defies such divisions. For example, to talk about the mission of the library in the first part and the collection in the last is to deny the interdependence of both for total, satisfactory reference service.

Bill Katz

PART I: THE COMMUNITY COLLEGE REFERENCE MISSION

COMMUNITY COLLEGE SERVICES

Derrie B. Roark

Community colleges come in various styles and sizes. There are small rural colleges where you will be *the* librarian—reference or any other kind. There are large multicollege districts and intermediate-size multicampus colleges. Sometimes librarians are faculty; sometime they are managers. Because of the nature of the comprehensive community college, you may work with or for professionals who do not have degrees in library science. As a newcomer to community college learning resources you will spend some of the most interesting time learning to work within the culture and organization of the institution.

The "junior" college concept began about 90 years ago in Joliet, Illinois. The idea then was to remove the first two years of undergraduate instruction from the university; the university was a place for scholars. In the first two years, students did not know their minds; the university wanted only serious students. Indeed, for many, the junior college was just what was needed. Students were closer to home, family and friends, and tuition was less expensive. In many cases, junior colleges were then considered an extension of the public school structure, handling grades 13 and 14. In many sites, junior colleges were actually found in high school districts (Monroe, 1972, p.12).

After World War II, the junior college concept changed dramatically. In 1947, President Truman established a commission on higher education (known now as the Truman Commission), which democratized education, making education a right rather than a privilege. "Equal educational opportunities for all persons, to the maximum of their individual abilities and without regard to economic status, race, creed, color, sex, national origin, or ancestry, is the major goal of American democracy" (*Higher Education. . . ,* 1947, v. 2, p.7). With that democratization process came the community college concept. This new institution would retain the junior college transfer of the first two years of college to the university; but it would become more than what was envisioned by just a few individuals 45 years ago.

The sixties and early seventies brought fantastic growth as the community college moved quickly away from the expanded postsecondary education system to become a unique and respected member of the higher education system. Community colleges were brought closer and closer to the people and to the communities they served. The leaders separated the community colleges from high school districts and established separate governing bodies to meet local community needs.

For the most part, governance through local control continues today. As an example, in the state of Florida there are 28 locally governed community colleges and more than 60 campuses serving 67 counties and feeding nine state universities and a myriad of private institutions. There is even a formal articulation agreement that guarantees community college graduates a place in of the state's public universities. Other states also have strong community college "systems": California, Illinois, Texas, Arizona, North Carolina, just to mention a few. Some stand alone and some are directly connected with universities—but all strive to serve their local communities.

The Learning Resources Program

The junior college library began as a "library." Out of the community college concept and post-World War II technology grew the concept of "learning resources." Community college faculty, renowned for their teaching abilities and concern for students, began to look to the library to provide audiovisual material for instruction. The intimacy of the community college, and the enthusiasm and excitement of those early years of the 1960s and 1970s, found library and instructional technology not just walking side by side, but actually merging! Before we knew it, audiovisual technology had found its way into libraries. As the two merged, not just figuratively, but physically—together on the shelves, books and AV material—the library became more than just a quiet place to find material for a paper or to study. With information and technology under one roof and considered an integral part of the curriculum, having the faculty look to the learning resources staff for instructional assistance was a natural for the time.

Three major areas—library, AV, and instructional development—merged to become the learning resources program. Today instructional development has not survived the budget cuts in many of our learning resources programs; but new technology has kept our LRCs (learning resources centers) the true centers of the institutions we serve. Technology is changing all libraries, and community colleges are no exceptions. In the recent revised standards (Standards. . . , 1990, pp. 766–767), more than 70 activities were cited as basic or special services that are or may be found within a learning resources program. These activities include telecourse administration and support, computer center, instructional design, radio and television stations, and testing and tutoring.

As a new librarian, the extent of your reference role will be determined in part by the size and structure of the institution, the organizational structure of the learning resources program itself, the status (faculty or nonfaculty) of the librarians, and the college bargaining agreement, if one exists. All these parameters need to be considered prior to answering the first reference question, maybe even before taking the position!

A board of trustees will probably hire you. This board is similar in function to a public library board in that the board of trustees may be comprised of members of the community who are elected or appointed. The members serve as a governing board, not an advisory board. This means that the president or chancellor of the institution must get approval for much of the business conducted by the college. There are state statutes, which are the legal guidelines, and state administrative rules, which interpret the statutes. Then the institution has its own policies and procedures that have to be followed, and they themselves must follow the state rules.

Generally speaking, academic libraries will report to the chief academic or instructional officer of the institution. The libraries/learning resources programs will normally be part of the academic or instructional side of the house—rather than the student, financial, or personnel side. The institution may refer to its learning resources program as a library or a learning resources center.

The head of the community college learning resources program may be referred to as director or dean of libraries or of learning resources. In a multicampus college (i.e., the college has one name, but several sites or campuses—the X, Y, Z campuses of ABC College), all campus libraries/LRCs may be managed by one district learning resources administrator (dean or director). In a multicollege district (i.e., the district has a generic name and each site is a separately named college), each college LRC may stand alone; technical services may or may not be a district operation. In this latter case, there may not be a central learning resources program administrator. (See Figures 1 and 2.)

The Technical Services Connection

One of the best things you can do for yourself as a "career" reference librarian is to find out all you can about the interactions of the different functions within the community college learning resources center. The technical services area should not be foreign land to you; walking through the back room should be as comfortable as walking through your reference collection. When you entertain at your home, you arrange for dinner to be cooked and served, the house to be straightened and cleaned, the bills to be paid, and the receipts to be filed. When the doorbell rings, you want to look your best and have everything ready to impress your guests. The technical services area is a public service area designed to serve you so you can serve the guests of the LRC. The technical services staff are as professional as the public service

EXAMPLES OF LEARNING RESOURCES ORGANIZATION

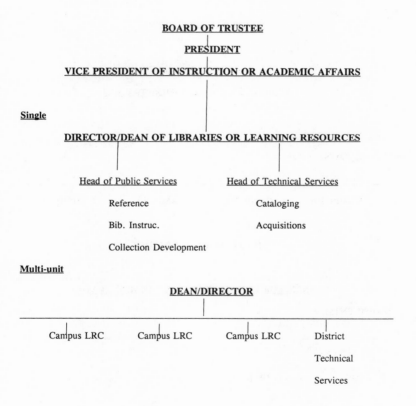

Figure 1. Examples of Learning Resources Organization

EXAMPLES OF MULTI-UNIT COMMUNITY COLLEGE ORGANIZATION

MULTI-CAMPUS COLLEGE

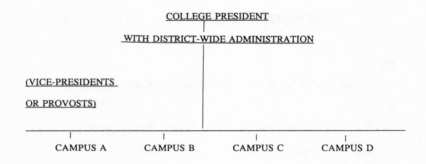

MULTI-COLLEGE DISTRICT

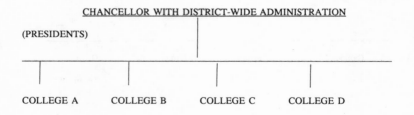

Figure 2. Examples of Multi-Unit Community College Organization

staff; each provides a different but important service. Just as you exist to serve the students and faculty reference needs, the technical services area exists to serve yours. This, however, does not relieve you of your responsibility to work with the technical services staff. Because it is the business end of the learning resources program, there are many rules and guidelines to follow, none of which are intended to make your life miserable. Rules and guidelines are intended only to manage fiscal and human resources, and to expedite the business process for your students and faculty. And as with any service area, the more pleasant you are and the more you know about what services are available, the smoother the operation will run. A reference librarian cannot know too much about the business end of libraries. Of course, the reverse is true of the technical services librarian as well—but that's another chapter in a different book!

Acquisitions librarians and staff are trained to order, receive, and pay for whatever you need. They are your link to getting material in a hurry. The materials budget may be found in the technical services area or in the director's office. To make operations run as smoothly as possible, become a colleague of the acquisitions staff and find out the acquisitions procedures of your LRC. The more technical services can do for you, the more time you will have for assisting faculty and teaching students. While your responsibilities may include selection and collection development, including weeding and working with faculty, the acquisitions area responsibilities include choosing the best vendor for the best price, processing and expediting orders, and following up with vendors, college purchasing, receiving, and accounts payable.

Technical services staff work with people all day. You should find them just as approachable as students and faculty find you. While you are balancing tours, bibliographic instruction classes, reference questions, term papers, and broken reader/printers, acquisitions staff are battling state and college rules, phoning or writing the college purchasing department, settling accounts with accounts receivable and accounts payable staff, negotiating with vendors to make sure the material you have selected is received in a timely manner, and assuring that paperwork is done to keep the vendors happy so they will respond to requests.

Collection development will be considered at the campus, college, or district level depending on the size and organization of your institution. It will also be affected by any cooperative agreements your institution has with other local libraries or regional/state consortia. Selection and collection development should not be taken lightly or given a token unit of your time at the end of the week. Money should be spent early in the fiscal year. Nationally, learning resources programs run the risk of losing money if shortfalls occur. The chance of losing funding at midyear means that the reference librarian/collection developer must stay ahead on selection requests and must work from some kind of formal collection development plan. A regular flow of requests or requests sent well in advance can assist the entire process by giving the acquisitions staff the flexibility to spend money and keep an even workflow. The process cannot be effective or efficient if acquisitions receives avalanches of rush requests at the end of the year. The acquisitions people protect your interests— your students and the collection you have to work with.

Cataloging and processing materials takes another big part of technical services staff time. A good cataloger is worth his/her weight in gold. They are getting scarcer than hen's teeth. If you really want to do yourself and the profession a favor, become a cataloger! Actually, it is a marvelous way to have an in-depth knowledge of the collection. Learn to use the cataloger's knowledge and interest to help make your job easier.

Once the acquisition staff has received material, the cataloging/processing librarian and staff will expedite the material to you. With hope, the material will be run through a bibliographic utility and be on its way. If not, other cataloging copy will have to be located or the material might need original cataloging. Alternatives for quick delivery to your site should be in place, even if the material must be returned later to technical services for completion. Rules and internal procedures should be reviewed so that you understand how questions and concerns need to be communicated. Remember, a cataloger is an expert in his/her specialty, just as you are in yours.

Learning resources organizational structure in a large institution could be elaborate. Review that with your department head or director. Usually, questions and concerns, and especially complaints, should go to your supervisor or to the person in charge of an area, not to technicians or clerks working there. Knowing cross-department protocol will endear you to your colleagues and can actually assist in the smoothness of an operation. If you are the librarian in charge of the public service area, your relationship with your technical services counterpart is important. That relationship could mean the difference between good and bad service in your LRC. The level of service is the reputation of your LRC. And because the LRC is an initial point of introduction to your institution, the reputation of the LRC could affect the reputation of the college. Do not allow personalities and lack of understanding of how the institution or LRC operates to stand in the way of the good service you must provide.

Automation and Instructional Technology

The automation librarian or specialist is another "technical" person you may encounter within your LRC. If you know little about the automation of the LRC you have just joined, the automation specialist is a good place to start. The professional, who may or may not be a librarian, probably acts as system manager for the automated system (OPAC, circulation, and so on) in your LRC. He/she may also have an expertise in personal computers, library applications of software programs, and office automation. If you know computers, work closely with this person. The learning resources program needs many advocates of new technology. If you find yourself knowing more than anyone in the LRC, capitalize on your specialty. You may be the person who can get technology into the LRC by selling its virtues to other staff, your director, and even your vice president or president.

Instructional (or educational) technology is actually a university program of study. In a large community college, instructional technology may be a unit of the learning resources program or it may be a separate area altogether. Instructional technology has been at home in community colleges for more than a generation. If you are fortunate to find yourself in a learning resources program that actively promotes media, there will be a special place for you. Instructional faculty may seek your input on audiovisual material and new formats, such as interactive videodiscs. If this is your specialty or interest, let your director know so you can expand this area as time permits. With or without the official title of "faculty" member, as a librarian you are in fact a professional colleague and will be sought out as such.

References
Higher Education for American Democracy. (1947). "Establishing the Goals: General Education," Washington, D.C.: G.P.O.
Monroe, C. R. (1972). *Profile of the community college*. San Francisco: Jossey-Bass.
"Standards for community, junior and technical college learning resources programs." (1990, September). *College and Research Libraries News*, pp. 757–767.

COMMUNITY COLLEGE LIBRARIANSHIP: A CHANGING FRONTIER

Marilyn Searson Lary

The library of the two-year college, be it called learning resource center, library resource center, or some other designation, is many things to many people and is presently being called upon to serve in an even greater variety of ways. The usual homogeneity that one finds in an educational institution—from the general socioeconomic background of its students and faculty, to the age of its first-year class, to the types of degrees that most students undertake—is no longer the rule in most post-secondary institutions, much less in two-year schools. The general student body and the users of the two-year college library are even more diverse than the general population because the two-year school itself serves such a palette of users, all with varying needs and dramatically different abilities.

The typical two-year college generally serves as diverse a community as one will find, one composed of its own students; students from other institutions; students often enrolled in graduate, off-campus programs sponsored by another institution; students in varying levels of continuing education activities, and those who are basically NOT students but who have informational needs to which the library must respond. This latter group is composed of many different types of people, with widely divergent skills: faculty members who are undertaking both lesson plans and research in their fields; retired individuals who want only best-sellers for recreational reading; immigrants who need to acquire skills in language, social skills and interaction, academic undertakings, and daily routines for survival; staff members who have personal informational needs—a child who needs some easy reading books, a wife who is scheduled for surgery, a businessman who hopes to enter the international market-place. Many two-year libraries encourage the use of the facility by the general public, creating the expectation of public library services in addition to the academic responsibil-ities inherent in the school's mission. If there is a single institution that seems to respond to all of the people, all of the time, the two-year college library is the institution most likely to qualify. The implications for reference services in such an environment are astounding.

For the two-year college library to be true to its mission, always within the context of its institution's mission, it MUST portray itself as a teaching unit. It is the library's responsibility to TEACH all its users the procedures and methods necessary to identify resources and to discover facts. Once the library begins retrieving answers for people, instead of teaching them how to find the facts themselves, the library abdicates its role in an academic institution. Often however—in the short run—it appears much more advantageous and much less stressful to provide the information, not to instruct users in finding information. The "service" philosophy that permeates the United States today does not connect with the "service philosophy" of traditional librarianship. Consumer service exemplifies the ideal of one's being taken care of, NOT of one's learning to take care of him/herself. The community college library *must encourage users to learn to take care of themselves.*

Instructional Services

Being responsible for one's own learning leads directly to the necessity of instruction, both formal sessions of biblio-graphic instruction (BI) and informal instruction with individ-ual users. Both types of instruction are necessary, especially the individual interaction. Because many community college students have limited educational backgrounds, a librarian must often work very closely with them, both to introduce basic library skills and to help improve the students' self-confidence in their developing abilities. And because the students' may have never used a library in the past, repetition of basic procedures is necessary. Many community college students must be clearly told the reason for consulting a particular title, be taken to the title and physically shown the best methods for using it. There is an advantage in suggesting that this source is useful for a comparable assignment in the same or another course.

Formal bibliographic instruction sessions are most effective when undertaken for a specific instructor and directed toward a specific assignment. General tours of the library and orientation talks do not often relate to the students' immediate needs and, therefore, are not remembered. Students are best able to use and retain "pieces" of the whole process of research, delivered at different times. For example, an instructor spends an entire class period in the library for periodical instruction. In addition to a librarian proceeding through the actual steps to follow in search of periodical articles, students should have time to spend in the library physically seeking an article and leaving with the article or information from it. There is much virtue in students' going through the procedure, with much less talking about it and a great deal of doing. Community college students need "hands on" activities to benefit from library instruction. The difficulty with this approach, of course, is the instructors' reluctance to devote such amounts of time to library training. Usually, an involved procedure such as this is used for one area of library instruction and one-on-one help is given for other areas of interest, for example, book sources or media materials. One rule to remember in dealing with community college students, and perhaps first-year students in general, is that they cannot absorb a string of verbal instructions. Give them too much, the process of identifying and retrieving a periodical reference, for instance, and the students will be lost from the beginning. One of the critical differences between community college students and other students is the community college students' lack of experience. Many of them have literally never been in a library before. And if they have, they have walked along the shelves and stopped when a particular binding or title caught their attention. Surely many have never attempted to identify or find a specific title that they may need. Imagine the overwhelmed feeling that comes from entering a typical library. Most of us assume some familiarity with the basic establishment. Most community college students have little or no familiarity with libraries or library usage.

Community college students really are at a disadvantage:

- they have no library skills;
- they have had little interest in acquiring data for themselves;
- there are no family members and/or friends who have attended post-secondary institutions;
- their time for school and school-related demands is at a premium;
- they have not previously been very successful in school;
- they are in an unknown environment.

The cardinal rule for reference services—in Bibliographic Instruction sessions, on the telephone with a student, or at the catalog with a first-year student—is *never assume.* One must not assume and one must not patronize. Do profess by demeanor and willingness that any question is legitimate and any unawareness (where are the books? what's on the second level? etc.) is just that: unawareness, not ignorance.

How long has one known the reason for a call number? Why doesn't a Who's Who volume contain information on American movie stars? It is not unusual for the typical librarian to be unable to imagine the lack of library awareness among the general student population. And it is not possible to try to remember one's own level of underexposure; too much time has passed. Students today literally may have never written more than a paragraph throughout their school years; they may have no books or magazines in their homes; the majority of information used to make decisions is that solicited from family and/or friends. As a group, they are underexposed to activities of the mind and, thus, to information awareness. Overwhelmed by information produced for mass consumption, they have had no need to identify specific data for themselves, nor have they generally questioned the information available to them. Therefore, retrieving information from specific sources is a new and primarily uncharted course for most community college students.

Dealing with individual students is the most effective method in making them aware of sources and in encouraging self-reliance. It is, of course, labor intensive and psychologically demanding; but it is the only method available to encourage responsibility for one's own learning, a novel idea for most recent high school graduates.

Community Users

About one half of the two-year colleges in the country extend community residents borrowing privileges in their libraries. Even if the community resident, as contrasted with the tuition-paying student, is not allowed to circulate materials, the residents are allowed—sometimes encouraged—to use the library's facilities. This, of course, covers reference services; interlibrary loan service may not be included in this.

Community usage of an academic library, unfortunately, creates a public library expectation within some individuals. Rather than enjoying the privileges that come from access to the college library, some individuals will demand services not usually provided by an academic institution: for example, physical retrieval of titles from the shelves, extensive help in identifying titles from the catalog, reserving of best-seller titles and notification of their status, and so on. These demands should be curtailed as quickly as possible, for the time devoted to such personal attention is neither justifiable nor available in the environment of a community college library. The community patron should understand the basic privilege granted to him/her in using the collection and abide by the type of service given to those for whom the library is supported.

The most currently observed conflict in community usage of an academic library is in the sometimes intensive use made by local high school students. Because of inadequate or unavailable school libraries, many high school students use a local college library as the library of preference. If the college is publicly supported, the problem is compounded by the students' belief that they have a "right" to use the facility. "We pay taxes" is the common rejoinder from these individuals, as well as from their parents. In fact, the public does not always pay taxes directly to support the local college or its library. Usually the state allocation to the college is for the support of college students and their curriculum. Again, public use is a privilege. Even when the local community is providing support for the college, that support is generally defined in light of college needs, not those of high school-age youth who have other agencies for support of their needs.

High school students, also, require considerable direction and explanation in using a college library. The most immediate difficulty is using the Library of Congress Classification System in an academic library; secondary school libraries are more likely to use the Dewey Decimal Classification system. Assignments, particularly in the literature area, in college and high school are often amazingly similar. Thus, two different groups are competing for the same core material. Conflicts are bound to arise and needs of both groups will not be met. Although some community college libraries do hold orientation sessions for high school students, it is not a particularly practical undertaking and it does place the burden of educating users on the wrong library facility.

A seldom noted fact is that in the typical college library there is much material that may not necessarily be appropriate for some high school students, especially younger students. This material is not usually in subjects that high schoolers will be investigating, (for instance, homosexuality, alternative life-styles, etc.), but it is material in which they have some interest. College libraries would prefer not to deal with potential censorship challenges, but the possibility exists in this situation.

Because they are not an integral part of the campus, high school students may not be as prompt in returning materials as one would wish. In that event, a number of days is required to retrieve materials that should be available for college students' use.

Other community users bring unique expectations to the college library: graduate students who are not able to support their courses; retired patrons who have expertise or in-depth knowledge in specific fields that the library collection does not especially support; individuals who want a smorgasbord of cookbooks, craft ideas, retirement planning, and so on. Two-year college libraries tend to attempt some measure of support for these groups, if they are using the library facilities. But, such expectations from these many diverse patrons place much pressure on the college library, undue and unfair pressure for a library that has a distinct, quantified mission. There is no easy or ready solution to the problems of non-college users. The tenor of the library's availability to these users is most often set by the college administrative staff and the library responds to the expectations created.

Technological Applications

Another aspect of the services provided by two-year college libraries is the extent to which the library offers computer-based resources. As a whole, two-year colleges have been quite progressive in applying computer technologies to their library operations. This opportunity/service is, however, a two-edged sword: technological applications are readily available and, comparatively speaking, reasonably priced; but there can be strong resistance to the new technology. Students themselves are wary of exchanging the card catalog for a printed index or a computer screen. Many students have had little exposure to computerized machines and are taken aback by automated activities within a library. More than the students, however, the faculty is reluctant to utilize information delivered by an unfamiliar method. College faculties, as a whole, are older and are wary of new technologies. Many traditional faculty actually enjoy using the card catalog and, surely, get some reinforcement of the research process from this procedure. It is strange that students appear to accept automated circulation with positive reactions, but an automated card catalog or periodical index is much more disconcerting. Perhaps such reaction is explained by the students' lack of interaction with most automated circulation activities; on-line catalogs and periodical indexes require more from the user.

Keep in mind that the automated activities that are such time-savers to librarians are not generally perceived nearly so positively by most library users. Whether there is an automated catalog, a CD-based periodical index, or an automated circulation facility, students and faculty must be introduced to them individually—and with patience. After an introduction, this is another opportunity for library users to become responsible for their own learning, for developing reasonable information-seeking behavior, NOT for librarians to do the work for them.

Let me hasten to add that there are library users for whom librarians must provide additional service. The number of these individuals, however, should be held to a minimum. It is probably the better part of discretion to retrieve the title from the second-floor stacks for the loud-talking, demanding patron who "has never used a library much before." Attempting to walk some users through a process is useless and will create public relations nightmares. Handicapped individuals may also require special considerations. A degree of judgment is necessary in dealing with all library users, though favoritism to particular individuals is certainly to be discouraged.

College students from other institutions will also use a local college library. They may wish only to use the facilities, not circulate materials. They can, however, be very vocal in their disappointment of the two-year college library holdings. These students may be enrolled in evening classes to acquire degrees beyond the two-year college curriculum, often courses at the graduate level. The two-year college is able to respond to these demands in a very limited way and has no recourse except to indicate that the two-year college library's responsibility does not provide for such "advanced" work.

Materials from Other Places

Two-year college libraries offer interlibrary loan services and on-line data base services to various types of people. Some limit requests to their faculty/staff; some extend one or both of these services to students and, even to community users. Some charge for these services; most do not. The individuals whom the college will support in these labor-intensive endeavors must be determined by the support staff available to provide the services or by the amount of money the library is capable of devoting to support such services. The library's membership in OCLC, DIALOG, BRS, and so on, will determine the cost of theses services, as well as the ease with which the services can be offered.

It is not uncommon for the two-year college library to attempt to provide support services for additional courses being offered by another college/university. Many colleges and universities offer off-campus courses in communities that are long distances from the college/university campuses. Although the two-year college library cannot respond well to this type of demand, the off-campus students, rather than making a trip to the distant college/university will attempt to fulfill course requirements in the most convenient library, invariably the nearby two-year college library. Not much can be done to improve this situation. If there are formal agreements between the two-year college and the other college/university that is offering courses, the two-year college library may be successful in initiating supporting links with the other institutions. They may, in some cases, even provide support for appropriate materials. There will, however, probably be no mention of staff or professional support—badly needed resources in situations serving completely different users. The best the two-year college library can do in these circumstances is to respond as well as possible; but library staff must indicate to the off-campus student the limitations of the library collection.

Community college libraries are literally all things to all people. It is a fact that two-year college students use the college library to the exclusion of every other type of library. That means that reference librarians must be experienced in dealing with all phases of information needs, not just those that relate to curriculum matters. It also stands to reason that the experience that the student has in the two-year college library will, surely, color the willingness to use the library again and, perhaps, the interest in using other libraries later. If this were not the only library that these students used, reference librarians in this environment would not be so critical. But, as it is, reference librarians most often set the temper of the individual's experience. The responsibility is often overwhelming.

There are various characteristics of the two-year college environment and of the two-year college library that are unique and that should play a significant role in one's decision to become a two-year college librarian. Firstly, two-year colleges—be they made up of 600 students or 10,000 students—strive for a family-type atmosphere. There is an effort by college instructors to know each student by name as quickly as possible and to be academically and personally supportive of each individual. Although this personal contact is not possible for the librarian, the supportive commitment underlies all activities on a community college campus.

Two-year colleges are exciting, challenging environments in which to work. They offer hope to those who most need encouragement and direction. Historically they have been on the forefront of change and creative solutions to academic concerns. Yet, they require dedicated personnel who respond well to individual interaction, who are not frightened of or resistant to change, and who are supportive of small successes for many diverse types of people. Two-year college librarianship embraces the challenges of all types of libraries: the academic, the public, and the school. Vive la différence!

TYPICAL IS ATYPICAL:
THE COMMUNITY COLLEGE STUDENT

Susan Anderson and Susanne E. Fischer

To be a typical student in a community college setting is synonymous with being atypical. Although there are numbers of students recently graduated from high school whose goal it is to achieve the Associate in Arts degree that will enable them to transfer to a more traditional four-year college or university, the students at community colleges run the gamut of ages, educational backgrounds, and assorted goals. They range from highly motivated teenagers, who are dual-enrolled in high school and college, to retired senior citizens; from adults actively engaged in successful occupations but looking to change careers, to single parents seeking improved employment skills to obtain financial security. More of them are part-time than full-time students; more of them are female than male. Some are academically talented; many are in need of remediation of basic skills and would not be admitted to traditional four-year colleges. And there are more students like these, especially in the southern region of the country.

A November 1990 report (*College Enrollment Trends in Southern Regional Education Board {SREB} States*), explains that although the number of high school graduates dropped, public higher education enrollment grew in the South, continuing a ten-year trend from 1978 to 1988, and growth in two-year private and public colleges accounted for much of the increase. In profiling the 1988 first-year students, SREB reported 45 percent of the region's students attended two-year colleges and 95 percent of those attended public two-year institutions, almost two thirds were part-time students, 58 percent were women, 13 percent were black, and about 8 percent were Hispanic.

The librarian who seeks to provide reference services and to develop collections serving the information needs of community college students needs to be cognizant of the differences in the types of students served and of the curricular requirements of the community college. Stewart Brand has said, "The only communicators taking *full* advantage of the electronic convergence of all media are the librarians, who owe allegiance to no single industry. In America, librarians are officially sanctioned outlaws. They truly believe information ought to be free and follow wherever it explores" *(American Libraries:* November 1990). The community college reference or public services librarian needs to be Brand's kind of "information outlaw" to assist the diverse categories of students who attend community colleges.

Colleges of Innovation

The community college is a uniquely American institution. Although its beginnings are in private junior colleges, the impetus for community colleges resulted from the need for inexpensive post-high school education for vocational and career training within commuting distance of student homes, a need that was prompted by societal conditions—the Depression, World War II, and the baby boomers. Many community colleges began as the thirteenth and fourteenth year of high school and still have administrative procedural ties to public school education. Others developed as junior colleges expanded their missions to provide more diverse curricula to an enlarged student population in the 1960s and 1970s—students who could not find admission to traditional four-year institutions because of crowding, increased cost, or less than optimal educational backgrounds. And as technology advanced, the community college was called upon to meet the training needs of the work force and to provide meaningful activities for increases in leisure time. The mission of the community college grew to respond to the needs of the people.

Libraries in traditional colleges and universities are repositories of the written word. They are designed to hold large collections of materials detailing both the latest in scientific knowledge as well as historical events, some long forgotten in volumes that are no longer in print. These libraries exist for research purposes and to a lesser extent to record the life and development of people and nations. The library models of traditional colleges and universities did not and do not fit the instructional support needs of this new type of college.

The role of the library expanded from a collection of books to an alternative instructional support system providing for diversity in learning styles to fit the needs of this new college. Thus, the development of the learning resource center or learning resources services designed to meet the instructional support needs of the heterogeneous student population at community colleges. Collections of audio and visual materials and the educational equipment to utilize these resources were added to the books.

For community college faculty, the emphasis is on teaching, not research. For the library or learning resource center, this means less emphasis on depth in the collections and more emphasis on currency of information and innovation in delivery systems. This role continues with community college informational support systems utilizing emerging technologies to enhance access to information. Community colleges have quickly embraced such services as on-line searching of bibliographic utilities, CD-ROM products, reprint services such as Social Issues Research Service (SIRS), and other avenues of facilitating access to information.

As the role of the library has changed, so has the role of the reference or public services librarian. The primary function of this position is not to maintain traditional methods of learning, but to provide an atmosphere of innovation and creativity for students and faculty. Seeking new ways to access information is a major component of the librarian's position in the community college. Being knowledgeable about new and improved delivery systems for instruction and being able to use them is a departure from the information base of the traditional librarian.

According to Fran Miksa at the University of Texas at Austin, "Technology has so expanded access to information, wherever it may be housed, that the system of delivering

Kankakee Community College
Learning Resource Center

information has become far more important than collections of material in individual libraries." *Chronicle of Higher Education:* August 1, 1990) Using technology, the community college reference librarian should focus on teaching students how to identify and locate material in a variety of formats. The past emphasis of traditional libraries in building local collections has changed to concern for resource sharing and cooperative collection development.

Programs of Instruction

Community college instructional support centers must respond to the informational needs of each of its different programs, which may have very different goals. Most community colleges offer at least four different types of instructional programs:

- University parallel education
- Vocational or employment skills education
- Remedial education
- Community or lifelong learning.

University Parallel Education

Community colleges are responding to an increased demand for university parallel programs. These programs, also known as college transfer programs, provide education equal to the first two years of post-high school education. Terminating in the Associate of Arts degree, they permit students to transfer to senior institutions at the junior year of the traditional four-year degree. The National Center for Education Statistics (*U. S. Department of Education,* NCES 90-692: September 1990) reported that from 1987 to 1988 the actual number of Associate degrees earned nationwide was 436,000. This number was projected to increase to 465,000 by 1991–1992. This acknowledgment of the responsibility to serve as transfer institutions is a return to the emphasis of the original junior college mission.

Completing two years of college work at community

colleges has obvious benefits to the student. First, there exist remedial courses on the campuses for those underprepared students who come to the college. Second, courses are taught by professional teachers in small class settings. Finally, the financial benefit of lower tuition and housing costs at community colleges is increased because the community college educational day is designed to accommodate students who work in addition to attending school.

The increasing emphasis on transfer or university parallel programs has augmented the emphasis on the teaching role of the community college library. Public services must provide for the immediate information needs to support the community college curriculum and an expanded requirement to teach research skills. Community college instructional experience has taught students to expect more individualized attention and this expectation has been extended to the library setting where there has been an expanded responsibility to teach research skills that will support students when they transfer to the four-year college and university.

Vocational and Career Training Programs

The vitality of community colleges is reflected in their response to the need for vocational and career training. Vocational education comprises those college credit programs that lead to the Associate in Science, a terminal two-year degree that trains professionals for employment in such areas as health-related occupations, business administration, criminal justice, engineering and construction technology. Also offered under the vocational umbrella are programs that train students for skilled and semiskilled occupations similar to training offered in vocational schools, which sometimes lead to a vocational education certificate, and those vocational courses designed to retrain or upgrade skills, but that are not organized as a program of study. If it is true, as the media tells us, that most Americans will have a minimum of three career changes during their working lives, providing training for these changes is a critical component of the community college educational mission.

Students enrolled in vocational courses range from the

recent high school graduate through the adult approaching senior citizen classification. They may be enrolled in courses leading toward a degree (credit courses) or not (noncredit courses). Responding to the informational needs of this second group of students requires special sensitivity to adult learners. Learners who may not have used libraries recently, who are often training for new careers while employed full time, and who may have family responsibilities that preclude long sessions of library use. Library policies and procedures should facilitate the instructional needs of these and other students enrolled in vocational courses.

Remedial Education

The roots of community colleges are firmly planted in an egalitarian foundation. A consequence is the open-door policy to which most community colleges subscribe and which requires only the high school diploma for admittance. This concept, however, does not preclude the maintenance of standards. To assure that students completing the A.A. and A.S. degrees are as capable as students attending the first two years of four-year institutions, there are extensive entry-level testing requirements. The results of these tests are not used to exclude students. Rather they are used for enrollment purposes, not as a basis for admission as in other types of institutions of higher education.

Test results are the basis for the placement of students in programs. Some students are placed directly in college-level courses, others are placed in remedial courses that will build basic skills in English, mathematics, and reading. The existence of remedial education courses, which usually do not exist at four-year colleges and universities, is an additional student benefit. In Florida, the state legislature has ordered only the community college system to provide remedial education at the post-secondary level and provides funds for its accomplishment.

In addition, English as a Second Language (ESL) programs are common as community colleges such as Miami-Dade in Florida respond to waves of immigration. Other colleges have special programs for the handicapped or the learning disabled. St. Petersburg Junior College, another public community college in Florida, has a hearing impaired program that also includes special help in terms of tutoring and counseling. Meeting the needs of these students for information requires a creative response from the library staff. Many community college libraries include electronic laboratories with computers, audiovisual equipment, and other tools to assist the learning experiences of these special students.

Community Education Programs

Meeting the varied needs of the community is an integral part of the community college mission. Four-year colleges and universities and technical schools exist to serve degree seeking students. Community colleges also serve this function and actively recruit nondegree seeking students. These students may enroll in college credit courses also or they may enroll in noncredit courses. Although these noncredit courses are post-secondary in content, they earn the student CEUs rather than college degree credits. They range from recreational activities, such as creative writing, sculpture, dance, art, and personal finance, to specially designed technical courses, for instance, time management, seminars for health-care professionals, and graphic design on the microcomputer. Courses developed at the request of corporations may be delivered at the college site, through cable vision at the student's home, or at the job site. This fourth aspect of the community college mission sets it apart from other types of higher education.

A review of the enrollment of students based on the purpose of enrollment, that is the four types of programs (college transfer, vocational, remedial, lifelong learning), reveals that those enrolled in vocational or employment skills education programs continue to be the strength of the community colleges. For example, Florida reported 964,366 students enrolled in community colleges in reporting year 1988 to 1989. Florida uses a reporting rather than an academic year for purposes of reporting to the Legislature. A reporting year equals the summer semester from the previous academic year plus the fall and spring semesters of the current academic year. For example, reporting year 1988 to 1989 equals the head count enrollment from summer semester

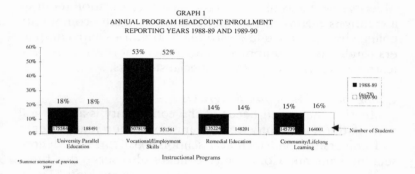

GRAPH 1
ANNUAL PROGRAM HEADCOUNT ENROLLMENT
REPORTING YEARS 1988-89 AND 1989-90

1987 to 1988 plus fall semester 1988 to 1989 plus spring semester 1988 to 1989. Graph 1 shows the distribution among programs. More than half of the head count enrollment was in vocational-related courses. Graph 2 shows the students without regard to program but rather by the type of course (credit/noncredit) in which they were enrolled. The majority of students were enrolled in credit courses seeking degrees. Those enrolled in non-credit courses, however,

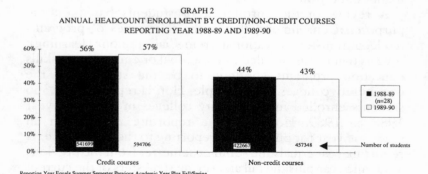

GRAPH 2
ANNUAL HEADCOUNT ENROLLMENT BY CREDIT/NON-CREDIT COURSES
REPORTING YEAR 1988-89 AND 1989-90

accounted for more than two-fifths of the total number served. At some colleges noncredit program enrollment far exceeds credit enrollment. The significance of this figure for institutions relates to funding, which is usually much lower for noncredit courses, and for libraries, because it indicates the types and numbers of actual library users.

Colleges of the Community

Diversity is the hallmark of community colleges. Because each community college is responsive to its own community, there is great variety in curriculum and instructional modes, student services, college organization in general and college internal units, and, in particular, the students. These differences can be seen clearly by comparing the enrollments and programs of urban to rural community colleges. large to small community colleges, and community colleges located near four-year institutions to those in locations where there are no other post-secondary institutions.

The information responsibility for community college libraries is also different. The community college library may be in some locations the only post-secondary library in the community. It may be the only source for research of any kind. In other locations, the community college may have other academic libraries nearby and may have established resource sharing activities with these libraries.

Florida as a Model

The community college system in Florida had its beginning in 1933 when Palm Beach Junior College was established as a public two-year college. It remained the only public two-year college in Florida until 1947 when St. Petersburg Junior College was changed from a private institution to a public one. The following year saw the establishment of a second public junior college and the change in status to public for a second two-year private college.

In 1955, the Florida legislature established the Community College Council, whose report *The Community Junior College in Florida's Future,* published two years later, contained recommendations for needed legal changes and a master plan for establishing a system of public community colleges throughout the state. Implementation of the plan would provide post-high school education within 50 miles commuting distance of Florida's population. The same year, the legislature authorized creation of the Division of Community Colleges in the State Department of Education and appropriated funds for six new community colleges. With the opening of the twenty-eighth college in 1972, Pasco-Hernando Community College, the master plan was consummated. The needs of the citizens of the state for post-secondary education had been served by the development of a community college system offering the first two years of a baccalaureate degree, vocational education, and adult continuing education.

With the realization of this plan, Florida became a national model for the development of a statewide system of community colleges. Moreover, in order to bring instruction still closer to students, colleges have developed more than 2,000 other instructional locations, such as churches, public schools, and community centers, and have established additional instructional centers and campuses to better serve student needs.

While the state was building to meet increases in the demand for more post-secondary education, the population itself was changing. The Division of Community Colleges in its annual publication *Report for Florida Community Colleges: The Fact Book*, (1989–1990) writes:

> Identifiable changes include an increase in the mean age of students, changes in enrollment patterns, population growth, changes in population patterns, increased emphasis on vocational education, increased emphasis on economic development, and entry of women into the work force in unprecedented numbers.

The Post-secondary Education Planning Commission (PEPC) was established by the Florida legislature in 1981 to provide overall guidance and direction for the improvement of post-secondary education. As part of the broad plan developed by PEPC, a new community college master plan was written in 1983, which addressed concerns such as the trend toward increased part-time enrollment, minority needs, and women's needs. Updated in 1988, the new five-year plan addresses areas such as quality education, economic development, and quality of life.

The diversity of mission and student body of Florida's community college are typical of community colleges nationwide. For this reason, the authors of this chapter used this system as a model to demonstrate the disparity among community college students and the resulting implications to which both the institutions and their libraries must respond. A brief survey was sent to the institutional research offices of each of the 28 public community colleges in Florida requesting head count enrollment data as of the opening of the Fall 1990 semester in order to obtain the most current information. Twenty-one of the colleges responded, for a return rate of 75 percent. The survey asked about student demographic information, gender, ethnic origin, and program enrollment. Since response from as many institutions as possible was desired, the survey instrument requested only information usually recorded by institutions and did not request the institutions to manipulate data or perform additional research. Even then, some colleges were not able to provide all the data requested. Because the development of the community college system in Florida was closely associated with the development of the universities and because the services requested of community college libraries vary upon the existence of other post-secondary libraries in the immediate area, the authors analyzed the data based on the criteria of a public university within 50 miles of the community college. Eleven of the colleges were identified as being within 50 miles of a university; ten were outside of the 50-mile limit.

When students enter the community college system, they are asked to identify their purpose for attending from among three choices. Either they wish to work for an A.A. degree, an A.S. degree or vocational certificate, or they are attending for some other reason classified as Other Personal Objective. Graph 3 shows that there were 200,521 students enrolled in the eleven colleges with universities nearby; there were 41,995 in the nine colleges without universities nearby. Although the majority of students at both groups of commu-

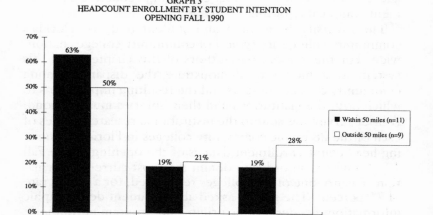

GRAPH 3
HEADCOUNT ENROLLMENT BY STUDENT INTENTION
OPENING FALL 1990

nity colleges indicated they were studying for the A.A. degree, more students in close proximity to universities were enrolled in that program of studies.

Colleges were asked to identify the number of students attending full-time versus part-time. All 21 colleges were able to report this data. Graph 4 shows about one-third of the 209,972 students attending colleges close to universities are attending full-time. The same is true of the 22,485 students attending colleges without nearby universities—about one-third are attending full-time. Only five colleges close to universities provided information on day versus evening attendance. This group reported almost two-thirds (65 percent) of their students attend in the day. This is at variance with the commonly held belief that only students attending college at night also attend part-time. Two of the colleges without nearby colleges reported time of day attendance. For these colleges, the average percentage of daytime attendance was less than one-half (46 percent). Combined with information about program of studies, the pattern of student attendance can assist in planning class schedules and assigning faculty, library acquisitions, and hours of service. This appears to be a serious omission in data collection for some of the colleges.

It is widely accepted that the number of females attending community colleges exceeds the number of males. Graph 5, based on the finding of the survey, supported this fact. About three-fifths of the student enrollment was female. This finding held whether or not students were attending a community college located close to a university. Gender might vary according to the balance of vocational versus transfer programs, community educational needs, and economic conditions of the community, however, colleges were not asked for the distribution among program types as this

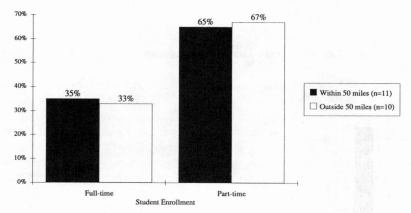

GRAPH 4
HEADCOUNT ENROLLMENT BY TYPE OF ATTENDANCE
OPENING FALL 1990

The Community College Reference Mission

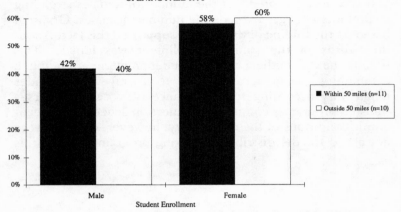

GRAPH 5
HEADCOUNT ENROLLMENT GENDER
OPENING FALL 1990

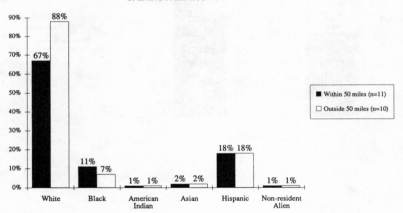

GRAPH 6
HEADCOUNT ENROLLMENT BY ETHNIC ORIGIN
OPENING FALL 1990

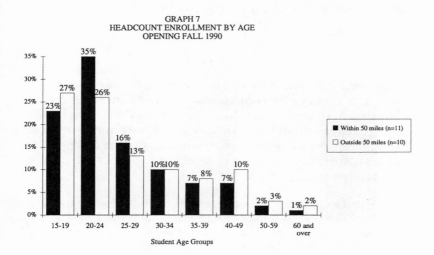

GRAPH 7
HEADCOUNT ENROLLMENT BY AGE
OPENING FALL 1990

information would, in all likelihood, have required the colleges to perform additional analysis.

Graph 6 displays the percentage of students by ethnic origin. In colleges with universities close by more than two-thirds (67 percent) of the students were white. This percentage was higher in colleges with no nearby university (88 percent). The high percentage of Hispanics enrolled in both groups of community colleges is consistent with the Spanish heritage of the state.

The average community college student is characterized as being white, female in her late twenties.

Graph 7 shows that the majority of Florida's community college students, while white and female, are closely aligned with the age bracket of traditional college students.

Reference Survey

Virginia Vail, reference librarian at Pensacola Junior College, developed a survey instrument in 1990 to seek information from Florida's community and junior colleges (Appendix 1). Vail requested information about reference hours, staff, bibliographic instruction, credit library instruction, data base access, intra and interlibrary loan, and library publicity.

Conclusion

General information about a community college system or even the concept of community colleges can be useful to libraries in planning services for users. Each community college library should investigate its own institution's student demographics and use this information to predict and provide library/information services in an effort to reflect the unique characteristics of each college.

> The LRC concept is unique, an ideal rich in promise for teaching and learning through many modes and media within the embracing context of the two-year community-oriented community junior college. [*College and Research Libraries*: November 1990].

References
American Libraries. "Thus Said." (November 1990), p. 939.
Bierbaum, Esther Green. "The Two-Year College LRC: Promise Deferred? *College and Research Libraries* (November 1990), 51, pp. 531–537.
Florida Department of Education: Division of Community Colleges. Report for Florida Community Colleges: The Fact Book 1989–1990. (Tallahassee, Florida), 1990.
Marcum, Deanna B. "For University Librarians of the Future, the Degree in Library Science, by Itself, Will Not Be Sufficient." The Chronicle of Higher Education (August 1, 1990), B2–3.

Southern Regional Education Board. College Enrollment Trends in SREB States (November 1990).

U.S. Department of Education: Office of Educational Research and Improvement: National Center for Educational Statistics (September 1990).

SURVEY OF REFERENCE SERVICES
IN COMMUNITY COLLEGE LIBRARIES/LRCs

College Responding
_____

Campus (if applicable)
_____

Name and title of respondent

1.   What are the Reference Desk hours? (manned by Librarian)
Monday-Thursday _____   _____ Friday
Saturday   _____   _____ Sunday

     Number of full-time Reference Librarians: _____
     Number of part-time Reference Librarians: _____
     Number of support staff (specify position): _____

     Do you at any time have 2 or more Reference Librarians
     scheduled for duty at the same time? _____
     When? _____

2.   (a) Do you provide bibliographic instruction? Yes___ No___
     If so, specify by type and patron category. Check all that
     apply.
            One on One   Tours/Classes   Workshops
Faculty: _____   _____   _____
Students: _____   _____   _____
Staff: _____   _____   _____
Community _____   _____   _____
 patrons:

     (b) Do you provide a credit library instruction course?
     Yes___ No___ Does that course fit the general education
     requirement? _____ How many credits does this provide and
     what is your average yearly enrollment?
Number of credits   Average yearly enrollment

_____   _____

3.   Type of CD-ROM Databases by type.
            Yes   No   Number of terminals
InfoTrac: _____   _____   _____
WilsonDisc: _____   _____   _____
PsychInfo: _____   _____   _____
Other: (specify type) _____ _____   _____
                      _____ _____   _____

Appendix 1. Example of Survey of Reference Services in Community Colleges/LRCs

4.   (a) Type of online database service subscription.
None _____
                  Yes   No   Number   of   terminals
searches/month
DIALOG: _____   ___   _____
BRS: _____   ___   _____
Wilsonline:_____   ___   _____
Other: (specify type) _____   ___   _____

      (b)   Do you charge for online database searches?   (specify
      by patron category and type of charge)
              Yes/No   Online cost?   Service charge? How much?
Faculty: ____   _____   _____
Students: ____   _____   _____
Staff: ____   _____   _____
Community   ____   _____   _____
  patrons:

5.   (a) Do you provide interlibrary loan services? (specify by
      patron category, type of material borrowed and charge)
              Yes/No   Type of material   Charge? How much?
Faculty: _____   _____   _____
Students: _____   _____   _____
Staff: _____   _____   _____
Community   _____   _____   _____
  patrons:

      (b) If you provide ILL for your students, do you encourage
      usage? ____ How many student ILL's do you request per month
      (average)? Books_____ Journal articles _____. Have you had
      problems with student ILL requests, i.e., failure to pick
      up, failure to pay, etc.)?_____ Please elaborate_____
      _____
      _____

      (c) Do you fill ILL requests for other institutions?_____ If
      so, what is the average number of requests filled per month?
      Books_____ Journal   articles   _____.   Are you a FLIN
      participant?_____ Are you a SOLINE participant?_____.

      (d) How many staff members handle ILL? (please specify
      position title, if part-time or full-time) What ILL system
      (manual, OCLC, etc) do you use?
Number of ILL staff   Position Titles   Full/Part Time
_____   _____   _____
Type of ILL system_____.

Appendix 1. Example of Survey of Reference Services (continued)

(e) If your college has various campuses, do you provide photocopies of articles from one campus to the other? (specify by patron category and charge) Do you have a telefax machine?____. If so, indicate whether you will telefax library material.

	Yes/No	Fax(yes/no)	Charge? How Much?
Faculty:	____	____	_____
Students:	____	____	_____
Staff:	____	____	_____
Community patrons:	____	____	_____

6. Do you publicize your services

	Yes/No
Campus wide?	____
to the Community?	____
to the schools?	____
to others(identify)?	____

If so, do you do this by:

(a) Publications?   No_____   Yes_____ If yes, please describe below.

Type	Yes/No	Distribution(whom)	Frequency
Newsletter	____	_____	_____
Handbook	____	_____	_____
Bibliographies	____	_____	_____
Pathfinders	____	_____	_____
Other (specify type)_____		_____	_____

(b) Personal contact with someone in authority (i.e. school district level supervisor, public library director, etc.) Yes____ No____ If yes, please explain.

(c) Radio/Television announcement, advertisment, etc.? Yes____ No____ If yes, please describe.

(d) Local newspaper announcement/column, etc.? Yes____ No____ If yes, please describe.

(e) Other. Please describe.

7. Do you provide any other reference service not mentioned above? If so, please explain.

I would like to receive a copy of the survey results (check)____.

PLEASE RETURN TO VIRGINIA VAIL IN THE SELF-ADDRESSED, STAMPED ENVELOPE PROVIDED. THANK YOU FOR YOUR COOPERATION. TELEPHONE: (904)484-2006, SUNCOM 681-2013.

Appendix 1. Example of Survey of Reference Services (continued)

AVAILABILITY: INFORMATION WHERE IT IS WANTED AND IT IS NEEDED

Al Carlson

Though I knew very little about community colleges, my first interview as my job hunting got under way was at one in a nice rural setting where it served a region of more than 100,000 population. I was impressed when I discovered it was a selective depository for government documents. Their only professional librarian had left the preceding June and this was their second effort to fill the position.

Apparently I satisfied the search committee. As I recall their only real concern was whether I could help a student find material after being out of library work for so long. I assured them I could because I had used libraries a lot even after I stopped working for one. When the dean offered me the job on the day I was interviewed, I could think of no reason to say no.

I visited a couple more times before I started work on July 1. They had just begun the Southern Association of Colleges and Schools (SACS) accreditation self-study and I got an early draft of it. I reviewed past budgets and was surprised that not much was spent on materials or staff. I expected to be involved in creating the new budget but wasn't. Initial steps toward hiring an LRC secretary were undertaken and the position filled during my first month. The library had been managed by a library assistant for the past year because the former coordinator of library services had left on June 30 of the preceding year. The college hired two young women at student wages to help the library assistant that year. One of these left, as planned, at the end of summer.

The LRC is a two-story building with a small basement. I occupied the office of the former coordinator of library services, which was located toward the back of the first floor. In addition to hiring a secretary, the first month saw completion of job descriptions and performance evaluation standards for the four LRC employees who reported to me. The state had just adopted this new system based on measurability and accountability. I soon phoned colleagues at other community colleges in the state whom I hadn't met and discovered that they were also understaffed and had small acquisitions budgets. They did give some help with the details of the reports I was preparing, sympathized about facing accreditation, and were generally encouraging. I was told that the state library association met in the fall, but not many community college librarians participated. There were several state organizations that could give me a chance to meet my colleagues and find out how they were solving similar problems. As I learned about them I usually joined.

In that first year I studied SACS, wrote memos about understaffing and lack of an acquisitions budget, and managed to get an IBM AT microcomputer instead of the 8088 processor most administrators received. Title III of the Higher Education Act provided the IBM in December. At the end of that month we also got a demonstration Bibliofile microcomputer so we could print cards. It turned out that Title III wouldn't pay for this, but eventually the college did approve paying for it as a periodical subscription. Another surprise came in April, when the Dean told me I could spend another $10,000 on materials. That was 50 percent of the initial budget. I guess acquisition librarians are used to this. We paid for the next year's periodical subscriptions and bought some sorely needed current encyclopedias. It didn't seem like it at the time, but that first year represented the good times. Action-filled and frustrating, it set the stage for all that has come.

Terrible, comic, and beneficial all describe my first accreditation experience. I took it seriously, spent a lot of time on it, wasn't intimidated by it (perhaps because I felt I was so new I didn't think I could be blamed for anything), but I certainly didn't get to shape the report the way I wanted it. I'm surprised that it seems to have impacted most of what I've done. The SACS guidelines look at library services. They make no effort to speak in the broader context of an integrated LRC. As this chapter reveals, that has pretty much become my focus, too. The local library subcommittee floundered in its efforts. The visitation LRC expert failed to understand us or even make clear recommendations. Yet, the rather large number of Visitation Committee recommendations for improvements in the LRC have served to justify many of the actions I've taken. The remainder of this chapter elaborates some of my efforts to provide acceptable reference and readers services, usually in the context of SACS criteria.

Professional Staff

Library standards state that libraries need both professional and support staff. Library schools teach that only people with a Master's degree in library or information science can be librarians. They imply that only such individuals can provide professional library service. I think that notion has been rejected. Specialized services, both in reference and technical processing, can often be performed very well by one without the Master's. I began my library career 30 years ago in such a paraprofessional position doing many of the same things librarians did.

In very small libraries with very small staffs the talents and characteristics of individual staff members should have a great impact on the professional–paraprofessional mix. Any requirement for professional staff that ignores these factors can be counterproductive. The local self-study committee ended up recommending and suggesting[1] that "steps be taken to increase the availability of professional LRC staff." In a memo to the self-study committee I responded:

> I do not deny that there would be benefits from having additional professional librarians on the staff. But for the committee to recommend such an approach gives this a higher priority than the many other needs we face. They are telling me, before you spend money on more materials, on more clerical assistance, on better computer literacy services, on video production, on automa-

tion, or on any other LRC service you must hire
additional professional librarians. They, presumably
unintentionally, are attempting to usurp the responsibility I have for balancing competing demands for limited
resources. There is no question that the library got the
short end of the stick in the few years prior to my arrival,
and things haven't improved a lot. So much remains to
be done that any recommendation that reduces my
flexibility in allocating limited resources is bound to
have adverse impacts. The most satisfactory recommendation would be: The committee recommends that
additional LRC staff be hired.

As I read this now I shudder because it is so much the
common plea of all administrators, but it is true. The
Visitation Committee recommended that additional professional staff trained in library or informational science be
hired. Eventually this led to a half-time hourly position as
reference library assistant. Hourly positions in Virginia don't
receive benefits, but are paid at the hourly rate established for
that classified position. It is not a professional position, but
some people in library assistant positions in Virginia community colleges do have a Master's in library science. Two
mature individuals enrolled in library science programs have
held that position in the past two and a half years. Not
surprisingly their goals have been to get their degree and a
full-time position as a librarian. Their primary responsibility
has been instruction in library use and reference services.
That has helped a lot, but I'm not convinced it made optimal
use of those dollars. Perhaps it would have helped if I had had
additional responsibilities for them to pursue when they were
not helping patrons. Because of the great flux we were in and
the temporary nature of their employment that wasn't realized. Of course, there are part-time librarians who work in
one position for a long time and make a valuable contribution.
Maybe that will happen here, but lack of benefits makes it
doubly difficult.

A position I held years ago as a science reference librarian
in a university illustrates that staffing reference can be
difficult. When I complained about the clerical nature of my
off-desk duties, I was told by my supervisor that what that

library needed was a library clerk, but my position was the only one that could be filled. My experience suggests that reference librarians (and their supervisors) should be asking whether they are there because the library can't hire a clerk. When that question is answered affirmatively, action is called for. I quit my university job after six months, but that may not be an easy option.

The process involved in filling the new half-time position here was tedious. Prior to its completion, I decided to simply move out of my office and work at the reference desk. This was facilitated by the arrival of a PS/2 computer that I can use when there is no user to assist. This is motivated by the philosophical realization that if the college can afford only one professional librarian, that person should be available to the students. I may be one of the few adequately paid reference librarians. Students and faculty have responded positively to my presence. Those instances when my professional skill allows me to help someone are rewarding. I know a little more about what is going on. Many of my administrative duties, and most of my acquisitions and computing activities, can be handled as easily from this public area. I do more circulation than I like, but that means other staff can concentrate more on their important support activities. There are still times when the library is staffed only by clerical assistants. I think users are just going to have to accept that today's economic climate requires it. I think they do accept it. Perhaps it reinforces my argument that the student must become a capable information finder.

The recommendation for additional professional staff has made it hard to get the needed additional support staff. Indeed, in the fall of 1990 the secretary I hired when I started resigned and the position was frozen because of the state's budget crunch. I was pleasantly surprised when the dean offered to allow the library a three-quarter-time hourly replacement. Even though we rely too heavily on hourly employees, that was very fair given the circumstances. Presently the library has two full-time employees and four hourly employees who work 100 hours per week. The hourly employees receive no health benefits, no sick leave, no paid vacation, and no state retirement benefits. I believe this is

unfair and is contrary to the intent of some federal legislation
that requires equal treatment of executives and other employees. The practice is rampant in state government and may be
disguised in some organizations by terms such as contract
employees. The effect is really to rip off the least powerful in
society. I have had little success combating it, and many
administrators can do little about it. But our elected officials
could. If you act on only one piece of advice in this chapter, I
hope it will be to remedy such gross unfairness if it is present
in your state.

My experience with work-study student employees has
been disappointing. Many have made important contributions, but such employees have inherent limitations. Often it
is well into the semester before ours begin work. Especially as
the semester ends they must give first priority to their classes.
Their contributions can be great if you don't depend on them,
but once you've gotten dependent on them you may be let
down. Some LRCs have had much better experiences. Perhaps the characteristics of the local economy have a lot to do
with what can be expected.

Collection Development

My dean says my job is to use the resources I'm given
wisely. I feel that is part of my job, but that I also must see
that we get resources we need. This conflict has included
staffing (he supported adding a half-time library assistant), but
has been more dramatic concerning materials. The collection
clearly aged during the Eighties. The 1987 accreditation
self-study made these comments:

> The 1976 self-study compared the PHCC library to
> eight other community colleges established in 1962.
> . . . The 1976 self-study stated that "Patrick Henry ranks
> favorably with the other schools." Since that time this
> college's ranking has declined in five of the six library
> categories. While data more recent than 1981–82 is not
> available to make similar national comparisons, local
> data collected since then causes concern. When library

expenditures for the three most recent years compared with the preceding years, [it] . . . depicts a decline in library expenditures as a percent of the college budget. *The committee recommends that a local formula be derived to ensure a consistent money supply for library expenditures so that the collection can be properly maintained.*

In the section on administrative studies the self-study committee "concluded that there are discrepancies in the distribution of funds to three specific areas and *therefore suggests that libraries, student services and operation and mainte-nance of plant be brought up to at least the second quartile of SACS Educational and General Expenditures of Member Institutions.* Unfortunately the SACS Visitation Committee ignored these ideas and made no recommendations or suggestions on funding for materials.

It took me awhile to find out why so little money was budgeted for library materials. But by November of the first year, I had pretty much pieced it together. Occasionally I find out a new detail, but I remain astounded and bewildered by the scenario. This is all happening in an age that stresses accounta-bility. Funding for higher education in Virginia must involve a state agency called the State Council for Higher Education in Virginia (SCHEV). They use a formula to decide what the need is in various categories (one is for library materials) based on programs offered at the higher education institution. Eventu-ally the governor[2] and legislature reduce these, but all institu-tions share in any reductions fairly. Individual community colleges unfortunately don't get an amount based on the SCHEV guidelines. All community college money goes to the central system office where it is distributed based on enroll-ment. Small community college library materials budgets are roughly 50 to 60 percent of what they would be if they got the legislative appropriation. Local presidents are given authority to spend the distributed money any way they like.[3]

My efforts to improve this included letters to the chancel-lor and visits with legislators. Local enrollment growth did mean some modest increases, but we are now in a time of limited state revenues, and library budgets have been slashed far more than most other areas. I have not been the loser in this battle; it is the students who don't have current resources for their college work who suffer. Recently a student asked for material on the Pakistan-India war of 1971. Of course we had encyclopedias, but the circulating books on India and Pakistan were all printed prior to that date. Bangladesh is not in our card catalog. Yet we want our students to have a global perspective! All librarians have a professional responsibility to make the case for adequate funding clear to anyone who will listen. Information service is pretty poor when funding to obtain current information resources is drastically reduced.

I have had more success in making the collections we do have more available. SACS suggested that the college have a collections development policy. I read several and tried to create one that contains the best features. It passed faculty review easily. I'm glad to have it because of the next activity I undertook: weeding. Systematic weeding is clearly called for in any twenty-five-year old academic library, but my prime motivation was the start of automation. I found *Books for College Libraries* to be extremely helpful. Its classified[4] arrangement makes it easy to use while at the shelf. In most subject areas I kept books less than twenty-five years old, but it is great to have a source to discriminate among the older titles. I provided faculty with lists of the more than 4,000 books removed. Many of them are now circulated from classrooms on an honor system.

I can't claim that automation is a success in our library, but if it isn't then it's my fault. We expect our CD-ROM public access catalog prepared by The Library Corporation later this month. The procedure by which we obtained it is not one to emulate. A computerized learning resource center was one of five activities proposed by the college in an application for assistance under Title III, Higher Education Act, Developing & Strengthening Institutions. The proposal was to hire a consultant to decide what was the best way for this library to proceed and then do it within the five years of the grant.

The grant was awarded, but because of limited funds the computerized LRC wasn't funded at all during the first year. About the time that decision reached us the Virginia Community College System decided that it would make one library information management system available to all the 23 community colleges on its computer network. Consequently, the continuation request we submitted for Title III funding for the second year of the grant took this into consideration. This turned out to be quite unimpressive to Washington. About $120,000 was requested over two years to do the activity. Washington decided that the activity should demonstrate only that computerization of the LRC would work and that that could be achieved in one year with $26,425. My arguments that no small library wants to maintain both a card catalog and an automated catalog and a manual and computerized circulation system made no impact.

By the time the grant year began it was clear that the VCCS ideas for a system-wide library management system had slowed. An initiative to get money from the state legislature failed because of the economic doldrums. A beta-test system had not lived up to expectations. I decided that we needed an implementation that would give us most of the capabilities I wanted locally now and that could later be upgraded to whatever central system was eventually adopted. Many proposed budget modifications for additional equipment were rejected, but halfway through the grant year Title III agreed that the half-time a college-paid library assistant was working on the activity as a contributed-service match would be picked up by Title III. The college agreed to use that money to buy equipment. We joined SOLINET as an associate user, obtained an OCLC workstation, identified MARC records for just over half the collection, bar coded and theft-protected those books, obtained three public CD-ROM catalogs, one CD-ROM for the circulation and reference desk and one CD-ROM for cataloging. My hope is that we will be so pleased that we complete the retrospective conversion by summer, even though we don't expect additional outside funding.

Government Documents

I've mentioned that the selective depository status clinched my acceptance of this job. I think that program means a lot to any library. I wouldn't seek to be a selective if another library down the street was already one, but a judicious selection of items can significantly enhance the collection in an isolated library. Unfortunately, being judicious isn't always easy. Presently we select about 10 percent of the items, but in the past this library had received far more than it needed. Such materials must be kept for five years before one can request permission to dispose of them. Such a request goes to the regional depository and then no longer needed documents can be listed for other libraries.

There was no question that weeding was needed. There was no room. I was fortunate to get some surplus metal cabinets to file microfiche. dBASE proved to be useful software for listing the documents. It took me more than one try, though, to write the sorting program to produce the lists in Superintendent of Documents order. Finally, in the fall of 1990 we were able to dispose of the last of the unneeded documents I inherited. I started over, of course, and was elated to finish examining the collection the day before Thanksgiving, just as this paper was being completed.

With its staffing changes, the library had abandoned its shelf-list check-in for documents. That was unacceptable, so I devised a computerized one, again using dBASE. Actually we checked in serials on one file and monographs on a file that provides a complete title. Those files make discarding a lot easier, too. For monographs I devised a KWIC index of words in the title. It is much less frustrating to use than the *Monthly Catalog* because most of the entries in the *Monthly Catalog* are for materials not in this library. But anyone who has depended on words in titles soon becomes frustrated because one doesn't have better subject access. We began getting OCLC GOVDOC MARC records with the start of that service in January 1990. Several Inter-Library Loan requests were received before we had local access to the records. In a couple of years I expect this access through the computerized catalog to prove that this community college should be a selective depository. Because we are just now getting local access to our GOVDOC tape records, I have not decided how our processing of new documents will be handled hereafter. They are a challenge, but the computer can make their management easier. I'm looking for funding to get MARC records for our documents received prior to 1990.

Shelving documents is a headache. Ours are on open stacks. Putting the SuDoc number vertically down the inside spine rather than horizontally across the top helps find the needed item. The weeding and a yeoman's effort by library staff prior to an inspection put the collection in pretty good condition. But it deteriorates readily. I have assumed more responsibility for the shelving. I can weed at the same time and my knowledge of the collection is enhanced.

Pamphlets

The library had abandoned its vertical file collection before I arrived. But I knew such items could be valuable. I waited awhile, but decided I wanted pamphlets shelved near the books on that subject. Each pamphlet is put into one of 39 Library of Congress classifications. Some are very specific; some very broad. About the time I started this, *Editorial Research Reports* changed size, so I have a lot of oversize pamphlets, too. Initially I proposed circulating these on an honor system. I was reminded of this when they became the first collection to be circulated with a new computerized system.[5] We have just over 1,000, which we circulate for a week. Of course, some have been lost. Many were purchased as sets. In reordering these it has often been cost-effective to order the set rather than the specific title. Thus we have three copies of several titles. Our circulation system is based on dBASE files. We were already using a dBASE file for the pamphlets so that we could have a KWIC index to pamphlet titles. The only time-consuming chore to get that collection ready to circulate was adding the bar code. I did this in a couple of weeks at the start of summer 1990. It has given us some experience working with the circulation system and is better than having the student write down the title on a daily list.

Periodicals

I was surprised to learn that community college libraries don't do much binding. Costs dictate this apparently second-rate approach. It does present problems, of course, but there are some benefits. Some community college libraries simply do not have room to shelve back issues of printed periodicals. These rely on microfilm, or increasingly, microfiche. I work in a fairly large building where one floor is devoted to books and the other to back issues of periodicals and government documents (and microcomputers, VCRs, AV department, and a Learning Assistance Center). For 20 years, very little binding of periodicals has taken place. A problem with this is keeping them in order. We've invested in a lot of labeled Princeton files. Significant staff time goes into this, too. Of course, we have some missing issues. An advantage our students get is that we allow loose issues to be checked out overnight. This is popular. Our missing issues and limited current subscriptions are also augmented by exchange lists. Many of the state's community colleges circulate lists of the materials they intend to dispose of. I check these assiduously. Of course, I make frequent trips upstairs to the shelves. But I am helped by our dBASE periodicals file. This is used to print our holdings list each fall. Each record has a note field where we can indicate missing issues. Using the computer to provide an accurate, timely listing helps make what we do have more available.

Although our only subscriptions to microfilm are for two newspapers, we do have a good collection of back issues of periodicals on microfilm. Sometimes these were acquired from exchange lists, too. When the college started a new academic program I did purchase back issues of one journal on microfilm. With the budget largesse in that first year we were able to fill a few gaps with microfilm purchases. Even though we have more room for periodicals than some community college libraries, it is limited. For several titles I have determined that back issues will be kept for only 5, 10, or 15 years.

We rely on the printed Wilson indexes, *CINAHL,* and *P.A.I.S.* to provide subject access to our collection. I'm not entirely satisfied with this arrangement, primarily because searches can mean looking through many annual volumes. I feel the initial cost of CD-ROM is too high for the relatively infrequent use we could make of it. I've used DIALOG, but the high unit cost has kept me from using it more. Of course, our costs for printed indexes are not insignificant, so maybe one day I'll cancel them and turn to technology.

Including government documents we get about 400 current periodicals. Until this year only about 100 of these could be displayed. I felt most students and faculty who visited the LRC did not know the real breadth of our holdings. Last year, for $1,542, we obtained two units of Gaylord display shelving that allow us to display 256 current titles near the reference area. I drove a van to the North Carolina Gaylord plant to defray the shipping costs. I believe students and faculty are better informed about what we have, and it even keeps me better informed about what's in our current periodicals.

Bibliographic Instruction

My job description, written by the college as a preliminary step to filling my position, says that I will design and implement a library instruction program, and that I will develop and implement a library orientation program. I have accepted this charge at face value and tried to do it. Both the local self-study and SACS Visitation Committee merely suggested that a more comprehensive orientation program be developed for the LRC. Although confirming its importance, the SACS criteria is admirably nonprescriptive:

> Basic library services must include: an orientation program designed to teach new users how to obtain individual assistance; access to bibliographic information; and access to materials. Any one of a variety of methods, or a combination of them, may be used for this purpose: formal instruction, lectures, library guides and user aids, self-paced instruction and computer-assisted instruction.[6]

My motivation to do better in this area is increased by the inclusion in the college's assessment plan for most programs a statement that students will know how to access, use, and appreciate information. Information has been important to me for my whole life, so I don't need much convincing.[7] Nonetheless the quantity of instruction and orientation that we give is still minimal. I hope the quality is good. Sometimes I may have asked too much of students: I feel the book *The Political Economy of Information* edited by Vincent Mosco and Janet Wasko is filled with material today's student needs, but distributing excerpts from it didn't seem to do much for my students.

Using the power of the computer has meant that the quizzes given all orientation students can be different and not require a lot of time to correct. Many students report they didn't know so much was available in this library. I expect that is a common reaction everywhere. It is my intention that library orientation be handled with a computer program, but that isn't yet the case. I believe that the computerized catalog will make such an approach even more logical and beneficial.

Conclusion

I've faced frustrations every week and fear that will continue. But I can't imagine a better library job than being director of a small library. I get the rewards of personally providing services to users and a good salary. Much of what I want to try I can try. Successes may affect relatively few people, but even a disastrous decision has limited consequences. There really is no excuse not to be bold in your efforts. An assessment instrument that would let one know if one is doing a good job would be helpful. That is probably true in bigger libraries, too. My judgment is that things are not yet exactly as I want them, but a lot of progress has been made.

Author's Note: This article describes the approach a veteran librarian, who had been a computer programmer for the preceding 12 years, has followed since 1986 when he was appointed director of the LRC at a small community college where he is the only professional librarian. I wanted to resume my career as a librarian because I felt I would have more contact with people and could apply the power of the computer to solving my problems rather than someone else's. While I now have several computers helping to provide efficient library services, I've discovered most of my problems can't be solved with the computer.

My philosophy of library service is predicated on the belief that a patron should be able to get the information wanted and/or needed.[7] This recounts my efforts to provide such library services to this somewhat isolated community college. Efforts to make professional staff, government documents, pamphlets, current and back periodicals, new books, bibliographic instruction, and on-line data bases available to students are detailed. Although often forced to make pragmatic choices I still like this job and the students.

References

[1] *Suggest* and *recommend* are technical SACS terms used in response to the verb *should* and *must* in its Criteria for Accreditation. Its 5.2.3 section on staff begins, "The library must be adequately staffed by professional librarians who hold professional degrees at the graduate level in library science or learning resources." In 5.2.1 it includes, "Professional assistance should be available at convenient locations when the library is open." I considered writing to the self-study committee chairman and asking that the intent of the committee be clarified, but decided the library wouldn't benefit from a clarification.

[2] As recently as November 1990, the Virginia Secretary of Education told the Governor's Conference on Libraries and Information Services that it is the governor's position that libraries in higher education needed to be protected in these times of budget reductions.

[3] Responding to criticism of this approach the VCCS chancellor mandated that presidents spend the distributed amount on library materials in 1988–1989. That is the only year during the Eighties when all the money appropriated for Virginia community college library materials was spent on library materials. PHCC spent 50 percent more on library materials in 1988–1989. The largest community college in Virginia spent 200 percent more on library materials in 1988–1989 than in 1987–1988.

[4] I also learned I detest the Library of Congress Classification System. It uses long numbers when a little planning would provide for short ones, and it has no unifying principles.

[5] We are using the AVAIL circulation system written in Turbo

Pascal by David Hillman, director of the library at Virginia
Western Community College. Since we started to use it about the
time I started writing this article, I think David deserves credit
for the name of this chapter, too.

[6] Southern Association of Colleges and Schools. Commission on
Colleges. *Criteria for Accreditation,* 1986. page 22; Section 5.2.1.

[7] Actually, I've realized this should be limited. I have refused, for
example, to borrow textbooks through interlibrary loan as some
patrons have requested. We can't provide free textbooks to our
students, so it doesn't make sense to provide such a service to
students taking a course elsewhere. There are, of course, lots of
information sources we don't provide. In these cases we fail to
live up to the standard I've espoused.

PART II: REFERENCE SERVICES

REFERENCE SERVICES AND INFORMATION LITERACY

Mary Adams Loomba

Reference services in community college learning resource centers reflect the overall mission of these special post-secondary higher education institutions. Because community colleges are partly controlled by local government, they are, therefore, responsive to local community needs. They generally advocate a philosophy of open access, and because tuition fees are moderate, students who under other circumstances would not be able to can enroll in college (ACRL 1).

Community colleges emphasize vocational and adult programs to provide employable skills. At the same time, academic programs in the liberal arts and sciences are offered, which allow students to transfer easily to four-year colleges. In addition, community colleges offer extensive remedial and tutorial assistance to help students remove academic deficiencies and to encourage good performance in higher college level courses (ACRL, 1). Community colleges are dedicated to the concept of lifelong learning through credit programs that lead to an associate degree or a certificate. They also offer noncredit courses that satisfy the intellectual and recreational interests of people of all ages, from all cultural backgrounds, and with various learning styles (WCC I 3–4).

This chapter will provide an overview of how reference services reflect the missions and policies of community college learning resource centers. It will also discuss reference service as it relates to information literacy. This includes instruction at the reference desk, bibliographic instruction, and computer and nonprint literacy. Related to this is collection development of reference sources. The next section will consider LRC reference staffs: their composition and hiring, training, and development, and evaluation of reference performance.

Library Resource Center Goals

The role of the library/LRC in a community college is determined by the philosophy and goals of the college. It is related to the stated mission, and each institution's individual curricula, size, location, and student body. Community college students are diverse, to say the least, and have widely differing needs. The learning resource center provides services for students who may be gifted, who may need remedial assistance, who may be recent high school graduates or high school students, who may be mature or older adults, who may be physically and/or emotionally disabled, who may have limited English abilities, and students who come from absolutely every cultural, socioeconomic background.

The goals of LRCs address the diversified interests and needs of the students, faculty, staff, and administration of the college, and to some extent those of the community at large. Necessarily, the services of the LRCs are comprehensive, and the different ages, abilities, and learning styles of its users are considered. Reference services are but a part of the LRC, albeit an important one.

There are three major objectives of a reference department: 1) to provide accurate answers to patrons' requests; 2) to build and maintain the collection to facilitate the answering of reference questions; and 3) to teach research strategies and effective use of the resources of the library (Batt 5). Perhaps the most important of these for a community college is the instructional objective. When a student arrives at a community college, it is generally assumed he/she knows very little about library research. Therefore, we view each student's request as an opportunity to teach.

Another objective is to serve the community: high-school students, older adults, people enrolled in special programs such as professional development education, workfare, or community service certificate courses. The variety of courses offered in a community college is short of amazing. The following courses can be taken at Westchester Community College this semester (fall 1990), for example: British Literature, Desktop Publishing using Word Perfect (noncredit), Differential Equations, American Registry and New York State Licensing Examination Review for Radiologic Technology, Italian for Children (noncredit), Marketing Management, Real Estate Investing and Tax Implications (noncredit), Twentieth Century U.S. History, Elder Health: Your Eating Plan (Mainstream program for adults), Business Law, Effective Speaking for Managers (professional development course), and an Orientation to American Life for Japanese Women (noncredit). The learning resource center attempts to support all the programs and courses that are offered.

Services provided by the reference department are determined by need and are framed in terms of policies. There are questions that can be termed general or ready reference and usually take less than 15 minutes. Examples are finding or identifying information in reference books, circulating books, periodicals, government documents, law cases or statutes, biographical or directory information, book reviews, literary criticism, technical information, and definitions (Young 3).

Extended reference service involves researching a topic that is either difficult to find, such as an obscure quotation, gathering material for an administrator's speech or for a college committee. Usually these questions take well over 15 minutes, and often a data-base search is required.

Instructional service is advice and instruction about how to use a reference book, a periodical index, or the on-line catalog (Young 3). Teaching research strategies, how to start the term paper or project, is especially important at the community college level.

Directional and telephone questions are numerous in LRCs because of the groups and types of students who attend the college. These questions become tedious at times, but community college librarians are aware that a polite, friendly response can make a great difference for students attending an open-door institution.

Many students have few academic skills, and many have had unsuccessful experiences in libraries and schools in the past. One of William Young's policy statements at the State

University of New York at Albany is, "Assistance to the individual library user is the chief responsibility of the reference librarian. In order to encourage users to seek assistance, it is imperative that reference librarians be approachable" (Young 10). In a community college the matter of being approachable is doubly imperative.

The goals and objectives of the LRC strongly influence the services that are offered by the reference department; and the services that are provided are formulated by reference service policies. A major emphasis for the community college library/ LRC has to do with the concept of information literacy, which will be described in the next section.

Reference Service and Information Literacy

Community College faculty are very concerned with the enormous issues of teaching and learning. The LRC philosophy parallels these concerns with its emphasis on information literacy. As mentioned previously, information literacy for reference services covers several different aspects: individual instruction at the reference desk, bibliographic instruction, and computer and nonprint information literacy. Related to these is collection development of both print and nonprint reference materials.

Information Literacy–What Is It?

During the 1980s the term "literacy" became defined as the possession of knowledge and skills that enable a person to function effectively. The concept of literacy skills has evolved to mean "communication," "computation," "problem solving," and "interpersonal relations" (Phifer 10). Community college LRCs' important contributions to these new ideas include: provision of materials for literacy teachers, tutors, and students; development of teaching and learning materials; and cooperation with community agencies already sponsoring literacy programs for adults (Phifer 12).

> "The community college library/LRC has been presented with the duty of supporting the community college in meeting the needs of its clientele. One of these needs, and a growing one, is the development of

basic literacy skills in the poorly prepared high-school graduate, the foreign born, and others who, lacking these skills, are unable to function adequately in today's increasingly complex society" (Phifer 20).

The latest ACRL Standards for Community, Junior and Technical College LR programs include a statement that concurs with the above quotation. Standard #5.7 states that there should be a program to provide a variety of services to support and expand the instructional capabilities of the LRC.

"LRs exist to facilitate and improve learning and expanding classroom instruction and to perform the instructional function of teaching students the information seeking skills for self-directed students and lifelong learning" (ACRL 12). . . . "There should be a program to provide students bibliographic instruction through a variety of techniques enabling them to become information literate" (ACRL 14).

Miami–Dade Community College has had administrative support to enhance the teaching role of librarians. President Robert S. McCabe has developed a program called "Information Skills for the Information Age" that is being used as a model for librarians involved in instruction throughout the United States (Breivik, *Information Literacy*, 9). The common focus of this program is that all academic libraries, especially the LRC, need to provide the essential resources and the services to help students be able to function in the world today.

Instruction at the Reference Desk

How does information literacy impact on reference instruction? Academic librarians have always been teachers. With the exception of directional questions, almost all questions we receive have to do with course assignments. If the assignment is new to the librarian, teaching skills are required to interpret the question. Then more instruction is needed to devise a research strategy and/or to explain the use of reference books, periodical indexes, or the on-line catalog (Schumacher 279).

What is significantly different for the community college library is the variety of student abilities the librarian encounters. One person might be a chemistry professor looking for ancient philosophers for his students to look up in connection with a special project. Another person may be a new, bright engineering student who can barely speak English; a home- less, unemployed mother in a grant program to upgrade employable skills; an honors student attending the commu- nity college for two years because it is less expensive; or a person with very limited academic ability doing an assignment with dictionaries for a noncredit developmental course.

Community college librarians need to be extremely flex- ible and able to adjust the method of instruction almost automatically, *without demeaning the student.* Excellent LRC reference librarians are similar to the reference staff at the St. Louis (Missouri) Community College. They offer personal- ized service by giving each student encouragement and the confidence to use their resources (Breivik, "Making," 50).

Bibliographic Instruction

Bibliographic instruction is often the most logical way to start teaching information literacy to students. Most students come to the library when they need to do a research paper, prepare a speech, complete a marketing plan, or work on some other assignment.

Because the teaching/learning process is the main focus of a college, the librarian's role is to enhance this process by striving to make student learning more effective. When library assignments are built into the content of the course, instruction and actual practice in the library/LRC occur at the time when it is most meaningful to students (Griffin 93–94).

Students become "empowered" when they realize that they can learn and conduct effective research methods. A good librarian in any kind of teaching environment can motivate students to draw on sources of information, knowledge, and ideas. In the process the student can become excited about it (Breivik, "Making," 40).

Many universities and four-year institutions teach credit courses in library research. A few community colleges have also begun offering these courses, some for credit, others not for credit. Frances Kelly at Suffolk County Community College in Selden, New York, has designed a manual that would be helpful for any librarian intending to offer this kind of service. The manual includes everything from reference sources and search strategies, to interlibrary loan and electronic data-base searches (Kelly 1–4).

More and more states are now focusing on the issues of competencies and assessment in higher education. Academic libraries/LRCs are also promoting competencies in connection with library instruction. The State University of New York Library Association's Task Force on Bibliographic Competencies completed their "Recommended Library Skills and Competencies for Graduates of Community Colleges in New York State" in 1988. These recommendations, written in the form of behavioral objectives, encourage critical thinking by asking that the student be able to evaluate sources, topics, and subject headings. The competencies also include the ability to develop an appropriate search strategy, as well as knowledge about how to use print and nonprint information sources. In addition, the competencies state that students will know how and when to consult a reference librarian ("Recommended Library Skills . . ." 1,2).

Because community colleges have large populations of international students, it is appropriate that some mention of BI for this special group be made. Clearly, foreign students have many more problems than the students who have grown up in this country. International students are not familiar with our systems of library organization and sometimes they face vast cultural adjustments. Most of all, these students tend to have difficulties in oral communication, they lack an adequate vocabulary, and some also have problems conceptualizing and applying the English alphabet (Goudy and Moushey 224).

Needless to say, a special program, working with small groups, is necessary to help them. It is important, however, to realize that their language problems have nothing to do with their academic abilities. They are highly motivated and, more often than not, become some of the best students when their language problems are solved.

The library/LRC's main goal for all users is self-reliance. Librarians would do well to keep in mind the simple, but often neglected, fact that libraries have become too complex for even librarians to be able to completely understand everything that is being offered in the world of information (Vincent 39–40). Furthermore, reference librarians/instructors are aiming toward the goal of information literacy. We are wise to remember that BI classes are composed of students who may never have used a library before. The quality of reference questions after BI sessions vastly improve. Also, the quantity of questions increases dramatically. Yet, reference librarians should not be surprised or disappointed by the inevitable number of students who missed the class or who were never offered a chance for an instructional session (Vincent 43–44).

Computer and Non-Print Information Literacy
During the 1980s there has been a proliferation of nonprint services in libraries of all types. Of course, microfilm and microfiche sources have been with us for years, as have the wonders of audiovisual media centers. We are also totally familiar with the periodical indexes developed by Information Access, the Academic Index, Business Index, etc. Who would have thought, however, that in such a short time even the smallest community college would have on-line catalogs, on-line data-base searching services, and CD-ROM services. Even the development of expert systems for answering reference questions is not far away. It is obvious that a student is no longer "information literate" by just knowing how to access print materials.

There are several reasons that community college students need to know about machine-readable and on-line sources. One has to do with lifelong learning. Soon every library will be fully automated. A second reason is for the student planning to transfer. As discussed before, two-year college students are increasingly expected to have specific competencies. Finally, electronic sources are useful right at the community college level.

Data-base searching is undoubtedly most useful for staff and faculty research. At Westchester Community College, for example, the data-base most often used is ERIC. In addition to providing searches upon request, a current awareness service could be developed. Faculty could be sent abstracts of publications in their field (Buus 50).

Data-base searching can also be helpful in everyday reference work. If demonstrations are performed in BI classes to make students aware of the service, answers to specific technical questions can be given more efficiently (e.g., the expected growth of the American market in electric cars, or the use of black-and-white 8mm films for the teaching of plastering, or finding an article on temperature transducers) (Buus 50).

Another possible use of data-base searching for community colleges is to supply non-English speaking students with research materials in their native languages (Buus 51). It should be reiterated that the trouble international students often have with language and communication has little to do with their basic intellectual interests and capabilities.

Only a few years ago, the on-line catalog seemed to be on the forefront of the library world. Today they seem almost commonplace. Many academic libraries have on-line systems, but relatively few are members of consortiums.

The Project for Automated Library System (PALS/ MPALS) began in 1985 at Westchester Community College in Valhalla, New York, and was developed by the Westchester County Data Processing Department. It has grown significantly because of the cooperation of WALDO, Westchester County's organization of Academic Library Directors. It now includes the catalogs of all the area academic libraries, including several outside Westchester County ("WCC Periodic Review Report," VII, 11).

In the last few years many additional applications have been added to PALS. We have access to the Westchester News Index (articles in Westchester Newspapers), the Westchester List of Serials (the holdings of all Westchester public, academic, and school libraries), GPO documents, ERIC documents, Peterson's College Guides, and Reader's Guide Abstracts, among others ("Westchester Periodic Review Report", VIII, 11). The present searching capabilities of this on-line system are a marvel to our students, faculty, and community users.

Data-base searching, CD-ROM capabilities, on-line catalogs, and the use of microcomputers for other uses in reference work are only the beginning. What reference librarians can do now is to develop a system whereby questions can be answered more accurately. An expert system, which is a knowledge base consisting of the facts and rules necessary to build this system, can significantly improve access to the information in a library collection (Richardson 231–32). An example of this might be as small as a product information guide for a marketing research assignment. The sources where information can be found would constitute the knowledge/fact base. (These could include reference sources, special issues of periodicals, specific product files, corporate files, periodical indexes, ILL services, etc.) Then the rules, or heuristics, would need to be applied. These are represented simply by "IF" and "THEN" statements (Richardson 233–34). An example might be IF the student needs to know the parent company, THEN use the *Directory of Corporate Affiliations*.

The development of expert systems is exciting and has the capabilities of very sophisticated features, including hypertext. Libraries are just beginning to become interested in this technology. Community colleges, with much of our curricula geared toward technology, will no doubt find these developments totally in keeping with its advocacy of information literacy.

Collection Development and Information Literacy

The objective of collection development for any reference department is to build and maintain a collection that will serve to answer the type of questions that are asked, and will contribute toward the ultimate goal of information literacy. An adequate collection of both print and on-line sources needs to be readily available. Materials also need to be on hand to help identify other collections, individuals, agencies, etc., to which users can be referred when appropriate (Batt 8).

The ACRL Standards state that

> "The reference collection shall include a wide selection of standard works, with subject bibliographies and periodical indexes in print and electronic formats. Reference is the core of every learning resource center and the beginning point for research. The reference collection should be of sufficient breadth and depth to serve the research and informational needs of the campus community" (ARCL 18).

Complementary to this general statement is the fact that each individual community college determines a collection policy to reflect its own instructional needs. At Westchester Community College, backup and supplementary material is provided in the reference collection for times when all other circulation materials are in use. We also attempt to fill the needs of a diverse ethnic population of various ages and abilities. This means we have the *World Book Encyclopedia* and *The World Nature Encyclopedia*, as well as the *Encyclopaedia Britannica* and the *McGraw-Hill Encyclopedia of Science and Technology*. In addition, we have the *Encyclopedia of Artificial Intelligence and other specialized materials*.

Community colleges generally have extensive collections of college transfer and career information. Our collections also have many sources that are technical in nature, such as the *The National Fire Codes*, the *National Electrical Code Handbook*, *The CAD/CAM Handbook*, *Time Saver Standards for Architectural Design Data*, and even such titles as *Hotel and Travel Index*. Finally, like all other American libraries, community colleges adhere to the ALA philosophy of intellectual freedom and the Library Bill of Rights.

In this library, the reference librarian shelves the new books and is thereby able to weed the reference shelves on a regular basis. Older volumes are placed in a nearby storage area. (If the information is not currently appropriate, the books are withdrawn.) The books in storage may circulate for a week unless the most recent volume happens to be missing. This system works well, and few backlogs occur for technical services.

We have a policy of sharing that is a boon for times of budget tightening. A corporation in White Plains sends us one-year-old editions of such titles as *The National Faculty Directory* and the *International Directory of Corporate Affiliations* and many of the Gale Research Company Publications such as *Research Centers Directory*.

We also receive the *Standard Rate and Data, Value Line,* and other business subscriptions, a few months old, from one of the large public libraries in Westchester. In turn, we send some of our reference sources to smaller public libraries in the area. In addition, we give older sets of encyclopedias to local schools or agencies, such as a drug treatment center.

Regarding the emphasis on information literacy, other community colleges collect items of a different nature. St. Louis Community College in Missouri buys and organizes materials that relate to specific programs. Selections of rocks for geology courses, fabrics for textile courses, and bones for anatomy courses are all made available through their Instructional Resources Department (Breivik, "Making . . .", 50). Though not strictly the reference collection, these types of collections are more apt to be found in a community college library than in a library at a four-year institution.

Some community colleges have many students who speak other languages. Pima Community College in Tucson, Arizona, has a large Spanish-speaking enrollment. A collection-development librarian at Pima selectively and carefully ordered Spanish reference materials to meet the needs of these students. The first step was to consider the number of students involved and to know what curricula they were studying.

A list of some of the most important materials are the following: *Libros en Venta en Hispanoamérica y España* (BIP), *Enciclopedia Barsa de Consulta Fácil, Almanaque Mundial, Forjadores del Mundo Contemperáneo, Enciclopedia de Mexico, Diccionario Comercial Español-Ingles, Ingles-Español, Encyclopedia of Business Letters in Four Languages, Simon and Schuster's International Dictionary: English–Spanish/ Spanish–English,* and the *English–Spanish / Spanish–English Dictionary of Technical Terms* (Buchanan 6-8). For more complete bibliographic information, the article by Nancy Buchanan listed in the references can be consulted.)

The goal of providing information literacy needs to be pursued in many directions. It includes individual instruction at the reference desk; bibliographic instruction, preferably at the time a major assignment or project needs to be completed; and instruction in the use of nonprint and electronic materials. Fundamental to all information literacy is the collection of materials that will meet informational and avocational needs.

No doubt, the most important link in promoting information literacy is the librarian. The reference librarian is the catalyst that connects the user to the information. If this process is performed with warmth and enthusiasm, the student will become literate in every sense of the word. Furthermore, the student will become a lifelong learner.

Librarians do not just happen, however. They need to be hired and trained, given chances for professional development, and provided with appropriate evaluation. The next section will deal with the community college reference librarian and how these special professionals affect information literacy.

Reference Staff

How are community college librarians different from other librarians? There are probably no quantifiable or even objective ways of describing us. It appears, however, that the community college librarian is truly an energetic jack-of-all-trades. There may also be a subtle difference in attitude shown toward students. Community college librarians are, almost always, very service oriented. They are used to dealing with a tremendous variety of students with different levels of abilities. We are almost always *truly* interested in the students' experiencing success.

Compared to academic librarians at four-year colleges and universities, there is usually less need for conducting in-depth scholarly research, except for the professors and administrative staff. But, reference work at community colleges requires the ability to put one's hands on a vast number and variety of sources quickly. Students are always running to a class or to a job, and they may live many miles from campus.

Because of the increasingly diverse ethnic character of our society it is advisable to have as many multicultural librarians as possible. This is true for any library, but especially important for the community college. Multicultural librarians can serve as role models and can also establish outreach programs for students (Dyson 953).

Reference librarians need to be empathetic in dealing with a culturally diverse student body. In fact, Errol Lam says that "focusing on better human interaction should be the goal of the whole interview process (Lam 391). He continues by

stating that when the reference librarian is white and the
student is black, an important opportunity to improve intercultural communication can take place. Positive interracial
and intercultural encounters can contribute toward better
human understanding among people (Lam 391-392). It goes
without saying that the same can be said when the librarian is
black and the student is white.

In light of what has been said previously about information
literacy, it is obvious that all reference librarians need to
recognize the importance of automated information retrieval.
Community college librarians need to have as many skills
about computers and on-line retrieval skills as traditional
reference book knowledge. We are able to provide information services effectively only with a thorough familiarity of
both types of information sources.

Community college librarians are hired when they have the
educational qualifications and the understanding of the mission of the college. After being hired, librarians need training
and myriad chances for professional development. These
opportunities need to be provided on a regular basis in order
that everyone can keep up-to-date and be reminded of the
expected level of service (Riechel 15). Furthermore, librarians need to be encouraged to establish an atmosphere of trust
and confidence in the reference interview, and the interview
needs to be concluded by encouraging the student to come
back if more help is needed (Riechel 21).

Beth Shapiro believes that ongoing training can help the
problem of "reference burnout and the seven-year itch"
(Shapiro, "Ongoing. . .", 75). Weekly training sessions can be
promoted to teach librarians about current information resources and to focus on improving reference skills. She also
advocates different levels of information desks: an information desk, a general reference desk, and a more specialized
reference desk (Shapiro, "Ongoing. . .", 76). This idea has
merit if the library is large and the number of staff is
sufficient.

Recently, the literature indicates that there is dissatisfaction
among academic reference librarians. Because of budget constraints and the proliferation of technological development, it

has placed a strain on librarians. They are finding it difficult to be everything to all people all of the time. A study at Michigan State University mentions that a tiered approach to reference service is helpful. A fast-fact drop-in information desk and an in-depth "gourmet" service desk have both been provided there (Shapiro, "Trying. . .", 287). She stresses, however, that whatever approach for problem solving is used, it is the solutions provided by the group that work the best. In other words, librarians can develop beyond the complaining stage into a "solving mode of operation" (Shapiro, "Trying. . .", 291).

Another aspect of reference service that is vitally important is evaluation. Much has been written about reference service evaluation, including a "Symposium" on reference service published by the *Journal of Academic Librarianship* in May 1987. An interesting debate about the issue of unobtrusive testing developed with the publication of Hernon and McClure's study. They found that only 55 percent of factual and bibliographic questions were answered correctly (Hernon and McClure, "Library. . .", 70).

It is unnecessary to discuss this type of evaluation fully or to belabor the fact that using paraprofessionals at the reference desk may have contributed to this low rate of correct answers (Christensen 482). What *is* important is that *some* kinds of ongoing evaluations take place.

It is important that all reference librarians ask themselves if the quality of reference service that is being provided is acceptable. Why do we believe it is acceptable or unacceptable? How successful are our ongoing evaluation and educational programs? In addition, does the reference staff have a clear-cut sense of the library objectives, of what the library is trying to accomplish (Hernon and McClure, "Where. . . ', 284)?

It should be emphasized that reference service for community college students is vitally important. So many of our students have had negative experiences and have experienced patterns of failure that even a simple directional answer can make a difference. At the beginning of the fall semester the number of directional questions we receive can be almost aggravating. How many times can one answer "Where is the bookstore?" or "Where is the academic arts building?" or "Where is the telephone?" We need to develop a mind-set that reminds us that displaying irritation can only make our students feel turned down once again. No matter how many Master's degrees or technological competencies we may have attained, *approachability* for the community college reference librarian is the bottom line.

Rosemarie Riechel has written an important book, *Personnel Needs and Changing Reference Service*. Among other things she discusses ways evaluation can take place. This can be effectively done by direct observation by supervisors to determine how well librarians connect users to the information they need. Supervisors can assess whether librarians are teaching effectively, establishing rapport, assisting patrons at the right level, and whether they are pointing too much when giving directions (Riechel 98).

Those in charge can also judge whether librarians are making efforts to expand their knowledge about electronic resources and whether they provide alternatives to questions when one source is unavailable. Are librarians getting to the patrons' real needs? Are their answers accurate and complete, and do they provide more current data when necessary (Riechel 98)?

Along with observation techniques, reference service evaluation can be conducted by surveys, at staff meetings, keeping statistics on patterns of use, constructive peer reviews, and self-evaluation (Riechel 103). Self-evaluation can be particularly useful if done conscientiously. Having two people in a department participate in an evaluation together is no doubt even more effective. We all need mentors and ways to help each other improve the quality of the service we provide. Moreover, we all need as many "pats on the back" as possible. As Charles Bunge has stated, we need "strong and supporting colleague relationships" (Bunge 131). This is particularly true in busy and often hectic community college reference departments, where it seems as though every student attending the college is in the library between 9:30 A.M. and 2:30 P.M. every day!

Conclusion

Reference services at two-year community colleges involve many components. First, it is related to the mission of the learning resource center/library, which in turn is related to the mission of each individual college. Providing good reference service is not an easy task, because as Ruth Fraley mentions, reference services have become increasingly complex. The reasons for this are the developments in automation, the growth of specialized subject information, the diversity of clientele, and the types of different questions that are asked (Katz and Fraley 3).

Most community college librarians are aware of the need to teach each student how to be information literate. One of the recommendations of the American Library Association Presidential Committee on Information Literacy is:

> "We all must reconsider ways we have organized information institutionally, structured information access, and defined information's role in our lives at home, in the community, and in the work place." . . . Colleges, schools, and businesses should pay special attention to the potential role of their libraries or information centers. These should be central, not peripheral; organizational redesigns should seek to empower students and adults through new kinds of access to information and new ways of creating, discovering, and sharing it" (American Library Association 11).

Reference service at community colleges, or at any academic institution, promotes information literacy in several concrete ways. First, it can be offered with individual instruction at the reference desk. It can also be accomplished through bibliographic instruction in classes, especially those geared to a specific research assignment. Along with these is the responsibility to impart electronic, on-line, and nonprint information literacy. These skills can be taught individually, in classes, and through an academic support learning resource department (media center). In addition, information literacy is dependent on collection development for reference materials, both print and nonprint.

Fred Batt suggests that successful reference service depends on many elements, all of which are essential: 1) a well-trained staff with a positive service-oriented attitude; 2) logically arranged work areas; 3) well-planned, clearly defined policies and procedures; 4) logically arranged service points; and 5) a reference collection that serves the needs of the faculty, students, and staff (Batt 10).

It goes without saying that no amount of materials or good instruction can take place without the reference staff. At community colleges, culturally diverse librarians and support staff are especially important to serve as role models for increasingly diverse student populations. Community college librarians need other special qualifications as well. Above all, they need to be approachable, service oriented, positive, adaptable, and energetic. They also need to have as broad an education as possible to be able to handle faculty informational requests as well as to help the students.

Community college librarians, like other librarians need ongoing training and professional development programs. We need to be apprised of new resources and other developments in the field. This is especially true for the ever-changing technological advancements related to information storage and retrieval.

Finally, a constructive program of evaluation is another feature of excellent reference service. For community college librarians it is vital, not only to improve service, but also to provide encouragement and to help alleviate burnout.

The 1986 Carnegie Foundation's report, *College,* mentions that the way to assess quality in a college is by the "resources for learning on campus and the extent to which students become independent self-directed learners" (Breivik "Making. . .", 44). At a 1987 Symposium "Libraries and the Search for Academic Excellence," sponsored by Columbia University and the University of Colorado, there was agreement that good undergraduate education requires the incorporation of library skills into the learning process (Breivik and Wedgeworth). The implications of these statements for community college reference services are manifest.

References

American Library Association Presidential Committee on Information Literacy. Chicago: American Library Association, 1989.

Association of College and Research Libraries. *Standards for Community, Junior and Technical College Learning Resources Programs.* Chicago: American Library Association, June 1990.

Baker, Robert K. *Doing Library Research: an Introduction for Community College Students.* Boulder, CO: Westview Press, 1981.

Batt, Fred. "Academic Library Reference Services." University of Oklahoma. ED284 556. 1986.

Breivik, Patricia Senn. Making the Most of Libraries: In Search of Academic Excellence." *Change* 19 (July/Aug. 1987), pp. 44–52.

Breivik, Patricia Senn, and E. Gordon Gee. *Information Literacy: Revolution in the Library.* New York: American Council on Education/Macmillan, 1989.

Breivik, Patricia Senn, and Robert Wedgeworth. *Libraries and the Search for Academic Excellence.* Metuchen, NJ: Scarecrow Press, 1988.

Buchanan, Nancy. "Recommended Reference Materials for Community College Libraries Serving Spanish-Speaking Students." *Community and Junior College Libraries.* 2 (Spring 1984), pp. 5–8.

Bunge, Charles A. "Potential and Reality at the Reference Desk: Reflections on a 'Return to the Field'." *Journal of Academic Librarianship* 10 (July 1984), pp. 128–133.

Buus, David B. "On-line Reference Searching in the Community College Library/LRC." *Community and Junior College Libraries* 1 (Fall 1982), pp. 45–52.

Christensen, John O., et al. "An Evaluation of Reference Desk Service." *College and Research Libraries* 50 (July 1989), pp. 468–483.

Dyson, Allan J. "Reaching Out for Outreach." *American Libraries* 20 (November 1989), pp. 952–954.

Goudy, Frank William and Eugene Moushey. "Library Instruction and Foreign Students: A Survey of Opinions and Practices Among Selected Libraries." *Library Instruction and Reference Services.* Ed. Bill Katz and Ruth A. Fraley. New York: Haworth Press, 1984.

Griffin, Mary L. "BI, Reference, and the Teaching/Learning Process." *RSR* 16 (1–2, 1988), pp. 93–94.

Hernon, Peter and Charles R. McClure. "Library Reference Service: An Unrecognized Crisis—A Symposium." *The Journal of Academic Librarianship* 13 (May 1987), pp. 69–80.

Hernon, Peter and Charles R. McClure. "Where Do We Go From Here? A Final Response." *The Journal of Academic Librarianship.* 13 (November 1987), pp. 282–284.

Katz, Bill and Ruth A. Fraley, eds. *Reference Services Today: From Interview to Burnout.* New York: Haworth Press, 1987.

Kelly, Frances. "Introduction to Library Research." Suffolk Community College. Selden, NY. ED 282 580, 1986.

Lam, R. Errol. "The Reference Interview: Some Intercultural Considerations." *RQ* 27 (Spring 1988), pp. 390–395.

Phifer, Kenneth O. and Ruth J. Person. "The Role of Community College Libraries and Learning Resource Centers in Literacy Education." *Community and Junior College Libraries* 2 (Fall 1983), pp. 9–21.

"Recommended Library Skills and Competencies for Graduates of Community Colleges in New York State." Prepared by the SUNYLA Bibliographic Competencies Task Force, 1988.

Richardson, John Jr. "Toward an Expert System for Reference Service: A Research Agenda for the 1990's." *College and Research Libraries* 50 (March 1989), pp. 231–237.

Riechel, Rosemarie. *Personnel Needs and Changing Reference Service.* Hamden, CT: Library Professional Publication (Shoe String Press, Inc.), 1989.

Schumacher, Mark. "The Continuing Debate on Library Reference Service: A Mini Symposium. A View From the Trenches." *The Journal of Academic Librarianship* 13 (November 1987), pp. 278–288.

Shapiro, Beth J. "Ongoing Training and Innovative Structural Approaches." *The Journal of Academic Librarianship.* 13 (May 1987), pp. 75–76.

Shapiro, Beth J. "Trying to Fix What's Wrong with Reference." *The Journal of Academic Librarianship.* 13 (November 1987), pp. 286–291.

Westchester Community College. *Library and Learning Resource Center Policies.* Valhalla, NY, 1980.

Westchester Community College. *Periodic Review Report—1990 for The Middle States Association.* Valhalla, NY, 1990.

Young, William F. "Reference Service Policy Statement." State University of New York, Albany University Libraries. Albany, NY. ED 260 736, 1985.

GENIUS TOOLS AND QUELLENFORSCHUNG

Mark Y. Herring

The title "Genius Tools and Quellenforschung" is not for the weakhearted. Some may think it pedantic. It was not chosen for that reason. Two quotes that every librarian is sure to know, and, in fact, may have made into phylacteries, come from Samuel Johnson. The first is the ever familiar, "[Either] we know a subject ourselves, or we know where we can find information upon it." If it isn't your motto as a reference librarian, it should be. The second supplies the first half of our title: "Genius is nothing more than the knowledge of the use of tools." Laying aside for now the difference in meaning of the word genius between the centuries, suffice it to say that all librarians should be geniuses. Okay, but what about that quellenforschung?

Quellenforschung is a German portmanteau word meaning, literally, source hunting, or a study of sources, a sport known to many researchers and the sport of choice among reference librarians. The problem is that we reference librarians are not very good at it. Not very good at all.[1]

The evidence of this charge rests, it appears, on the dismal statistic that at best we can muster correctly answered reference questions about 55 percent of the time. Of course we can palliate that offense. But when we do, we begin to sound like educators trying to justify a 30 percent dropout rate, illiterate students, and fierce discipline problems. When we try to obviate the charge, we begin to argue about the ambiguity of patrons, the incomprehensibility of requests, the snipe-hunting nature of some questions, and so forth. We point the finger at everyone and everything but ourselves. But, "The fault, dear Brutus, is not in our stars, But in ourselves."

When it comes to source hunting, almost anyone could do better than a librarian, or, perhaps I should say, at least equally well. A reasonably intelligent student (say with an IQ one and a half standard deviations above the norm) might be able to find one of two questions, or two of four. Where the problem affronts our integrity is at the heart of who we are: *reference* librarians.

For example, suppose you went to the doctor with a headache, general malaise, erratic chills, and fatigue. Suppose he examined you, confirmed your complaints, and then flopped down on the desk before you the *Merck Manual.* "There," he'd say with a sigh. "The symptoms you have just given me indicate that you may have more than one thousand possible diseases. You really can't expect me to pick out the right one, can you?" Or take another example. You go before your tax accountant and he shakes his head and says, "If you only knew how much there was to remember, and how many places I have to look, you wouldn't get mad about this two thousand dollar late penalty."

Of course you would not accept either of these scenarios any more than I would. And yes, there are problems faced by doctors and accountants not terribly dissimilar from our own—mountains of data from which must come sense. Moreover, doctors and lawyers are often treated in similar ways as reference librarians. Patients often mask symptoms because they fear the worst; and, well, sometimes clients have been known, unwittingly or not, to withhold evidence from the accountant for their own good. Nevertheless, we *expect* them to unravel the problem and give us the best possible service.

The same is true, or should be true, of source-hunting librarians. We should expect of ourselves a better than 50-50 hit rate. And we should also hope our patrons come to us with great expectations. If they do not, then they are perfectly right in saying, "Oh, the dickens," and going elsewhere. If you are honest, you know you feel the same way.

Several reasons spring to mind why our hit rate is so bad. Three, to be exact, posit themselves as more than strong suspects: librarian preparation, technology, and work ethic. Let us examine them more closely.

Librarian Preparation

One problem that lies at the heart of this issue is our training for reference or source hunting. While some schools have begun to take aim at this problem with the two-year program, not enough is being done. The fact of the matter is that most library schools offer courses in the humanities, the social sciences, the sciences, and perhaps another one or two courses. But what these courses amount to is an astonishing amount of memory work out of Sheehy, but little else.

This is not to criticize that approach—we simply can't be expected to know everything. But it does have a fast-food attitude about it that is sure to lead to bad taste. It is impossible to say how many reference librarians have actually read the prefaces of the major reference tools they use daily, but many with whom I deal and have dealt have obviously not gotten far past Sheehy. While the truncated, vitamin-pill approach Sheehy offers to the weary librarian is a must, it is not, or shouldn't be, the be-all and end-all of reference.

If we haven't noticed our sheer lack of training clout, both in and out of the profession, then certainly we have noticed the weakness of our training by a simple scan of the *Chronicle of Higher Education*. How many ads have you found lately where the educational qualifications for a reference librarian end with the ALA approved MLS? Isn't it far more likely that the ad requires, not prefers, a second Master's in a subject area and even a second language? Moreover, it is not by accident that *scholars* are selected over librarians for the catbird seat at the Library of Congress. It takes one to know one, you see.

Such glaring realities make one pause. Of what use is the MLS if not to qualify its recipient for library work? It would appear that the degree merely makes one eligible for *consideration*. It is the second Master's that must *prepare* him. This is a most telling and damning point. Obviously employers feel that the second Master's is the one in which real study and research is performed, making one more capable for the task at hand.

Librarians must become more involved with the reference tool. Learn its ins and outs. Find out what the eccentricities are. Look for its omissions. This advice is hardly anything earth-breaking, but, as Johnson, naturally, said, "What is known is not always obvious, and what is obvious is not always known." It is time, high time, that reference librarians changed the image people have of them as vending machines with answers: Select knob AA for geographical question. While that does occur, it should not be the guiding philosophy of our approach to solving patron questions. Because some vending machine mentality has been present in our approach for the last few decades, we are now experiencing others hammering on the sides of our heads for better service. If we do not improve, the swift kick is sure to come.

Bits and Bytes

A second fault in our makeup, after education, is automation. We have this notion that we have to be like computers. Input a few phrases via Boolean logic and voilà! you have an answer. Unfortunately, computers have become the reference source, not the reference assistant they were intended to be. This is not a departure from what I have said in another place. There, computers were praised for their relief from overpriced reference sources. They can be a very present help in times of financial trouble. But ceteris paribus they should not be the first resort for the reference librarian, unless the patron asks specifically for that help. By relying on the computer-first approach, we force our patrons into thinking that *every* question will be an easy one-two-three solution. While many questions lend themselves to that approach, we must not provide patrons with the impression that this is the only approach for all questions, especially those questions that fall under the rubric of true research.

Some questions, like some books, as Bacon pointed out, have to be digested slowly. A computer may provide the initial starting point, but it is up to the reference librarian to make the connections, or to provide the synapses, to change the metaphor. Those synapses can be made by a reference librarian who really understands the nature of research, has done research himself or herself, and who appreciates the untold number of hours required for making those synapses correctly. We must guard against making the task appear too bovine, but we must take special care in making the whole task seem like short-order librarians cooking up answers while they wait patron tables at circulation.

Librarian Prerequisites

Lastly, there is this matter of love of reference work. Some years ago, in a major library journal, myths of librarianship were presented. One of the "top ten" listed was "a love of books." Such a love was, according to the author of these myths, unnecessary. Such sentiments, the writer believed, had gone out with Noah and his ark, or Cutter and his table. This attitude—a mere disregard for books, but a love for all things technical—is the very attitude that has landed us in this mess, this morass of reference service that isn't half bad—or half good—depending on how you look at it. Fifty-five percent is hardly anything to get excited about. Having an attitude that disregards the importance of books, or places them on some level of abstractions that says, "These are aspects of the job that you have to put up with," will surely be poisonous to the profession overall, and certainly begin decay from within.

What we do need are reference librarians who understand the importance of both. This is not an either-or philosophical choice. We reference librarians have to be both technical and aesthetical, if I may be permitted a wide skein to catch all the fish intended here. It is not enough to know shortspeak definitions to reference tools, nor is it enough to have a curriculum vita that posits all the necessary courses for the title "Reference Librarian." It is going to take more if we are ever to overcome this professional embarrassment of 55 percent right. To say we're half-baked is to say the mortal truth of what we face as professionals. We must do better.

A La Recherche du Temps Perdu

I do not mean to praise past things because they are past, or to remember past times because they are better, but if you cast your mind back to the heyday of modern librarianship, you get a completely different picture. Where, today, are the John Cotton Danas, the Frances Neel Cheneys, the Sir Anthony Panizzis, and the Isadore Gilbert Mudges of the reference world? Of course, such notables were not the "mean" of reference service. But neither were they the exceptions to the rule. These names, and others like them, brought to reference service a professional mein, a character or attitude, if you like, that reference service was something that continued from the time the skills were first learned, until retirement, or death. Reference service was a process, a development in which skills were honed and new techniques mastered. But above all, it was an approach or attitude about reference service that was upheld for all to ascribe to. Can you name 10 librarians who also are known for their scholarship in the same manner as the previously mentioned three? I do not mean library scholarship of fact and figures, but scholarship in the form of monographs on subject areas, or bibliographies and biographies that extend the ken beyond the circulation of books.

I do not mean to make it sound as sacrosanct as all that, but there was a sense about research that can today, in most cases anyway, only be learned through books. Old books. Pick up almost any article about reference service, and if you are not bewildered by Pearson's Coefficients, Cronbach's alphas and Venn Diagrams, then you are reading better journals than I. What we are treated to are technical definitions of a specialist language, nearly hierophantic in tone and quality. Then pick up Altick's *Scholar Adventurers,* or Graff and Barzun's *The Modern Researcher.* In both you will find mention of the computer. But in both you will also find an approach to research that is nearly unheard of in library circles. While it may make Art Plotnik[2] feel better about reference to know that the batting average is .550, or that it exceeds newspaper predictions, it should not satisfy the rest of us. The last time I checked, neither baseball players nor newspapers had the sort of image any other profession would want. What we have lost in today's reference market is what English professors call mood in stories. We have lost the sense of aesthetic. To put a fine point on it, in the play *A Company of Wayward Saints,* the actors and actresses find they are acting out of force of habit and ego and have therefore lost the ability to make the audience feel, their main goal. For librarians, the shoe is a tight fit, but it is a fit, nonetheless.

We have lost that sense of mood that caused our clan to approach research in the same manner as scholars. This is not advocacy for eggheadism. On the contrary, it is advocacy for approaching reference not as a commodity, but as an art, as a way of finding out.

"[Either] we know a subject ourselves, or we know where we can find information upon it." This is hardly the case with reference librarians today. Rather we could say, "Either we know a thing, or we have a fifty-fifty chance of knowing where to find it." Having lost the sense of reference as an art, we have proceeded to make it a commodity, thereby making ourselves unnecessary to the process. This, coupled with our overtechnicalization of the process and our weak professional training, adds up to service that is not only unnecessary, but even superfluous.

Consider for a moment the following image of the librarian as it appeared in a recent publication:

> I needed to do some research for an article I was writing, so I called New York City's library information service. A woman whose mellifluous voice I've recognized for years came on. Her willingness to help has been boundless. "What do you want?" she asked.
>
> "I don't think you have it. It's sheet music. I need lyrics."
>
> "Which?"
>
> "It's a forties song: 'Spring Will Be a Little Late This Year.' "
>
> "Oh, yes. That's from a Deanna Durbin movie."
>
> Pause. And then, would you believe it, she started singing it to me. Mind you, *sing,* not recite. The lyrics tripped along swiftly.
>
> They took me back to the London I was writing about. September 1944. V-2s in blossom. We met in Strand Palace Hotel bar. We were both lonely and nineteen. We went to see *Christmas Holiday* with Deanna Durbin. She sang, "Spring Will Be a Little Late This Year."

> End of flashback. Back to the Singing Librarian. At
> song's end, I said: "That was beautiful. You broke my
> heart. But you'll have to say the words slowly so I can
> write them down."
> She did, I wrote, then I asked, "What's your name?"
> "We're not allowed to give that information."
> "That's okay," I said. "I know you."

Purely accidental? I don't think so. This is a reference
librarian who understands the meaning of reference. Of
course, I do not believe for a moment that she would know
every song asked of her. But this should make the picture of
what I have been trying to say more clear. Obviously this is a
librarian who makes it a point to *know*. This is not some stale,
cold information she memorized. It is facts speaking to mind
through imagination. It is mood, aesthetic, power of words,
emotion. It is understanding that the divine gift of language
and letters was designed to outlive us all. Because it is
intended to continue on indefinitely and it will, research is no
mere commodity that is churned out of machines, but instead
it is harbored in the mind, cataloged, and carefully stored for
the right moment. It is genius.

"Genius is nothing more than the knowledge of the use of
tools." We can come back to this quote now, for we are ready.
Genius, in eighteenth-century usage meant more than it does
today. Today it is a mere headful quantity of intelligence. But
then it combined something of the idea of native intelligence
and more. Genius was a tutelary god or attendant spirit that
governed a person's fortunes, his character, and his conduct,
both in and out of this world. Johnson seems to be saying this
tongue-in-cheek, as if to say that when knowledge of the use
of tools has been mastered, one is well on his way to
understanding the notion of this attendant spirit.

Understanding Reference—How-to

Now, what can be done about all this? Three very general
recommendations and five rather specific ones obtain. First
the general ones.

Better Reference Librarian Training Needed—As obvious from the first criticism, this recommendation flows quite naturally. Library schools—of the few that still exist as such—need to undertake a huge reform of their training programs. The reforms must be in the direction of a more factual understanding of reference in general, and research in specific. It may be necessary to break down the general reference course into two parts. Extra course work may also be needed in other areas of reference. Moreover, the tendency of schools to require the memorization (or something quite like it) of Sheehy's (or Winchell's) reference guide must be *added to*. The words are italicized because the memorization needs to be held in place, but additional knowledge is necessary.

It is very trendy these days to excoriate rote memory and lionize conceptual (i.e., higher order) thinking, the one because it is too hard and easily abused, the other, because most anything will pass for it. But this is *not* what is recommended here. Rather, what I am recommending is that reference librarians learn the very broad descriptions of coverage of the 200 reference tools that are often posited in library school courses, but add to those mere adumbrations a more substantive understanding of what is covered. How does coverage in PAIS differ substantively from SSI? This kind of question will lead to a better search process and a higher likelihood of patron success.

Design Apprenticeships in Reference—While not the first to recommend such a procedure, and most assuredly not the last, such a recommendation needs to be made. One of the main objectives of the two-year programs, at least in their initial incarnations, was to stress that the second year be something of an apprenticeship in a number of library work areas. Many library school students do work in a library, but many of them spend vast amounts of time doing clerical work. While realizing that this is a requirement of the libraries in which these students are employed, we cannot afford to neglect the expansion and preservation of the profession. Clerical work hardly increases library search skills.

Apprenticeships should not be designed as only part of the course work of would-be librarians, but it would also be a good idea to expand this concept to a mentoring one when the entry-level professional makes his debut in the library. Pairing a young reference worker with an older, mature, and highly successful worker, whenever possible, will reap many dividends for libraries, patrons, and professionals.

Apprenticeships during library school should be designed so that they expose budding reference workers to more than one way of skinning the reference cat. Such practice is necessary and profitable. Of course, this recommendation requires that library schools be attached to larger research libraries. This is not always the case, as many professionals know. But if the work of librarians is to be considered professional, we will have to take a more professional attitude toward the professional's education.

Can anyone really postulate that a good librarian can emerge from a library school where only minimal library facilities are present? Yes, one can. But it is highly unlikely that many librarians will come from such schools. Everyone points to the Abraham Lincoln story of a lantern and the one-room school, or the Horatio Alger story. But it is instructive to bear in mind that while these figures keep us humble in an age of vast technology, they are easily remembered because they are so few, and so exceptional.

Stress Reference Librarian Accountability—In everyday words say, "Place a greater emphasis on results." Now, this is not a call for the bottom line or any such nonsense as that. We must remember what history teaches about large numbers: Hitler, Stalin, and Mao all had large followings—they also have many tombstones to their names. By stressing the results of reference work, I mean that we should instill in students who are working to become reference librarians that results do matter, and that getting close should never be a point of satisfaction. We must inculcate the necessity of handling patron requests, from wherever they originate, with the utmost speed and success. Were today's reference librarians in our military, we would be in mortal danger. Hitting 50 percent of one's targets would place us all in peril.

Throughout the reference training, stress on success should be made at every point. Questions that test reference skills should progress from easy to hard. Too much of my own training focused on the easy—a book on this, or a figure about that. While it is true that some reference work does include this, there are also reference questions that are extremely hard and must be ferreted out. Every time I teach a reference class, I am always careful to place at least one question in which there is a bum steer, or a way of getting lost. It is instructive for students to know that they will get close to the prey, even hear its snorting and pawing, but will find it, like the unicorn, ever elusive. This must quicken in them a desire to find—to push source hunting to its limits. Anything less and success will never be achieved.

Having said that success must be stressed, that results are important, it must also be pointed out that failures should be expected, but never to the 50 percent range. Failures should be kept and looked at from time to time. My own experience has taught me that when I could not find what was needed at the time, and I persisted long after the request had expired, my subsequent discoveries taught me much about the harder reference hunts. Usually, when you have been successful finding one very difficult question, it will equip you better for a similar hunt later.

These three recommendations, while not masquerading as profundity, do offer the profession a worthy goal. But they focus entirely, or nearly so, on the entering reference librarian. What about the reference librarian already in the profession, perhaps three to five years deep in the reference fray? What can be said to him or to her? Five observations strike me as equally important here.

1. **Gain a Fuller Understanding of Research**—Whether you take research from the French *recherche*, a quest or a pursuit, or from the combined meaning of re- and search, the answer is the same. Research is a process, or, as the OED has it, "A search or investigation of some fact by careful consideration or study of a subject; a course of critical or scientific inquiry." What is missing from modern reference is that aspect of critical inquiry. Very few reference librarians are aware of the nature of research or of its requirements. In order to do better by their clientele, they will have to learn more about this process of critical inquiry.

But wait a minute! you say. Aren't we talking about

reference, not research? Indeed we are, and no, I am not confusing the two. We are looking at the nature of the reference librarian. He or she is referred to, is come to as an *authority.* How can one be an authority on a subject one knows little about? How is it possible to find the animal your patron wants when you, as guide, have never seen it? Understanding better the confines of research, its intricacies, the minutiae, and the broad generalities of it will help reference librarians provide more instructive reference success for patrons.

2. **Make the 80/20 Principle Work for You**—Much research has been done on the 80/20 principle, meaning, of course, that about 80 percent of patron need is supplied by 20 percent of the collection. Something like these figures are very true about reference. Although it is quite true that each library reference course attempts to focus on that 20 percent, each *library* will have the same principle at work. It will most likely not be the same for every library.

As a practicing librarian you should find out which reference books answer most of your clients' questions and learn more about those books. These are probably *not* the same books contained in your ready reference collection, though they will surely be some of them. This will require that you pay attention to your library work, that you make notes after each reference search, and that you take the time—dare I say it—unpaid time, to bone up on those tools that are most helpful to your clients. This will require some study conducted in a quasi-scientific manner, but its rewards will be manifold and its successes truly manifold.

3. **Acquire a Specialty**—As a reference librarian you surely have tastes and propensities in one area that are better suited to you than those you have in others. Perhaps that area of specialty has changed since you were an undergraduate. Whatever it now is, focus on building it up. Gather as much information as you can about that specialty. Learn the many reference tools of that specialty, and, above all, *read* as many of the journals in that specialty area as you possibly can.

It is astonishing to me how many librarians in general write and speak about reading as démodé. It is the lifeblood of a reference librarian, and if you are not doing much of it, you cannot possibly hope to achieve more than a 50 percent "hit" rate. Learning is interconnected. If it were not, we would be able to learn only one thing each. But because our minds are able to make connections with other areas of learning, what we learn in one area will help us with learning in another. Education experts did much to outlaw this notion, eliminating Latin and Greek on the basis that both were useless languages and did nothing for the mind. If anyone has not had second thoughts about that, they must never have studied either of those languages.

Becoming something of an expert in one area will not, of course, make you an automatic expert in another—a common modern fallacy that allows scientific experts automatically to become theologians. But a deep understanding of one area of research will help you enormously with the reference work in other areas. It will train you on how to look and where to look for it. It will also help you to acquire a tenacity that is so desperately needed in library reference work today, but so lamentably absent.

4. **Develop an Awareness of Current Events**—By now some readers may be thinking I just stepped off the boat from the eighteenth century. I've heard worse. Nevertheless, it must be maintained that a current awareness of what is going on in the world is an absolute necessity for librarians, especially reference librarians. This understanding must not be superficial either, limited to what one finds in *Library Journal* or another library magazine.

As I have written elsewhere, reference librarians would be much better off reading *New Republic* and *National Review* than *Time* and *Newsweek*. I say this because *New Republic* and *National Review* are unabashedly biased in favor of the left and the right, respectively. *Time* and *Newsweek* masquerade as magazines that are balanced, or neutral, but in fact are decidedly biased, as most nearly every human, or every human production is. The intellectual rigor of *New Republic* and *National Review* are also much more to be desired than the popular weeklies because of the power of mind needed to read them.

Of course, it does not have to be *New Republic* and *National Review*, but two other magazines, equally biased in their coverage, but in two different directions. I chose these two magazines because they are the most familiar. Such an approach will help the reference librarian gain a fuller understanding of what is going on in the world, what important issues may be coming up for research in the near future, and they are abundant in reference facts. Religion, politics, art, drama, and social issues are a part of each of these journals, and a careful reading will return an astonishing amount of knowledge that plays into the reference librarian's hands (or should I say *head*?) when needed.

5. **Do Original Research**—In a recent survey of professional librarians doing research, it was discovered that most of us are not doing it at all. It is inconceivable how we expect to help others do something we have very little interest in, are not very familiar with, or have never done ourselves. But do not jump to conclusions. I am not calling on all reference librarians to be scholars. But some general interest in a field that calls on the librarian to undertake investigations of his own is bound to be of benefit.

It does not have to be earthshaking, or even momentous, but it should be original and should come under the heading of research. In the same manner that not everyone is cut out for cataloging as a career, not all librarians are reference librarians. But those who dare to take the title should also be responsible for the attendant tasks. It is not possible to become very good at reference work without becoming somewhat useful at what reference work ultimately becomes. It is unconscionable, or should be, that reference librarians would presume to be able to function as such without ever having undertaken the rigors of research. You will note carefully that I did not say "published research." It is the fact of research, not its sometime resulting glory, that makes the difference.

Conclusions

Pick up almost any journal of opinion and you will find something about students and their dismal performance in public schools or in colleges and universities. While this should alarm all of us and make us open to any plausible suggestion of reform, it should be especially alarming to librarians.

With the rate of success at 50 percent, and with students graduating from high schools and colleges with less and less abilities, one can only forecast that the worst is yet to come. In the case of reference librarians, the same is true. A large part of what reference librarians know is based on a liberal arts background. With the foundation weak and getting weaker, we can only suppose that it will soon crumble unless we can fortify its weaknesses. While this is not the provenance of librarians or library schools, we should at least make our contributions where we can—in the library schools, and with ourselves.

If genius is, as Johnson said, nothing more than the knowledge of the use of tools, then we should approach that genius unwavering. Recommended herein is hardly the usual one-two-three approach of most how-to articles. But if reference could be corrected with a one-two-three approach, then perhaps anyone could be a reference librarian. Some of the recommendations, it is true, assume a special attribute or propensity of the librarian, i.e., a love of learning and a desire to know. Other recommendations assume a love of the hunt, of *quellenforschung,* if you will. I meant the assumption. Not everyone is cut out for the work, in the same way that not all of us can be, or are, leaders. But if these attributes are combined in the reference librarian, he will have the necessary tools to improve performance, augment old skills, and satisfy clients. One could not ask for a great deal more.

References

[1] See for example, Terence Crowley, "Half-Right Reference: Is it True?" *RQ* (Fall 1985), pp. 59–67; Tom Eadie, "Immodest Proposals: User-Instruction for Students Does Not Work," *Library Journal* (October 15, 1990), pp. 43–45; and Charles A. Bunge, "Factors Relating to Reference Question Answering Success: The Development of a Data-Gathering Form," *RQ* (Summer 1985), pp. 482–486.

[2] "Half Right Reference." *American Libraries* 16 (May 1985), p. 277.

LEAN AND MEAN: REFERENCE SERVICE IN THE SMALL COMMUNITY COLLEGE

Richard N. Shaw

Community college library budgets are such that all services, including reference, must be lean and mean if they are to survive in a useful way.[1] In the case of reference services I take "lean and mean" to define services that are extremely cost effective and that are of demonstrable and substantial value to library users.

A defining characteristic of the reference service environment in the small community college library is huge variation in library user abilities and skills. This can range from highly skilled faculty needing to do sophisticated research to users who may be barely literate. For a significant number of students enrolled in the small community college, their only adult experience with libraries may very well be in their college library. While success in using the library may not be critical to student retention or to ultimate student success, it can nevertheless be an important factor, especially in shaping the student's general view of the institution. It is imperative, therefore, that all library services, but especially reference, be delivered to users in a competent and caring manner.

As for defining the character of the small community college library itself, some readers may quarrel with the term "library" and prefer to replace it with "learning resource center." I have no wish to add fuel to this particular fire.[2] Reference service has been recognized in the *ACRL/AECT Standards for Community, Junior, and Technical College Learning Resources Programs* as an essential service of the learning resources program, along with other traditional "library" services. Accordingly, the small community college library may be defined as an academic library, which shares characteristics of the small public library, some school libraries, and even special libraries. It differs from these other types of libraries largely in providing services that are not usually found in them, such as audiovisual production services. For the purposes of this article the term "community college library" includes technical colleges, and is defined as a library, learning resources center, instructional resources center, or similar unit, which employs not more than two professionals.

There are numerous small community or technical college libraries around the country. *Peterson's Guide to Two-Year Colleges, 1990* lists 601 colleges having technical or community in their names. A check of these against the *American Library Association Directory, 1990* showed that 356, or 42.6 percent, employed one or two professionals. In some cases the number of library professionals at a given technical or community college could not readily be determined.

The implications of service in a small community college learning resources center or library are familiar to those of us who serve in them. We know that it is entirely routine for a librarian to move quickly from carrying out an administrative function, to providing audiovisual service, to providing reference service, to loading paper in the copier, to technical processing, and back to any of the preceding areas. Reference service is, therefore, only one of many library services provided by one or two professionals in the small learning resources center. It is axiomatic that much of the reference service provided in the small community college library will be provided by nonlibrarians. A major concern will be, therefore, to ensure that any staff who do provide reference service to users have been appropriately trained to carry out this function.

It is also important to note that some small community college libraries are "smaller" than others. A small library or learning resources center that participates in an active local consortium or other interlibrary cooperative arrangement may provide an entirely different variety of reference service than does a library that is geographically isolated or that does not participate in such cooperative arrangements. The implications of such cooperative arrangements, or the implications of their absence, must be carefully considered in planning reference service in the small community college library.

Reference Collections

Effective reference service in any library depends first and foremost on the availability of a carefully selected reference collection that is extremely well-suited to the needs of library users. This collection will usually consist of both print materials and appropriate automated resources such as CD-ROM indexes. Reference collection contents will necessarily vary according to the local institution's program and mission. Collection development in general is beyond the scope of this article, but it is enough to say that it is a fundamental professional responsibility to ensure that the reference collection maintains an appropriate balance between identified user needs and institutional or programmatic requirements.

The reference collection demands ongoing evaluation and maintenance; the reference cows do not stay milked.[3] Each small community college library will have to develop a schedule for updating and replacing reference materials. This replacement schedule may be simple or complex, but it must be tied to budget realities. It also should be sufficiently flexible to allow for curriculum changes or other programmatic changes that may affect reference collection development practices.

As with other areas of collection development, building the reference collection must be done with significant input from the college faculty. The means for gathering this necessary input may include conferences with individual faculty members and/or an advisory committee, as well as circulation to faculty of bibliographies, publishers' lists, or approval slips. Any combination of means that will ensure meaningful faculty participation in building the reference collection, as well as library collections generally, is appropriate. Faculty input will tend to produce a reference collection that is better suited to faculty and student research needs and that is therefore more likely to be used than it otherwise would be. Further, faculty participation in library collection building is mandated by most accrediting agencies. Input for library collection building must also be obtained from administrators, students, and other groups that are served by the library.

There are, of course, standard sources and bibliographies

for selecting print reference materials, all of which must be used in a highly selective fashion in the small community college library. Sheehy's *Guide to Reference Books* continues to be the standard reference bibliography. Supplements are issued between editions, and annual updates are listed in *College and Research Libraries*. ALA's *Reference Sources for Small and Medium-Sized Libraries* is useful, although a new edition is needed. This is updated annually in *American Libraries*. *Library Journal* also runs an annual compilation of best reference books, as does *Choice: Reviews for College Libraries*. *Books for College Libraries* is an essential collection development tool that can be used in part for reference. Bowker's *Reader's Advisor* is also a valuable tool for reference collection building, especially in libraries that are beginning to offer humanities curricula. Some library vendors are also beginning to make available CD-ROM and software packages for collection analysis and comparison, although I am as yet unaware of any that are well-suited to the needs of small community college libraries. This will likely change, however.

There are many specialized bibliographies that will be useful in most small community college libraries. Special Libraries Association publishes *Tools of the Profession*, which can be used for reference selection. This bibliography includes recommended CD-ROMs. A very useful bibliography for Nursing and Allied Health is the so-called Brandon-Hill list[4], which can be obtained from Rittenhouse Book Distributors; many titles are appropriate for reference. Any number of associations make bibliographies available. A check of the *Encyclopedia of Associations* or *Associations' Publications in Print* will suggest some good possibilities in various subject areas.

Special Reference Services

The need for highly specialized, unusually expensive, or unique reference services must be weighed very carefully in the small community college library. While the decision process regarding the provision of new or specialized reference services is likely to be similar in any size library, the effect of such decisions is likely to be much more immediate in a small library with its correspondingly small staff. The most important test for any proposed new reference service or technology is whether it will effectively meet the needs of users. If the proposed service or technology meets this fundamental test, it must pass many others, including a determination of its probable impact on other library services, and on the people who provide them. Issues such as cost, space requirements, ease or difficulty of hardware installation (if any), availability of user support, and staff training must all be considered.

An increasingly common decision for small LRCs is whether to offer CD-ROM resources, and if so, which ones. Library literature is replete with articles on evaluating and selecting CD-ROMs[5], and I do not propose to review those. Rather, I wish to emphasize that it is critically important in a small library not to lose sight of basic and fundamental service concerns. When the printer at the CD-ROM station jams, who will service it? How will you deal with the noise from the printer? Is there adequate space for the CD-ROM station? Is there any need for networking CD-ROMs? If so, are suitable licenses available for the CD-ROM products? Does technical support exist to accomplish the networking? Other questions will be concerned with how much assistance will be rendered to users at the CD-ROM station and who will provide that assistance. In the case of CD-ROMs it is highly desirable to examine the product on-site before purchase, and many vendors now make such on-site trials available. These trials should enable the librarian to determine how much support a particular product will require and what effect the use of the product will have on other library services. The product trial will also place the librarian in a better position to plan for any necessary user or staff training. Product trials are also available with resources other than CD-ROMs (some microform products, for example), and librarians may wish to take advantage of these possibilities.

A library's participation, or lack of it, in local consortia or in other cooperative arrangements will obviously influence many decisions regarding the provision of special reference services. It is certainly possible to develop collaborative arrangements for sharing both the financial and service burdens of new or expensive reference services. Cooperation in reference collection development may be desirable in many situations, especially in regard to avoiding needless duplication of expensive CD-ROM or on-line search services. Networking solutions can also be pursued where appropriate.

Training Users and Staff

Even the best reference collection and the most modern technological resources are of little value if library patrons and library staff do not know how to use them. There is no substitute for (and no excuse for lack of) personal knowledge of the reference collection by the library staff, especially in a small library. Similarly, staff must be fully knowledgeable in the use of whatever technological resources are available. A good method for learning the collection or for gaining familiarity with automated resources is to have staff members give practice reference questions to one another. These can be "made up" questions or they can be based on actual experience. Staff members can then discuss their success or lack of it in finding the answers. Such questions may or may not be geared to the library's actual resources. Gordon Wade has suggested that a subject approach may be a useful way to organize such staff training.[6] Examination and discussion of the use of new reference materials before they go on the shelf is also a good idea.

More formal staff development activities such as attending reference workshops sponsored by area colleges or universities, or by library professional associations, may also be appropriate. Vendors may sponsor training sessions on CD-ROM or similar products, which staff may attend. Professional reading regarding reference service is obviously important for the librarian, although much of what is currently available is not very applicable to the small community college library.

Staff training materials may be available through a state library, a consortium, or may be ordered direct from vendors[7]. In some situations it will be desirable to develop training materials in-house. Marty Bloomberg's *Introduction to Public Services for Library Technicians* will be a valuable text in many small LRCs[8]. Periodic assignments can be made in the text and then discussed. Librarians should select or develop training materials for staff that emphasize positive and effective communication with users rather than specific knowledge of reference sources. Staff members who can communicate effectively with users will provide better reference service than those who cannot do so. It is also important that reference training be understood and planned as an ongoing process and not as a one-time event.

Even in small reference collections some materials may cause particular problems or may require additional attention in the training process. Many community and technical colleges offer, for example, paralegal programs that require their students to make use of a variety of legal materials. Staff must therefore become familiar with these materials, their arrangement, and their use. At the same time, it is important to ensure that most training time is devoted to instruction in answering accurately those kinds of questions that are asked much more frequently than those questions that are not asked so frequently. This is admittedly a difficult balancing act, but it is also an important one.

Dealing with the difficult reference question is a problem in any library setting. In the small community college library it will be necessary to establish guidelines for determining which reference questions should be dealt with by the librarian. This will obviously vary locally, but the critical element is the ability of the staff to produce an accurate answer. Staff members must also be sensitive to any policy implications that might be generated from a reference transaction. A successful search by a faculty member for a video title on AIDS may lead to a policy question regarding the use of audiovisual equipment that must be dealt with by the librarian.

Abundant literature is available on the art of the reference interview[9] and there is no need to review that here. Suffice it to say that carrying out an effective reference interview may be absolutely crucial in a community or technical college library setting where many library users are likely to be relative strangers to libraries. A significant number of community or technical college students are adults who may not have used libraries for several years, or who may have experienced problems in using them earlier[10].

This points clearly and emphatically to the need for an effective bibliographic instruction and orientation program. Here again nonlibrarians will be directly involved in providing this service, so appropriate training is necessary. Not only does such a program perform the useful function of instructing students in using common (or even specialized) reference tools (thereby relieving the library staff of answering at least some of the more routine questions), it may also serve a grander purpose. Some students will, for the first time, find themselves empowered to use information resources they were scarcely aware even existed. The library staff may play a direct role in helping to produce a better informed and more productive citizen. That has, in fact, been for me one of the joys of small community college librarianship.

Evaluation of Services

A final and vital component of effective reference service is ongoing evaluation of the service as a whole. Jo Whitlatch's book *The Role of the Academic Reference Librarian*[11] provides several useful models for examining the process of reference service evaluation. This title also provides a useful survey of research dealing with reference service effectiveness. Whitlatch notes that effective evaluation of reference service depends on both user input and on objective service measures.

In addition, a new resource is available that will assist not only in the evaluation of reference services but of many other library services as well. Recently published as of this writing is ALA's *Academic Library Performance: A Practical Approach*[12]. This volume offers recommended approaches and sample forms for evaluating reference and other library services. The ideas and forms found in the volume can be easily modified to meet the needs of individual libraries. Not only is the volume useful in terms of providing concrete suggestions for evaluat-

ing services, it can also function as a guideline for responding
to state requirements regarding institutional effectiveness,
establishment of performance measures, or providing accountability, whatever the local language may happen to be.

Evaluating services is not enough, however; one must act
effectively on the basis of the evaluation. The librarian must
be prepared to use the results of careful evaluation to change
reference practices that do not work to ones that do work.
The librarian must also be prepared to use the results of
evaluation to negotiate with administrators for budgetary
support of services that have been documented as effective.

References

[1] I am indebted to Lee Hisle at Austin (Texas) Community College
for the title of this article. It was Lee whom I first heard use the
phrase "lean and mean" to describe community college library
services, and it struck me as most apt. See Lee W. Hisle,
"Learning Resources Services in the Community College: On the
Road to the Emerald City," *College & Research Libraries*, 50
(November 1989), pp. 613–625, for an excellent review of both
the history and trends in learning resources services.

[2] See Esther Green Bierbaum, "The Two-Year College LRC:
Promise Deferred?", *College and Research Libraries*, 51 (November 1990), pp. 531–538, for a review of the LRC-library debate.

[3] See *The Reference Librarian (Number 29): Weeding and Maintenance
of Reference Collections*, ed. Sydney J. Pierce (Binghamton: The
Haworth Press, 1990) for a useful survey of the title topic. Steven
Vincent's article "Let's Get Rid of It: a Reference Librarian's
Battle Cry," pp. 145–157, is especially helpful.

[4] Alfred N. Brandon and Dorothy R. Hill, "Selected List of Books
and Journals in Allied Health Sciences," *Bulletin of the Medical
Library Association*, 78, No. 3 (July 1990), pp. 233–251.

[5] Several helpful articles on CD-ROM issues were published in
Library Journal, Vol. 115, No. 2 (1 February 1990).

[6] Gordon W. Wade, "Managing Reference Services in the Smaller
Public Library," *Reference Services Administration and Management,*
ed. B. Katz and R. Fraley (New York: The Haworth Press, 1982),
p. 111.

[7] See *Does This Answer Your Question?* (Baltimore: Library Video
Network/American Library Association, 1985), VHS videorecording, 16 min., or *The Difficult Reference Question* (Baltimore:

Library Video Network/American Library Association, 1986), VHS videorecording, 19 min.

[8]Marty Bloomberg, *Introduction to Public Services for Library Technicians,* 4th ed. (Littleton: Libraries Unlimited, 1985).

[9]See Elaine Z. and Edward J. Jennerich, *The Reference Interview as a Creative Art* (Littleton: Libraries Unlimited, 1987) or three useful articles in *Reference Services Today: From Interview to Burnout,* ed. B. Katz and R. Fraley (New York: The Haworth Press, 1987).

[10]See Jane C. Heiser, "Libraries, Literacy and Lifelong Learning: The Reference Connection," *Reference Services Today,* pp. 109–124, for a useful examination of adult literacy issues in the reference context.

[11]Jo Bell Whitlatch, *The Role of the Academic Reference Librarian* (New York: Greenwood Press, 1990), pp. 19–29.

[12]Nancy A. Van House, Beth T. Weil, and Charles R. McClure, *Measuring Academic Library Performance: A Practical Approach* (Chicago: American Library Association, 1990).

DEVELOPING THE REFERENCE COLLECTION

Dale Luchsinger

The reference collection in the community college library exists to meet the information needs of the academic community that the library serves. To meet these needs requires an understanding of the institution and the educational program. The academic program, individual instructor needs, and student requests all must be considered in developing the reference collection. The reference collection serves as a primary source of information for the users of the community college library.

A core collection of information sources, including indexes, encyclopedias, government documents, dictionaries, handbooks, atlases, bibliographies, and other reference sources, must be available to provide a wide spectrum of information that will facilitate and support the educational purpose and process of the institution. The following bibliographic sources may be used to develop the core collection in community college libraries.

Blazek, Ron, and Elizabeth Aversa. *The Humanities: a Selective Guide to Information Sources,* 3rd ed. Englewood, CO: Libraries Unlimited, 1988. Use this work for reference sources in philosophy, religion, language, literature, and the performing and visual arts.

Books for College Libraries: a Core Collection of 50,000 Titles. 6 volumes. 3rd ed. Chicago: American Library Association, 1988. This is an invaluable source for identifying basic reference sources that are useful in the two-year college library. Although this is a basic listing of titles for the four-year undergraduate college library, many of the same titles are necessary for the community college library. Librarians should use this extensive bibliography as an authority for identifying retrospective titles that would strengthen selected subject areas of the collection.

Gates, Jean K. *Guide to the Use of Libraries and Information Sources.* 6th ed. New York: McGraw-Hill, 1989. Intended to help college students learn about libraries, Gates includes many bibliographic citations to reference sources that community college libraries will find useful. It is an excellent listing of reference materials for first-priority purchase for small and developing reference collections.

Katz, William. *Introduction to Reference Work.* 2 volumes. 6th ed. New York: McGraw-Hill, 1992. A basic guide to equally basic reference works and reference services. It is employed in most library schools and many libraries of all types and sizes.

Herron, Nancy L., ed. *The Social Sciences: a Cross- Disciplinary Guide to Selected Sources.* Englewood, CO: Libraries Unlimited, 1989. Along with essays for each of the social science fields, this title is an excellent source for social science materials that the users of the community college library might find useful. Good detailed annotations add to the value of this book.

Readers's Adviser: a Layman's Guide to Literature. 6 volumes. 13th ed. New York: Bowker, 1986. Librarians should use this source as a book selection tool for developing the community college library in the subject areas of the humanities and the social sciences. This venerable publication from Bowker has served readers and librarians alike for many years to identify the best reading and information sources.

Sader, Marion, ed. *General Reference Books for Adults: Authoritative Evaluations of Encyclopedias, Atlases, and Dictionaries.* New York: R.R. Bowker, 1988. Especially useful because this source covers the evaluation of encyclopedias, atlases, and dictionaries, plus detailed analyses of titles common to many libraries.

Sheehy, Eugene P., ed. *Guide to Reference Books.* 10th ed. Chicago: American Library Association, 1986. This is a comprehensive bibliographic work that lists reference works available in most subject areas. Use it to identify titles in specific areas where the reference collection is weak.

Webb, William H. *Sources of Information in the Social*

Sciences: a Guide to the Literature. 3rd ed. Chicago: American Library Association, 1986. This is a helpful source for reference titles in history, geography, economics, sociology, anthropology, psychology, education, and political science.

Wynar, Bohdan S., ed. *American Reference Books Annual.* Englewood, CO: Libraries Unlimited, 1970– . Annually, this series comprehensively reviews U.S. and Canadian English-language reference titles in all subject areas. The detailed reviews make this a worthwhile selection tool.

Wynar, Bohdan S., ed. *ARBA Guide to Subject Encyclopedias and Dictionaries.* Littleton, CO: Libraries Unlimited, 1986. An annotated guide to subject encyclopedias and dictionaries selected from *American Reference Books Annual* provides help with selections of specialized reference materials.

Selection of Titles

There is not a single published core collection of reference sources that the community college librarian may use that will satisfy the information needs of every community college library user. Although there are similarities among community college libraries that necessitate some common reference materials, there are individual differences in courses, strengths of each institution, and academic programs that require librarians to make judgment calls on which titles should be purchased to meet the needs of a single library. Budget limitations require the judicious expenditure of funds to cover not only reference sources, but other materials for the library as well. Rarely are there enough funds to purchase everything that might be useful in a community college library.

Decisions must be made to ensure that retrospective titles provide the core of information that the college librarian needs to meet the informational needs of students and instructors. Keeping brief written records of library information requests provides documentation of how well actual requests for information are handled. An atmosphere within the library that permits input from all staff who work at providing information to have a voice in the selection of new reference materials will help balance the collection with needs of clients.

Let instructors and students know that you encourage their input for materials needed for assignments. Faculty in two-year institutions have heavy teaching loads, sometimes having all their work time assigned to classrooms and laboratories with students. There are few opportunities for them to spend time selecting library materials. Their emphasis is on teaching students rather than research and publishing. The astute librarian keeps them informed about significant library reference purchases and consults with them on library expenditures as time allows.

Keep abreast of current enrollment numbers in every academic area so that growing areas of the curriculum will be reflected in an expanding collection of reference materials. It is always useful for the librarian to be an ex officio member of the curriculum committee so that as changes in the academic program and curriculum are known, library needs may be anticipated and met.

A network of reference librarians within a state or region is useful for the librarian working in a community college. Networks contribute ideas about library operations and facilitate the development and sharing of library resources. Recommended lists of reference titles for the start-up library along with collection development policies may be shared to give beginner librarians ideas on how to proceed to develop their own institutional libraries.

Reviews of reference sources in current periodicals will provide access to information about new titles, new editions of previously published titles, and new volumes of reference sets published at regular intervals. Among those titles that should be regularly read for new reviews of reference materials are *Booklist, Library Journal, Reference & Research Book News, RQ,* and *Wilson Library Bulletin.*

Some of these journals provide a bonus by giving readers recommendations of the best reference titles published during the year. Both *Library Journal,* with its "Best Reference Books of the Year," and *American Libraries,* with its annual report of the ALA/RASD Reference Sources Committee's "Outstanding Reference Sources," provide high-quality lists and bibliographic notes on the titles to aid in the selection of reference titles. New titles and updated editions provide information in many areas that will be useful in the community college library. These surveys of reference titles provide a helpful way to be certain that no significant reference books published during the past year were overlooked by the selector.

One periodical geared to the reference professional, *Reference Services Review,* offers survey articles covering the reference information area. It includes bibliographic essays that give excellent overviews of popular reference subject areas. Use these fine essays to improve reference skills as well as to obtain knowledge of basic reference sources in selected areas.

Probably no one individual can develop the collection solely on that person's knowledge of what the information needs are in a library. An individual librarian may direct the development of the reference collection by assessing needs and identifying which reference sources will help meet the needs for information. The librarian responsible for reference source decisions in collection building has a special responsibility to bring together the informational needs of the institution and translate these needs into intelligent decisions on additions to the reference collection. Reference collection development is both an art and a science tempered with knowledge of the institution and a willingness to select resources that will help clients effectively use information for their own personal and academic development.

Evaluation of the Reference Collection

It is not unusual for an experienced librarian to visit another library and to know instinctively that the reference collection is dated with older reference materials that should have been discarded or replaced with the latest editions of reference titles. A dated reference collection may be an indication that funds are not available to purchase up-to-date materials or that the library staff puts little emphasis on maintaining a collection that is current. Although this is a bit of a superficial judgment on the currency of a collection, librarians should make every effort to replace information sources that change and appear with new information annually. General encyclopedias should be placed on a purchasing schedule so that sets will be replaced approximately every three to five years. Each year one new set of encyclopedias should be purchased to replace the same older set that may be from three to five years old. Funds should be allocated to replace older editions of other reference titles that appear annually with substantial amounts of new information.

Along with timeliness of information available in reference sources, the librarian must consider the changing nature of the academic programs in the community college. As colleges grow and change direction, it is easy to overlook these program changes when new materials are purchased. On an annual basis the librarian should assess the direction of the institutional academic program and attempt to maintain a reference collection that meets the needs of the developing curriculum. As dated materials or materials that are no longer appropriate for the reference collection are evident, decisions must be made on withdrawing the materials and discarding them, placing them in the circulating collection, or offering them to another library in the region where the materials might be more useful. Funds should be budgeted for replacing outdated reference materials as well as for the purchase of materials to build and fill gaps in the collection.

Library evaluation with both instructor and student input may identify weak areas of the collection that can be addressed in future purchase decisions. Those who work in and use the community college library must feel that they are helping to build the collection with sources that will provide information to facilitate the educational mission of the institution.

By keeping careful but brief records of successful and unsuccessful reference question transactions, the librarian can gain insight into whether the collection is meeting information needs of students and instructors. A daily reference log that lists the brief information requests and whether the information was satisfactorily provided is a useful tool for ascertaining how well the reference collection provides information to users.

Periodicals are an essential source of current information in the community college library. For the user to quickly locate needed information in periodicals, indexes must be used to access these publications. Although the *Readers' Guide to Periodical Literature* is often the standard index that many students would first mention as the one with which they are most familiar, there are a variety of printed subject indexes in most of the areas that users need information. The cost of indexes may be high but the cost is less significant if you consider that indexes are the most efficient means of locating information in hundreds of periodical titles.

The community college librarian has a responsibility to expose students to a variety of periodical indexes to provide information for academic programs in the community college. The librarian also needs to provide students who may transfer to a four-year college with a foundation for using the resources of a larger library including periodicals that may be more specialized. Students working on bachelor degrees often require specialized resources for writing papers or giving reports in their last two years of study. The two-year college library must be able to introduce students to these specialized indexes and help students use them with ease.

This is the time and place for students to become effective users of libraries. When bibliographic instruction is used to introduce students to the library, indexes are useful tools to demonstrate how information is accessed. Along with other reference sources and the public catalog, avenues of information are opened for students. As students pursue their undergraduate education, the value of libraries as information providers will become evident. The challenge for librarians is to provide community college students with every opportunity to use and become familiar with the broad spectrum of reference sources.

FEE-BASED INFORMATION SERVICES: SERVING BUSINESS/STRENGTHENING THE LRC

Diane Grund

Links between community colleges and business have been in evidence for more than a decade, but the last few years have seen the increased involvement of more traditional college departments with off-campus concerns. In response to the recession of the early 1980s, all areas at Moraine Valley Community College were challenged to seek ways to assist companies in the district in order to strengthen the economic base of the community. The learning resources center responded to this challenge with the creation of the Business-Oriented Search Service (BOSS), a full-service information center that functions as a corporate library for businesses that have neither the financial nor human resources to perform these services in-house. BOSS assists companies with their information needs by providing reference and research, on-line data-base searches, document delivery via photocopy of interlibrary loan, corporate borrowing privileges, and facsimile transmission service—all on a cost-recovery basis.

It is often assumed that fee-based information services are only possible within large, research-oriented institutions. Experience with BOSS has shown that this is not necessarily true. In responding to some inquiries, the more extensive collections available at a university library would prove beneficial. Yet, the questions posed by most small and medium-sized businesses are well within the abilities of a competent reference librarian utilizing a solid community college LRC, on-line sources, and the telephone. In general, the information needs of this clientele are based on day-to-day business needs, not on complex research issues. In most instances the service is consulted because the firm is unaware of resources and/or does not have the time or staff available to locate the information.

It does not necessarily follow, however, that because all LRCs have resources and provide information that every LRC should establish a fee-based service. The initial consideration regarding the possible development of this program at any institution should revolve around two essential questions. First of all, does the institutional mission statement support the development of this type of service? The mission statement should be examined to determine if the program is compatible with the stated purpose of the college. At Moraine Valley the philosophical basis for BOSS can be found in the statement that indicates that it is a tenet of the college to "provide services to the community which are appropriate and beneficial." Meetings with administration to review the proposal throughout its development assured that this objective was met. It also provided an opportunity to respond to questions and build support for the program prior to its final presentation and acceptance by the administration. Without a commitment by the college, the project would not have been possible.

Second, implementation of the service can provide benefits to both the client and the LRC, but does the staff as a whole want to take on this project? If they do, it must be with the realization that serving the corporate sector on a fee basis will at some time impact individuals and work areas throughout the entire LRC. Considerations include the fact that working for a fee often requires that the activity take precedence over others. It may mean that there will need to be adjustments in schedules with little or no notice in order to meet deadlines. BOSS is not a difficult program to replicate in terms of the services being supplied, but it may require the assistance of staff not normally involved with the program: Are they willing? Even if the mission statement permitted the development of the service, it would not be possible to proceed without staff support. If that is forthcoming, then it is appropriate to begin development of the program.

Planning the Service

Although the "fees for service" concept is not in itself new to LRCs, implementation of a program of this complexity requires extensive planning. Because the LRC will, in essence, be operating a small business, approaching the process via the development of a business plan is not unrealistic. This method also provides the benefit of familiarizing staff with the problems that are encountered by their potential clients. There are a number of tools available that can detail the business plan approach; all cover the essential elements that must be considered.

As with all new undertakings, the first issue to be addressed is purpose. A mission statement must be written that delineates why the LRC wants to undertake this activity. This statement will help to clarify the purpose of service as well as to define the clientele and identify appropriate services.

The proposal itself will cover all aspects of the operation. It should identify the clientele and the basic geographic area to be served. A market survey will be essential if the LRC does not have access to recent demographic data on proposed service area businesses and research about the information needs of these firms. In some institutions this information is readily available through the college research office. If it is not, research staff may be available to assist in the construction of a survey instrument. In the development of the BOSS proposal, the LRC utilized an industrial retention study, which had been conducted the previous year. This survey revealed that only a few of the 1,000 in-district firms responding to the survey had any in-house information facility and that access to information was essential if these companies were going to compete effectively in today's marketplace.

The plan should also address the types and levels of service to be offered. There is no single approach. LRCs, their institutions, and the communities they serve are not alike; thus, the services that are offered should not be alike. The decision regarding which to offer should be based on the needs of the businesses in the service area as well as an analysis of the strengths and weaknesses of the LRC and the institution. Components to be considered include staff (from the standpoint of both skills and number), time availability, and institutional policies and procedures. The contributions that could be made by non-LRC departments and staff should also be considered when identifying potential services. In planning BOSS, document translation was discussed with appropriate faculty members, and BOSS has been able to provide this option to clients utilizing non-BOSS personnel. In addition, the LRC and the graphics department discussed the possibility of offering signage and other graphics services to clients. Although these were not implemented, this activity remains a possibility for the future.

Once the services are identified, a determination can be made regarding personnel needs. One individual should be identified and given responsibility for all aspects of the service. Organizational skills are of great importance because of the coordination necessary to respond to client requests and at the same time keep the administrative functions of the service operating—billing, mailings, marketing, and so on. In many operations this administrator is the sole contact person for clients even though he or she may not be the total service provider. Great care should be taken in identifying the "right" individual. The ability to work with corporate clients, to speak the language of business rather than academe, and to grasp the immediacy of client needs is essential. While it might be assumed that a business reference background is important, experience with BOSS has shown this not necessary. The types of questions posed by companies often are not business-based. Listed below are some of the inquiries that BOSS has responded to in the last few years:

> "When was the _____ Building in Galena completed, and for what purpose was it used originally?"

> "I need background information on the impact of asbestos; can you get me some good books or articles?"

> "Our condominium association is fighting a proposed helipad site on a nearby building; we want to know all

about emergency helicopters and FAA regulations governing their use. . . . Can we also get newspaper articles
on any helicopter crashes that have occurred within the
city during the last five years?"

It should be obvious that any good reference librarian could
readily respond to questions of this nature; business reference
experience is a plus, not an essential.

In smaller volume operations, the service administrator
could provide most of the reference service, with other
members of the LRC professional staff serving as backup in an
as-needed capacity. In responding to client inquiries BOSS
has also called upon instructional technologies technical staff,
faculty, and administrators, who have fulfilled the role of
consultants on several projects.

Technical and/or secretarial support is also needed on a
regular basis for word processing, photocopying, and record
keeping and billing, as well as any other clerical activity. In
some instances it may prove possible for the fee-based service
activities to plug into and use existing LRC operations.
Perhaps the best example of this within BOSS is with
interlibrary loan requests; client requests are channeled into
the existing procedures and processed in the same manner as
any other patron request. Separate BOSS statistics are kept
by staff in that department to determine the level of demand
attributable to BOSS.

Other basic considerations to review in planning the
service include housing, hours, and general access. A decision
must be made regarding the physical location of the service
and its availability to the public. Some services are available
on a walk-in basis; others operate by appointment only. All
have a direct telephone line. It has been the experience at
BOSS that some clients will feel more comfortable in using
the service after a face-to-face meeting; therefore, an office,
however small, is a necessity in order to establish an atmosphere of professionalism and assure confidentiality. Hours
of operation can be tailored to the institution, but most clients
will expect the service to maintain standard business hours.
An answering service/machine can aid in extending coverage
both during and after scheduled hours.

Addressing Complex Issues

In addition to these basic components of the program, a number of very complex issues need to be addressed. As each one of these could be the subject of an entire chapter, we will simply allude to the need to consider these aspects of the service in the planning process. The resource materials listed at the conclusion of the chapter will be of assistance in establishing local policies and procedures.

One issue that causes much discussion is the fee structure. Operating on a nonprofit, cost-recovery basis sounds simple, but what elements will be involved in determining cost recovery: salaries, data-base fees, heat, telephone, supplies, postage, equipment maintenance, custodial fees, and so on? Will inclusion of all elements price your service beyond the reach of potential clientele? How should services be priced: by the hour, the type of service provided, or a combination of the two?

Another question involves copyright law, an issue that remains open to interpretation and discussion. Will the service pay royalties to the copyright owner or are the documents provided under fair-use guidelines? What notification will be given to clientele regarding copyright law? It may prove necessary to consult institutional legal counsel to determine the position of the college and the service with regard to this very complex matter.

Quality control will also be a problem regardless of the size of the staff. What mechanisms will be used to allow the administrator to determine if the response to any inquiry was timely, provided sufficient material, and was appropriate to the needs of the client? Without internal checks and feedback from clients it will be impossible to assess the quality of the service.

To this point administrative decisions that primarily involve only the LRC staff have been examined, but there are others that require outside assistance. The research department should be contacted to assist in the development of the survey, which will help to identify target markets. The publications department will need to be apprised of the need for marketing materials. The fee-based aspect will require that arrangements be made with the accounting department regarding account codes, invoicing procedures, noncollectible accounts, and so on. It will take time and effort to resolve the interdepartmental issues that arise because of the uniqueness of this program, but there are definite benefits provided from the ability to tap into the existing specialized services and the expertise that already exists on many campuses.

Operating a Fee-based Service

It should be apparent that implementing and operating a fee-based information service within the community college LRC increases the workload at all levels. In assessing this program, it is our belief that the benefits accrued far outweigh any disadvantages. As a service entity, BOSS complements the mission of the college, the mission of the LRC, and our mission as librarians. It builds on the processes and procedures already in place to support regular clientele to serve an essentially unserved population in a unique manner. We are comfortable with the fee aspect because we provide specialized, personal service, which clients can avail themselves of without leaving the office. Many businesses hire accounting firms to manage their financial problems and law firms to deal with their legal questions; is it a far stretch to hire information specialists to solve information problems? The program is not in competition with public libraries. Most cannot provide the type of service BOSS provides, and referrals from this group are common.

In addition, these partnerships with the business community have served to extend the visibility of the institution within the community as well as to enhance the image of the LRC within the college. A service such as BOSS provides an excellent opportunity for public relations: articles have appeared in the local and metropolitan area press, including *Crain's Chicago Business*, the manager has appeared on a television interview program, and presentations have been made at national conferences. Incubator businesses have been attracted to the campus due in part to the availability of specialized services like BOSS.

BOSS has also provided the opportunity for the LRC to assert its role within the institution. In-house usage of the LRC by administrative offices and faculty has increased. The fact that the LRC is paid fees by noncampus clients has served to heighten awareness of the competency of the LRC staff throughout the college; librarians have become valued for their knowledge, not just for the tools that they use.

The existence of BOSS has done much to enhance our ability to respond to LRC and patron needs. Twenty years ago the library was viewed as the heart of the educational institution. Today the LRC is competing with other departments for more limited budget allocations, and it often seems that the mission to provide solid bibliographic and audiovisual assistance to students, staff, and community does not automatically bring the same levels of financial support as were previously available. Monies from BOSS have enabled the LRC to purchase specialized business resources that benefit both the clients and the students; a fax machine that is utilized by the entire campus was purchased from BOSS revenues. Based on the LRC's contact with the business community, one high-technology materials vendor placed his expensive product at the college at no cost.

Operating a fee-based information service continues to be a daily challenge. Would the LRC take on this project again? Probably yes. At a time when community colleges across the country stress the importance they play in fostering the economic development of an area, services like BOSS underscore an institution's commitment to that effort. In addition, BOSS has provided the LRC with the means to enhance its image, extend its collection, and strengthen its budget—all without abandoning its basic service mission.

References

BOOKS

Conference on Fee-Based Research in College & University Libraries, *Proceedings.* June 17–18, 1982. Center for Business Research, Greenvale, NY, 1982.

Fee-Based Services: Issues & Answers. Second Conference on Fee-Based Research in College and University Libraries, Proceedings. May 10–12, 1987. Michigan Information Transfer Source, Ann Arbor, MI, 1987.

Maranjian, L. and R. W. Boss. *Fee-based Information Services: a Study of a Growing Industry,* New York: Bowker, 1980.

Operating and Marketing Fee-Based Services in Academic Libraries: a Small Business Approach. Chicago: Association of College and Research Libraries, 1986.

Warner, A. S. *Making Money: Fees for Library Services.* New York: Neal-Schuman, 1988.

ARTICLES

Broadbent, C. "Pricing Information Products and Services." *Drexel Library Quarterly* 17 (Spring 1981), pp. 99–107.

Donnellan, A. M. and L. Rasmussen, "Fee-based Services in Academic Libraries: Preliminary Results of a Survey." *Drexel Library Quarterly* 19 (Fall 1983), pp. 68–79.

Heller, J. S. "Copyright and Fee-based Copying Services." *College and Research Libraries* 47 (January 1986), pp. 28–37.

INTEREST GROUPS

Contact the American Library Association for the name of the current chair.

BRASS (Business Reference and Services)

FISCAL (Fee-Based Information Service Centers in Academic Libraries)

SOUTH CAROLINA TECHNICAL COMMUNITY COLLEGES AND TECHNOLOGY TRANSFER

L. Gene Elliott

Businesses and industries sometimes fail because new technology is not located and applied. Management often fails to stay current on new methodology and products. At the same time, the federal research and development sector invests millions of dollars in developing new technology, which is available to business and industry.

An efficient delivery system between the two sectors affords sizable savings and greater efficiency for firms taking advantage of existing technology. Traditionally, community colleges have not been involved in this exchange at the national level. But with improving computer technology coupled with accessible data bases, these institutions are being encouraged to participate in information delivery to local businesses and entrepreneurs.

NASA (National Aeronautics and Space Administration) has had a technology transfer process operating for close to 30 years. It was established with the objective of having NASA-sponsored or -produced research and technology transferred to the public and private sectors. Technology passes from NASA research and development centers such as Langley Research Center to organizations such as STAC (Southern Technology Applications Center).

Southern Technology Applications Center

STAC is an organization consisting of a network of resources and expertise sponsored by the Florida State University System and NASA. It is headquartered in Gainesville, Florida, at the University of Florida.

Another component of the NASA Technology System consists of Industrial Applications Centers located on various university campuses or at nonprofit corporations. These provide regional access to NASA technology and build links among NASA, universities, and the private sector by recruiting consultants.

Another component is the Application Team, located at Research Triangle Park in Raleigh, North Carolina. This arm attempts to design ways to take NASA technology into the marketplace.

STAC maintains offices in various Florida universities, in their colleges of engineering or business. In Georgia, STAC affiliates with Georgia Institute of Technology; in Alabama, with the University of Alabama in Huntsville; in Tennessee, with the University of Tennessee and Memphis State University. In Arkansas, it is located at the University of Arkansas at Little Rock, and in South Carolina, it affiliates with the State Board of Technical and Comprehensive Education (SBTCE), the umbrella organization of the state's 16 technical community colleges.

In South Carolina it was decided that the SBTCE was the best place for transfer to be facilitated, since the 16 technical community colleges were electronically networked and geographically situated so as to provide efficient information flow statewide to prospective business clients.

The foundation of the transfer program is the use of worldwide computer data-bases, including the NASA Recon data-base, DIALOG, Department of Energy Recon, BRS, SDC, and Pergamon.

Clients are afforded access not only to data-bases and document delivery, but networks of consultants and experts. Florida provided a data-base of all university and college faculty, together with their respective specialties, and called it Florida Research Profiles. South Carolina has plans to provide a similar data-base.

The South Carolina State Tech Board created a management guide for technology transfer in 1987. The contact office at the colleges for clients interested in technology is the library, or specifically, the director or reference librarian. The librarians network the clients with STAC, while first providing local reference services.

Marketing of the services began both at the state and local levels. The State Board provided a descriptive color brochure describing the transfer process and the opportunities it afforded. These brochures were made available for distribution by the colleges. Other means of advertising used included articles in periodicals, newspaper ads, and exhibits at trade shows.

Local marketing efforts involve direct mail, paid ads, continuing education activities, Chambers of Commerce, and other economic development groups, and personal telephone calls to prospective clients.

The plan states that each college that elects to handle requests locally should have at least two librarians trained in on-line data-base searching. To facilitate this, the SBTCE provides introductory and advanced DIALOG search training for as many librarians as finances will permit.

Once a client requests services from the college library staff, an interview is held with a librarian. A *Search Definition Form* is filled out, which defines the search, determines its confidentiality, lists search descriptors, and provides limits on information and cost. (See the sample form on pages 126–127.) The director or designated librarian determines if the search is within local capabilities. If a decision is made to forward the request to STAC, the Search Definition is also forwarded, and the STAC personnel will contact the client if additional information is needed to satisfy the request. Once the search is complete, the results are to be given to the client in such a way as to enhance the credibility of NASA, State Technical Education system, and the individual college. That is, the answers to the research problem move from STAC to the local college, and finally back to the client.

To show the possibilities that this process affords the local businessperson or would-be entrepreneur, we can illustrate by describing a situation that took place at Greenville Technical College, Greenville, South Carolina. An organization that meets regularly at the college is the Carolina

Inventor's Council (CIC). This group consists of members who hold at least one patent or are interested in developing an idea into a possible patent. Organization meetings are geared to providing information on how to get inventions patented, marketed, and sold. During one of these meetings, the library director explained to the membership the opportunities afforded with technology transfer and reference assistance available from the college library.

Joyce Selph joined the CIC and began to make use of these opportunities. She had invented a pet car carrier, which she called a Pooch Pouch. This device kept dogs and cats from crawling all over the car's interior while the vehicle was in transit. She was having difficulty knowing how to obtain a patent to protect her idea and in finding a prospective manufacturer. About a year after having invented this device, she heard about the CIC and joined. The members explained the patent process to her and explained how technology transfer could help her.

By consulting U.S. and world patent indexes, she might discover materials already patented that could be used in manufacturing her product. She could discover if a similar product existed. Other data-bases could tell her which advertisers would be best suited to support her product.

The name Pooch Pouch might be a potential problem. Would there be a better name for her product? A search of the data-base Trademarkscan could turn up any products using similar names. Other data-bases, such as Electronic Yellow Pages, could help with a mailing list of potential customers.

Joyce found that the name Pooch Pouch was being used, so she changed her potential product's name to Park-a-Pooch. She was then able to apply for a patent, find a local manufacturer, advertise in several pet magazines, and begin marketing her product. Joyce's needs were met by the local inventors' group and Greenville Tech's Library, and in this instance, the services of STAC were not needed. Other examples are plentiful.

At Apollo Beach, Florida, Andrew Leonard found that he could not do without STAC. Leonard designed a direct-current electrical power system used in hospitals. Self-

```
                        SEARCH DEFINITION FORM
Date:_____   Job#:_____    P.O.#_____

Client Name:_____  Title:_____

Company Name:_____  Phone #:_____

Address:_____

        _____

Completion Date:_____   Searcher:_____

Search Cost:_____ Results:_____

_____

*****************************************************************

1. What is the topic of your search?_____

   _____

2. Is this confidential?   ☐ Yes   ☐ No

3. What would you like us to find?_____

   _____

   _____

   _____

4. Who will ultimately use the information we find?_____

   _____

5. How and where will it be used? _____

   _____

6. Have you (client) already done any research on the topic? ☐ Y ☐ N

7. How old is the information you have?_____

8. Are there any authors you know of whose work is of special interest
   to you in this field?   ☐ Yes   ☐ No

9. What are these authors' names? _____

                                  _____

                                  _____
```

Search Definition Form

10. In what publications would you expect to find this information?

    _____

    _____

11. What are some synonyms or closely related terms for your ideas,
    terms, processes, products, methods or techniques?_____

    _____

    _____

12. Is there alternate spelling for any of these synonyms? ☐ Yes ☐ No
    What are they?_____

13. How much information do you expect us to find?_____

    _____

14. How many citations would you like?   ☐ Under 25   ☐ 25-50   ☐ Over 50

15. Are there any language restrictions?_____

16. What time span should be covered?_____

17. If we find less information than you requested, can we broaden the
    search strategy? ☐ Yes ☐ No
    How?_____

18. If we find more than you requested, how can we narrow the search?

    _____

    _____

19. What are your financial limitations?_____

20. What is your deadline (date) for receiving this information?_____

21. Will you order the full-text documents?   ☐ Yes ☐ No

22. Do you want to be kept up on this topic in the future? ☐ Yes ☐ No

23. Would you like help finding an "expert" on this topic either as a
    consultant or to conduct research and development? ☐ Yes ☐ No

Search Definition Form (continued)

regulated by a PC-driven expert system, the invention maintains electrical power balances in different modules at all times. This can be lifesaving when power outages occur.

Through contacts at STAC's Tampa office and small-business organization meetings, it was determined that the product had space station applications as well. STAC officials then steered Leonard to experts in the Florida university system. The resulting network of individuals has ultimately contributed to the success of his new company, Critical Power Consultants, Inc. Andrew Leonard vows to use STAC for testing the market for the new product, and he is appreciative of the success of his venture at relatively low cost due to the presence of STAC.

Jeffrey Warren of Engineering Design and Testing Corporation near Columbia, South Carolina, benefited from technology transfer. His firm was working with a client who was attempting to automate a plant for processing nuclear materials. They needed to know what types of air cylinders and valves could be used, as well as how robots would function in such an atmosphere. He contacted Midlands Technical College Library after finding at a trade show that the service was available. An appropriate data-base was found, which provided the answers.[1]

Since 1988, when South Carolina's technical community colleges became involved in technology transfer, requests for assistance from STAC have not been numerous. In the first year of 1988, there were 18 searches referred to STAC by nine of the colleges. These nine produced 77 searches for industry, 279 for faculty, and 15 for students, which along with the 18 for STAC, totaled 371 for the calendar year.

Even though the referrals to STAC have not been great in number, those in the community college system are hopeful that the service will be increasingly used as it becomes better known. Having the technology transfer service as an alternative at the local college level makes it easier for the college library to advertise reference and on-line search services to local business and industry. This adds to the public's confidence that if the local college cannot deliver, there is a more extensive and expert service available. At the same time, local publicity about each college's services has produced more requests for reference and on-line searches. Thus the colleges have helped to create a better climate for business in South Carolina.

References

[1]Frank D. Durham, "STAC launches entrepreneur into space industry," *Florida Spotlight on Technology,* (January-February 1989), p. 5.

PART III: COMPUTERIZED REFERENCE SERVICES

A TRIP DOWN CD-ROM LANE

Douglas K. Lehman

Once upon a time there were no CD-ROMs in this world. I know this seems impossible to comprehend now, but it is true. Why, only as far back in the mists of time as the early 1980s, those creatures did not exist. How in the world did we ever survive as librarians? Or have we sold our souls for life in the fast lane? After all, with the *Readers' Guide* available on CD-ROM, why should a student ever learn to use the paper copy? For that matter, why should your library even continue to subscribe to the paper copy? I think there are more questions than answers to this problem, and librarians have been struggling to come up with solutions since those little shiny disks first appeared at our doorsteps.

Of course, it is not just the small silver platters that we have to contend with, is it? No, now we have to mess with computers and monitors and CD-ROM drives and printers and software. Software that usually does not like any other software residing on the same computer with it and so causes all kinds of headaches for the librarian. It seems like there has to be a simpler way of life. In some parts of the United States, there are groups of people known as the Amish. They live without electricity, automobiles, tractors, and indoor plumbing. They lead life the way we did 100 years ago. Perhaps they are happier because of their lifestyle, but think of everything they are missing out on. Sort of like life before CD-ROMs for librarians.

When did these CD-ROM products start invading our libraries? And where did they all come from? Who is responsible for this?

Well, the whole thing started back many, many years ago. As far back as the 1940s Vannevar Bush, in an article for *The Atlantic Monthly,* envisioned a device he named the "memex" for lack of a better term. The machine proposed by Bush would be similar to a desk but would have several screens, a keyboard, and buttons and levers. Part of the memex would be used to store information. Bush conceived of a device in which we would continually add information as we came across it via a microfilm camera in the desk, as well as adding contents already available through microfilm. The major drawback in the 1940s was that microfilm technology did not possess the optics required to reduce and then enlarge documents as required by the memex. In fact micrographics have still not reached the level of development in common usage required for the memex, but the concept put forth by Bush in 1945 certainly sounds like a step on the pathway we are walking today.

Of course, the years since 1945 have not been a wasteland. Micrographics has continued to grow and expand. While commonly distributed microfiche is in the 24X to 48X reduction category, ultrafiche made its appearance requiring extremely high-powered magnification to return the document to a readable format. Still and all, these formats left much to be desired for the common user. Perhaps the major patron complaint concerning microformat documents is the propensity of the user to get headaches or dizziness. Headaches usually are caused by a patron spending many hours looking at a reverse-image document. All those little white lights shining through the dark background could give anyone a headache. Dizziness usually comes when the patron tries to read the microfilm (I believe dizziness is confined to microfilm, not the other varieties) at a slow speed or watches it as it traverses the screen. This is not a pleasant feeling, and only through practice can one develop the technique of not watching the screen or trying to read the moving image.

So for years micrographics, particularly microfilm and microfiche, remained the main, if not the only, mass full-text storage medium available to the library public.

The Videodiscs Appear

Sometime in the latter part of the twentieth century, oh, around 1980, scientists working long and hard in their little laboratories came up with the technology that would allow them to take a disk that looked like a long-playing record album that had been spray-painted by a vandal with silver paint. Only something wasn't quite right here. This thing was shiny. It didn't quite glow in the dark, but it sure was different. These strange-looking devices first showed up in video stores, and they claimed there were movies on them. It seems some scientists had devised a means of putting images on the shiny undersurface of these refuges from someone's home movie of UFOs. Not only were there movies there, but these movies looked better than anything you had seen (including if you had seen it in the theater) or heard. Of course they did, because they were digitized. Ah, but would they sell? Unfortunately, no. Why? Because you had to buy an expensive piece of equipment to play them on and besides videocassette recorders (VCRs) were coming on the market, and guess what? You could record a movie at home from television and play it back with one of those VCR devices. The shiny silver platter, also called videodiscs (a creative bunch named them) could not record anything. You could only watch the movie and watch it again, but you could never record a movie. Ah, the fatal flaw.

In the early 1980s, we saw the rise and demise of an industry in such a short period of time that many of us even forget it ever existed. Sort of like the Iowa Baseball Confederacy. But those videodiscs did not just go away. No, they stayed around and some people continued experimenting with them. In fact, the Library of Congress in Washington, D.C., decided that maybe they could make use of these disks. Maybe you could store information on them? Perhaps there was hope yet for the memex.

While people were experimenting with the various capabilities of the videodisc, there was another group of scientists trying to figure out how to do two things with the platters. First, how could we make them even smaller? Maybe they could be made small enough to fit into a shirt pocket or a notebook. That would be handy. Who wants to carry a 12-inch disk around the planet with them. Oh, they're fine if you want to play Frisbee, but not for trucking across campus. Second, can we make them so we can not only play back what is recorded on the disk, but can we record our own information on them? What if I decide I don't like that particular movie and there is a new movie on the television that I should like to record. Why can't I?

For the first question the scientists finally made a startling discovery. They could make these babies about the size of a computer floppy diskette. The 5.25-inch size. Remember when Tandy computers first came out, the external drives for floppies were eight-inch drives. Then we got those 5.25-inch floppies (which never were very floppy), and now we have the 3.5-inch diskettes, which aren't floppy at all. So, now we have a "compact music disk," or CMD, which could fit into your shirt pocket. Actually, they are 120 millimeters, or 4.75 inches, across, but who's counting. A new term came into being. No longer were they videodiscs, which only contained videos. These new discs were "compact" and they could contain full-text, graphics and audio. Now, this was about 1982, and of course, we all said, what is this world coming to? None of us had seen these things yet, but we had heard about them. Surely, they could not have the clarity and storage capacity of their big brothers, the laser videodisc. Alas, it was true for the storage capacity, but the clarity was the same. After all, it was the same technology. In fact, we now have compact disks in the same size as the 3.5-inch computer diskettes, but that's getting ahead of the story.

Just for the record the statistics on the CD-ROM are pretty standard. They are 4.75 inches across and weigh in at 0.7 ounces. The amazing thing is that they can store 540 million ASCII alphanumeric characters. If you use a standard page of 2,000 characters, then a CD-ROM can store about 270,000 pages worth of characters. Taking this one step further, you can see that the CD-ROM would equal 1,500 double-side/double-density 5.25-inch floppy disks, each with a capacity of about 360,000 characters.

So, problem number one has been solved, but what about problem number two? You could record your favorite record on cassette deck, or even your favorite movie with a videocassette recorder, but how could you solve the problem of recording your favorite movie on a laser disk? Well, you couldn't. Oh, you could if you could spend big bucks to purchase the latest expensive digital recorder, but who has the money for that, and besides they didn't exist on the commercial market in 1983. True, several vendors had a WORM (a Write-Once Read-Many device), but what was truly needed was a machine that allowed you to write-many and read-many and those are still few and far between. So even today we haven't solved this problem to anyone's real satisfaction.

Now, the day of the laser disk had come and gone in the early 1980s (although there still are pockets of the movement and occasionally it rears its head and looks as if it may make a comeback), but still the scientists experimented with the compact disk. Another event was occurring at about the same time as the development of the compact disk, or CD-ROM (Compact Disk-Read Only Memory) as it came to be known in its non-audio life. This was the development of the personal computer and the marketing of the IBM PC. While there had been personal computers since the mid-1970s, they were typically the province of electronics wizards. A normal person on the street seldom owned a PC. This all changed in 1983 when IBM introduced the IBM PC. Soon several vendors were marketing personal computers, and before you knew what happened it seemed like everyone had one at home. Well, the PC was just what the doctor ordered for the further development of the CD-ROM. Compact disk technology had gone down two roads. One was that of using the technology for the reproduction of audio sounds. This path, which I will call audio compact disk, has burgeoned to the point where the 33-1/3 long-play album is a dinosaur and nearly as hard to find. I am not interested in audio compact disks here. What I am interested in is the CD-ROM and the impact this technology has had on reference services.

The CD-ROM Revolution

The early 1980s were a time of great promise for librarians. During the 1960s and 1970s several attempts had been made to develop the perfect integrated on-line library automation system. We are still waiting. Most of these behemoths were designed to run on a mainframe computer and they really could do little more than what could be done manually. Not only that, sometimes it took longer to get the information than it did the old way. Typically only institutions with lots of spare change could afford to purchase a system.

By the 1980s the landscape was changing. More than 2,000 libraries used OCLC for cataloging purposes. OCLC had become the de facto national union catalog. Still, it was not available to everyone. You needed to have some money to use the system. Seems like there is a common thread here.

Several events started occurring within very close proximity to one another that was about to change this. As mentioned above the personal computer was about to burst onto the scene and blaze like a bright start. While there had been PCs since the mid-70s, it really took IBM to make the PC the big success story it is today. Also emerging was the compact disk industry. While audio compact disks appeared first, soon the technology improved enough to allow the digitizing of text and graphics onto those little disks. Of course, appropriate hardware had to be developed to play this information back. During the early years of the Eighties this occupied a lot of time and effort and when the PC and the CD-ROM player met, it was like a match made in heaven, sort of.

Of course, many decisions had to be made as to what information should we store on the compact disks. It also became evident that we had to have some kind of software that would allow a person to retrieve this information. Oh, it was a very complex problem.

There were a couple of ideas about what should be put on the disks. One was that the disks could be used to store books and journals. Another was that this would provide a cheap means of distributing cataloging information to libraries that could not belong to one of the national bibliographic utilities. Yet another idea was that with the right search software you could put print indexes on the disks and make them available to the public. Now we were moving in the right direction.

In the wink of an eye Information Access Corporation announced INFOTRAC in early 1985. This product would combine a personal computer and four laser disks to produce a high-tech answer to searching indexes. Using search software, a patron could enter a subject heading and within seconds the screen would reveal the results of the search. Only one small problem. This really was not a CD-ROM. Remember it had laser disks. The big fellas.

Finally the CD-ROM systems and disks made an appearance at a major trade show in the United States. In November 1984 at COMDEX (Computer Dealers Exposition) in Las Vegas. Philips and Sony were two of the early developers of the CMD technology and its expansion to accommodate data and programs.

The CD-ROM actually made their library debut at the ALA annual conference in 1985 in Chicago. Even then it was only a prototype. IMLAC of Needham, Massachusetts, marketed SilverPlatter. The original product included the data bases on compact disk, a microcomputer workstation, including monitor and keyboard, a CD reader, and the necessary search software. Some of the data bases shown at ALA were PsycLit, ERIC, PAIS, and LISA.

By the end of 1985, it was obvious that a revolution was underway and at least 50 disks were being marketed. Some of the data bases available by then included: Current Biotechnology Abstracts, Chemical Engineering (COMPENDEX), Compact Disclosure, Academic American Encyclopedia, a sampling of the H. W. Wilson company indexes, and Books in Print. The Academic American Encyclopedia by Grolier Electronic Publishing was interesting because it was not an index, but rather a full-text data base. The entire text of the print version of the *Academic American Encyclopedia* was available on a CD and could be searched for any term. While graphics were a bit much to ask of the primitive technology, it certainly was a step in a different direction.

By now the problem of storing the data and retrieving the data had been solved. Obviously print indexes were a thing of the past and could just be pitched. Soon libraries would be populated with PCs and CD-ROM drives, and patrons could virtually search for their information on their own with nearly instantaneous responses. This saved patrons a great deal of time perusing indexes like the *Readers' Guide,* but it created an entirely new problem for the reference librarian.

The Reference Librarian as Mechanic

Most of us have varying reasons for becoming librarians, and of course reference librarians have even different reasons. Some become librarians because they like books (ooh, the old stereotype), others because they like helping people—it's just part of their nature—and still others because they couldn't figure out what to do with a history bachelor of arts degree. Anyway, it is doubtful that many reference librarians made this their chosen profession because they wanted to spend all day explaining why the computer was not working, or how to do a field search in an index that had only arrived and been set up this morning, or, worse yet, clearing paper jams in those infernal printers. No, sir, I did not graduate from one of the great universities of the Midwest to become a "mechanic."

Yet, that is how some reference staff view their new role. Simply that of a mechanic. They have to start the computer in the morning, they have to replace the ink jets on the ink jet printers or ribbons on the dot matrix printers. They have to put paper in the printers, and then when the darn thing jams—usually because the patron didn't know what they were doing, right?—they have to clear the jam, using no specialized tools, except maybe a jumbo paperclip, bent into all kinds of new angles.

Where is the teaching? Where is the marvel of watching the light turn on in a student's head when he or she has finally mastered the *MLA Bibliography,* if indeed it is possible for anyone to master? How can we possibly send these students on to the great universities in the Midwest if they cannot find Lord Byron in the *MLA?* Did we ever do so, anyway?

Be not afraid and timid of these plastic and metal one-eyed monsters with the shiny little disks. No, I say march up to it and learn, because the world has turned, and will turn yet again, and he who is on top today will be on the bottom tomorrow.

There are several problems inherent with bringing personal computers and CD-ROMs into your library. Foremost may be the cost, but that is not an issue addressed in this chapter. Okay, there are still costs to be dealt with. Human costs. This too can be divided into yet more finite areas. The cost of training and the cost of staff as they play with the new technology. Then too there is the cost of those who are reticent and reluctant to even touch one of those infernal machines. Yes, these librarians do exist, and we must find them and show them that while CD-ROMs are not something you may cuddle up with in bed at night, they do have a certain warmth and charm.

Training has long been a problem with computers and CD-ROMs in libraries. Do you recall when your first computer arrived? Well, probably not if you became a librarian after about 1985, or if your library is still waiting for the first. Remember how someone came and set it up so carefully and you stood around marveling and wondering when it was going to do something? I come from the prepersonal computer generation of librarians myself, but I recall our first OCLC M300. For a few weeks we used it only for OCLC. Finally, we got some software and I sat down and taught myself a popular word processing program. No training, just do it.

The same problem has existed with CD-ROM products. Frequently the computer and CD-ROM arrive one morning unannounced, and a reference librarian's first exposure to it is at 8:05 A.M. when a patron says: "How does this work?" Then it's time to hem and haw, "Well, let's see what we have here. Hmm. I guess you just enter what it is you want to search for." And the librarian looks like exactly what we have struggled for years to avoid: an idiot. If we have learned anything from the past five years it should be when you introduce new technology into the library, give the staff a little chance to play with it before letting the public have a go at it.

But how do you get the staff member who does not want to touch the computer to learn to love it? I don't know. Some people take to them like a fish to water, while others view them as some poisonous serpent to be avoided at all costs. Folks from that persuasion believe that the patron must learn to use the paper copy. What would happen if we had an electrical outage and then the computers would not work? Well, neither would the lights so you couldn't read the indexes. Well, the student should learn how to use the paper indexes. They may go to a library where they don't have a

CD-ROM and then where would they be? The same place as if they go to a library without an on-line catalog. They would learn to use the paper indexes and you have done nothing to lessen your importance as a part of the student's learning process.

So, where are we? Well, we need to plan a little when thinking about bringing CD-ROM technology into your library. Even if you have already done so, you need to stand back and see what you could have done differently. You need to discuss the issue with the reference staff, particularly as to which data bases to get. They are the staff on the front lines and they can help make the correct decision for your library. Allow them to help in the evaluation process. How easy is the search software? How easy are the citations to decipher? Most search software products have very basic, simple searching capability, with another level for the advanced searcher. How easy can you move up to the advanced level? Get the input of the reference staff. After all, that's what we pay them for.

You need to plan for training for staff, before letting the CD-ROM go public. Nothing is more embarrassing for a reference librarian than to be confronted by a new piece of hardware with a student breathing down his or her neck. Plan formal training well in advance. How do you deal with reluctant librarians? Unfortunately, there are no clear-cut answers. Encourage them to experiment with the new technology. Try a search using the paper index and then try it on the CD-ROM. Be creative with what you suggest to them. Take time to discuss the new technology so they are more comfortable.

What Does the Future Hold?

Now we jump to the future. We all know that CD-ROM is here and will probably stay for several years. There are some concerns being expressed about the life of a CD-ROM product, especially in the audio field. What is the problem? Basically the feeling is that a CD-ROM will have a lifespan of only about 10 years. As no CD-ROM has been in existence this long we have no conclusive data to show that this is true.

Whether this concern will ultimately apply to library applications is yet to be seen. As many of the products currently produced for libraries are indexes and abstracts, they are not in use for years. Typically they are updated on a monthly, quarterly, or annual basis. Unless we start using CD-ROM as a method of storing books and journals for the long haul, as we currently use microfilm, it may not be material whether the medium can last for decades.

Let's look at the idea of using a CD-ROM for "permanent" storage of data. Can they work in this application? Theoretically, there should be no reason why not. Yet, in reality we are all aware of reasons why they will not. On the positive side is the capability of being able to physically reproduce the item. If we have the right type of printer we would be able to print the item on paper and have it bound. We could even store images and have them reproduced. Of course, the amount of storage required for digitizing images may use so much space that little space may be left for text. The Grolier *Academic American Encyclopedia* does not include images for this very reason. Obviously, the quality of reproduction, both on-screen and in print, would be at a higher quality than that of microfilm, but at what cost for storage.

On the negative side of the coin we have the same problem we currently have with microfilm. When a roll of film is in use, only one person can use that roll and that reader-printer. The same problem would apply to CD-ROM. At present, most of the products are one-user products. In many libraries there are lines waiting to use the CD-ROM, or the libraries have put time limits on use of the workstations. How does one solve this problem? The answer is: not easily. Many attempts have and are being made in the area of networking CD-ROM. Several vendors have come out with a jukebox arrangement where more than one CD-ROM can be used at the same workstation, but while this saves the library money in hardware, it really exacerbates the situation because now only one person can tie up the use of two, three, four or more CD-ROM products. This is not networking.

A network is a group of workstations that have the ability to access the data on any of the other workstations in that group. There are several different means of networking computers.

A local area network (LAN) is the most typical and may include any number of workstations and has no truly established geographic limitations. For the purposes of this discussion, however, let's limit the geography to the library. These workstations are typically connected by twisted-pair telephone wire, although coaxial cable and fiber optics may be used. A software package is used to allow the computers to talk with one another.

In a CD-ROM network the number of users is multiplied by the number of workstations on the network. Several vendors are working on developing this technology. SEFLIN, in Fort Lauderdale, Florida, is a multitype library network serving a three-county area in southeast Florida. This organization is developing a CD-ROM network using technology developed by CBIS. In addition to accessing the CD-ROM on the network, the user will be able to access data on the hard drive of the server and transparently move to the Internet. This interface opens many doors to the user in the area of information retrieval.

There are, of course, concerns and knotty problems to be untangled with this process. One is price. Vendors have typically seen CD-ROM as a one-user item and have priced it accordingly. The issue of pricing CD-ROM for a multiuser environment is a whole new ball game. Another problem is trying to get the different search software packages to coexist peacefully on the same computer. Software can be very temperamental, and in the CD-ROM environment everything must work together properly for just one CD-ROM to work. Imagine trying to get several different types of systems working properly. It can result in gnashing of teeth and rending of clothes. But, as with everything else, progress is being made and we are seeing a move toward standardization of search software, which should result in greater compatibility among products.

Now that CD-ROM technology is firmly among us, will it spell the demise of on-line data bases? Probably not. The size of some of the data bases is so great that only a large network of CD-ROM drives could make it operational. Some large data bases have already been mastered to CD-ROM and are now being marketed, but they come with forty to fifty CDs.

The cost in hardware becomes substantial, even if it is possible to purchase enough multidisk changers. Time also becomes an issue at this point. Most changers allow only the user to search the currently selected disk. There is no searching across disks. This requires a user to search one disk, then the next, and so on. Searching in an on-line environment allows the user to search the entire data base with one fell swoop. While it can be anticipated that search software will be developed and marketed that will solve this problem, it has not been done on a mass-market basis. What is happening is that several of the library automation vendors, DRA in particular, are developing the capability for a library using their system to mount data tapes on their computer and then make the tapes searchable via the on-line public-access catalog. While this can be an expensive proposition, it certainly opens many doors from the reference librarian's view. Every OPAC suddenly can search the Information Access *Academic Index* or the Wilson data bases. It is even possible to mount full-text data bases like the *Academic American Encyclopedia*. This changes the entire nature of reference work even more than CD-ROM did. No longer must the reference librarian be concerned about how this CD-ROM operates or this particular search software. Now it is all available via the OPAC. But is this the best solution? Probably not. What happens is that the OPAC is no longer simply used to access information about books in the library. It now is used for accessing indexes or full-text documents. What happens to demands on the terminals? While you can project that students will locate material quicker because of the speed of the computer, it may well be that by utilizing keyword/Boolean searching a student will spend more time at the terminal than at the card catalog because many new paths open up before their eyes. No longer will they be constrained by the subject headings and cross-references in the drawer they are using. They will be able to branch off in all different directions. Eventually we will see catalogs that will search the library data base of material, indexes, and full-text data bases and respond with, YOUR SEARCH WAS LOCATED IN 5 BOOKS, 18 MAGAZINE ARTICLES, 4 GOVERNMENT DOCUMENTS, AND 6 FULL-TEXT DOCUMENTS. And it will respond by voice.

Where does this leave the CD-ROM? Obviously, not every library will be able to purchase data tapes and create their own on-line files. Nor would every library want to. Part of the solution will be found in the process of networking CD-ROM. This will occur even in those libraries that do purchase data tapes. Sometimes it will be just too expensive to get the tapes, so a CD-ROM network will have to suffice. If networking does not occur, CD-ROM will still remain in many libraries as stand-alone workstations.

The limitation comes with data storage and access time. While 750 megabytes sounds like a lot of storage, the process of digitizing, especially images, is a very storage-intensive process. Not many images can be stored on a CD-ROM. For this purpose the laser videodiscs discussed earlier are still a better solution. Whether demand will become great enough that they will become a viable alternative remains to be seen. The Library of Congress is working on a project called the American Memory Project, which uses the laser videodiscs to store images from various graphic collections. It is still difficult to beat this product for storing images.

The issue of access time for a CD-ROM versus an on-line data base must be considered also. The CD-ROM does not fare well in tests against the on-line system, but you must keep in mind what you are getting and what you are trying to do. The CD-ROM comes at a much lower cost, and for many libraries that is a major factor in a decision. If you have money to burn, then it makes sense to go with the on-line data bases, but money is in short supply these days.

The decade of the Nineties will bring as many changes for the library profession as the Eighties did, if not more. We may never reach the library of the future like we saw on the *Star Trek* television shows where there were no books, only cartridges that had to be viewed on a machine. The paperless library and society predicted for years is yet to appear, but we are moving in that direction. Just as Vannevar Bush saw his memex as a step in that direction, we see CD-ROM and other optical storage devices as rungs on the ladder, leading us nearer the day when we will be able to retrieve full-text documents via a terminal. Personally, I will be a little disappointed when that happens (if I am still around). I guess

I am old-fashioned enough to enjoy walking into the reading room of one of the large, turn-of-the-century university libraries and feel the books around me. The very smell, the texture of the walls lined with print material takes be back to an earlier day. Yet, we cannot escape the future, and another part of me would not want to. I want to see what the future will bring to this profession. It has been a most interesting past.

THE ELECTRONIC LIBRARY'S IMPACT ON REFERENCE SERVICE

V. Sue Hatfield

Junior and community colleges occupy a unique role in higher education. Since the formation of the concept of two-year colleges in the early part of this century, these institutions have assumed the responsibility for providing easy access to higher education for all citizens. The 1947 President's Commission on Higher Education for American Democracy, known as the Truman Commission, strengthened the future of the community college when it called for open access to education two years beyond high school. The commission suggested that the role of the community college should be the provision of education for all citizens of the community regardless of race, sex, religion, color, geographic location, or financial status.[1] This open-door philosophy has been expanded to also include those citizens who may be underprepared academically. Thus, two-year colleges have emerged not only as institutions providing trade and career programs, but by offering transfer programs with an emphasis on traditional undergraduate liberal arts courses, they have also become bridges to four-year institutions.

In the early 1950s there was recognition that special services geared to first-generation college students were needed if universities were going to deal successfully with this unique and rapidly growing population. Library-user education programs sprouted during this period. The undergraduate library became the "Teaching Library."[2] The two-year college libraries had also recognized this early on, and the role of the library was expanded to include library instruction. Reference librarians became one-on-one teachers who not only answered specific questions but attempted to teach everyone how to use card catalogs and periodical indexes as well as how to develop search strategies and use specific reference tools. Pathfinders, work sheets, and various self-help handouts were developed. Formal bibliographic instruction classes became the norm. This was done with the belief that an individual who understood and could fully use a library would be able to pursue a lifetime of independent learning.

Now as we enter the Information Age this is all the more true. People must be prepared for a society where the use of and need for information is essential. This is the information age and an information society, a world where one's lack of information and inability to locate and decipher new information is a major handicap.

Computerization of the Library

In the past the undergraduate's research needs have been met by the traditional array of indexes and bibliographies typically found in most academic library reference departments as well as through the book collection access via the card catalog. Through structured programs of bibliographic instruction, both general and specific, and through class assignments requiring library use, reference librarians focused their energies on teaching the undergraduate how to use the bibliographic resources in that library. Although always available for specific or continuing consultation with students, our goal was self-sufficiency for the student.[3]

But in the 1980s when the actual computerization of some of the library's traditional information sources became a reality, many new problems arose. On-line searching of remote data bases, such as the ones provided by DIALOG, initiated one of our first dilemmas. Should the end user be allowed to directly search expensive remote data bases, or was this expertise better left in the control of the librarian? Should they even be searched at all for the student, especially the two-year undergraduate at the technical school level? Weren't those data bases reserved for those doing "research" in graduate or postgraduate courses? Certainly there was enough information in the local institution's library for the student. Should the student even be told that there might be resources available outside the home institution? Also, what about the cost? This type of data base searching was expensive. Who was to pay for it—the student, the faculty member, or the library? And finally, to actually access the material, we would have to use interlibrary loan. Who would pay for that?

What happened to the concept of the student being self-sufficient? Suddenly the librarians had become the gatekeepers of information again. In some ways it was fun to be the gurus of information. We had the key and it was kept well hidden. A mystique arose around on-line searching even among our own profession. Somehow those who were selected to be trained in searching techniques had a special power that those untrained must rely on to find information. A division among librarians' skills became very real. Shouldn't we all be able to perform searches? Why only one or two select individuals? We struggled with the answers to these questions for the better part of the decade. Due to the financial considerations and in some part to security, most libraries continued to act as the mediators of on-line searching and continued to designate one or two librarians to perform those searches.

Then, in the latter part of the 1980s, many libraries computerized their catalogs. All of a sudden their students were using computer terminals to search the local holdings of the libraries, learning Boolean logic, combining sets, full-text searching, and applying many of the same techniques that librarians had been using for years to search remote data bases. The students and faculty learned very rapidly and discovered that they had the ability to search the catalog more thoroughly and efficiently. They no longer needed the librarian to interpret the Library of Congress Subject Headings. With a few keystrokes they could see on the screen the specific book they wanted and if it was available.

As we enter the 1990s, affordable compact disk data bases have emerged and are replacing printed indexes. These tools not only give the user the citation, but in many cases an abstract. Students no longer have to write the citation—they can simply print it out on paper or onto their own disk to take home. Where they used to select the first few citations out of the paper index, photocopy the articles, and be satisfied, now they are finding whole screens of citations, which, with a touch of a key, will be printed out for them. The sophistication required to master high-tech information resources is certainly within the grasp of many of our students. In fact, they are usually more adept than we in grasping new techniques. There are barriers, however, along the path toward making true end users of our students. Among these barriers are our reluctance to admit that students have the abilities and capabilities of becoming bona fide end users.[4] We must, at this point in reference service, set aside our egos and give back to the user the self-sufficiency we have always believed they needed, and, in fact, must have to be productive in this information-driven world.

The Student as an End User

The door that used to hold back the flood of information has been forced open and a torrent has been released. The library users love the power the computers give them. They wonder in their independence and in their ability to quickly find so many citations when just a few years before (or months in many cases) they would have had to spend hours and hours poring through paper indexes and card catalogs looking for just the right word or subject heading.

I myself relish watching the ease with which the patrons use the on-line catalog and the CD-ROM indexes. The thrill they experience when the screen fills with the citation they need is exciting. Some almost clap when the printer spits out the list of sources. They feel confident, self-assured, and comfortable in a library, maybe for the first time in their lives.

"Librarians should take into account the delight of the user in this technology. Perhaps a little reminiscent of joy-sticking through Space Invaders, the user opens new worlds of information with the touch of a few buttons. It is the knowledge seeker's own ship to be flown single-handedly and freely to any subject in the universe on information on the disk."[5]

So, why do I feel uncomfortable and uneasy when I walk through the reference room and see the students happily hacking away on computer terminals or walking through the stacks with sheets of computer printout trailing behind them?

Don't take anything for granted and never assume that the student knows how to use all the new toys that are rapidly being introduced into our libraries. Some years ago most reference librarians assumed that the introduction of auto-mated reference resources would mean a diminution of the need for labor-intensive instruction. It is now apparent that for the most part the opposite is true.[6] Currently we are finding that the command language is different in almost every data base. Search strategy is rarely the same. Depend-ing on the data base, the function keys may or may not work. The holdings on the disk vary greatly. Abstracts may be available if you know to go deep enough into the citation. Printers may work from screen/print command, citation/print command, or on a command to print all the citations (which, at the librarian's discretion, might be disabled or limited). The data base may be indexed on every word of the entry or only on specified indexing terms like subject headings. You might get a list of those headings or you might not. You might be able to initiate a search from that list or perhaps you have to reenter the appropriate terms. As the librarian knows, very few data bases are designed the same. But do the students know this? I don't believe they do, nor should we expect them to know. We can never assume that they know. Thus, some of my discomfort. Every day I see uninitiated students wander over to a workstation and begin searching. Sometimes they read the messages on the screens, but for the most part if a librarian, friend, or simply anyone who looks like they might know walks close to them they will ask a question about using the workstation or the data base. They don't seem to have any embarrassment or reluctance to admit that they don't know how to use the computers as they did when using the card catalog or paper indexes.

As a result of these factors, automation of reference may not always save librarians appreciable amounts of time, although it has undoubtedly made their work more effective in many cases. Its effect on bibliographic instruction has resulted in the promotion and use of new modes of instruction. New questions about instructional strategies and a new "curriculum" of instructional content areas are also being raised.[7] The formal, organized in-depth tour of the library and traditional bibliographic instruction are proving ineffective methods for training on computer data bases. Hands-on experience is necessary to learn these resources, and this requires many hours of personalized training and instruction. Thus, the librarians role has changed from information provider and mediator to workstation trainer. As with the acquisition of any new equipment, we find ourselves involved in the hands-on training of the users. In some cases, this scenario is the same as when we introduced photocopiers or microfilm readers and printers. We are now training people how to use equipment rather than teaching them the search strategies and critical analytical skills necessary to wade through all the citations presented and select only those appropriate. After automation, we see circulation statistics skyrocket with the patrons checking out everything that possibly could relate to their subject. Also, many more journals are used. The users are retrieving everything. They are checking out, photocopying, duplicating, reading microfilm, and using reader printers with a much greater frequency than before automation. They leave the library with masses of information and probably use only half of it, if that.

Librarians now need to concentrate on data-base discretion rather than equipment-use training. The student who is looking in the Humanities Index on disk for a general article about AIDS for a social science class is going to find a citation like the one in Figure 1. These are obviously not what the student wants, and he or she must start again. The labeling of the contents of these library resources must be more explicit and more informative. They all look the same and are usually in white or off-white computers with screens that are very much the same. As Beth Weilage, my head of reference, says, "It would be a lot easier if the Humanities Index was in a pink computer and Academic Index in a black one, and *Readers' Guide* in yellow." At least at that point the user might get the idea that they are not all the same. As it is they look exactly the same. The trick lies in getting the student to read the help

```
#1
Nelson, Emmanuel S.
AIDS and the American Novel
Journal of American Culture v13 p47-53 Spring '90
bibl

SUBJECTS COVERED:
American fiction/20th century
AIDS (Disease) in literature
Homosexual authors
```

Figure 1. Example of citation in a Humanities Index on disk.

information or to ask which one to use. Remember, they love the computers and feel very powerful using them. Once they know how to use the computers they believe that they no longer have to ask the librarians how or where to look, but that with a simple keystroke they can find it all. And they do! But they really don't want it all. They especially don't want it all when all relates to literature and they are doing a social science paper. Instructing these users in the appropriate choice of data-bases seems to require an in-depth, one-on-one approach. We will have to be willing to spend much more time with each student for not only will we have to teach them the content of each data-base but also how to discern which article or book they want.

Certainly, the world of information has opened to the user. I do not believe that any of the above considerations outweigh the advantages of the computerized sources and the fact that the users feel very comfortable with the technology. I do believe, however, that we must be careful and must not assume that patrons who act like they know what they are doing really do. Never take for granted that they know the equipment. We must not allow ourselves to be lulled into the false belief that because the users don't ask, they know what they are doing.

Provision of Materials

Now that the door is opened completely, do we forbid the crossing of the threshold? We are encouraging the students to be self-sufficient and independent learners, but once again we hold all the keys. We tease them only enough to make a few very angry and the others simply frustrated. No, we don't have everything on that printout, which they so proudly drag around the library. How can that be? They ask, "It's in the computer over there, so you must have it." This is another big dilemma. If we are going to buy the data-bases and we are going to put them in the public's hands (which we have done), then how are we going to supply them with the information they find there? Do we subscribe to all the journals indexed and all the books cited? Do we supply through interlibrary loan? Do we send them to the research institution down the road? These questions may have more of an impact on the two-year community college-type libraries than any other academic libraries. We normally have more limited collections and have usually been able to satisfy our students and faculty with those materials. Now we are probably going to be faced with the possibilities that we need to expand our serial collections to meet our users' needs, expand our interlibrary loan services, or find some other creative means to meet this need.

It is imperative that we inform the user up front what our policies are on acquisition of materials indexed in these data bases. This situation should be similar to that of the printed indexes, but for some reason once again the computer has defied the logic of libraries. We were rarely faced with the belief that we would own everything that appeared in a printed index. Then, why would we have everything in the computer? I don't know. All I know is that the patron expects it and is usually very surprised and upset to discover we don't own everything.

I believe that if we are going to provide these indexes and

through them open these vistas of information, then we should be responsible for ensuring that the users can in some manner acquire access to the information. This could be accomplished by expanding collections, (although this alternative is rarely attractive to most libraries), interlibrary loans, or reciprocal borrowing privileges. There are no easy answers to this dilemma. I certainly do not have the answers, I simply state that it is one of the major concerns for reference departments as we enter this age of automation. All libraries will have to determine which method or plan works best for them. They may be forced to use a mix of them. We simply cannot slam the door to information in the faces of our users.

The proliferation of high-tech data-bases and the rapidly descending prices are creating confusion within the reference departments in all types of libraries. It seems that each day we receive at least one flyer or telephone call from a publisher claiming to have created a new CD product that far surpasses anything on the market. They will want to demonstrate it to all the librarians and then place it in the library for a trial period. We try one data-base after another and know that tomorrow more will hit the market. We do analyses of these data-bases, we talk to other librarians to get their responses, we do user surveys, and still we are confused about what to buy. The only solace is the fact that unlike our paper indexes, if we don't like the product of one company, we can switch fairly easily. The disks contain only a limited amount of material and are superseded by the next accumulation. This gives us unexpected flexibility.

Having been through many changes in the last several years, some of the anxiety librarians experienced due to change has worn off. Innately we now know that the market will eventually settle down or perhaps the technology will change completely. So we keep trying more and different products. What we must remember is that we cannot continually change data-bases simply to test them. The user once again will not know the difference. This type of technology all appears the same to the patron. Constantly changing computerized indexes will lead to frustration for the user and ultimately require many more hours of one-on-one instruction. Therefore, we should choose certain data-bases and remain fairly consistent at least throughout the academic year, so as not to confuse the users. We must not become CD disc jockeys.

Additionally, the need to choose those materials we will continue to receive in paper copy is probably more challenging to the two-year academic library than any other. Unlike our four-year and research library counterparts, we don't normally need to provide major retrospective collections. We will have long runs of some types of journals and other library materials but not nearly as extensive as other types of academic libraries.

We currently will have to continue to buy some indexes in paper format so that we can provide access in ten years to the materials that we keep in long runs. This choice of indexes, unlike the choice of ROM indexes, is fairly irrevocable and will need to be made with much attention to all traditional factors, including curriculum, usability, cost, frequency, and content, which affect our purchasing decisions. We should always remember that sometime in the future we will probably be able to replace even the retrospective paper indexes with disk technology or another even more futuristic computerized method.

Thus, our major concern in the selection of reference materials today and in the future revolves around the consistency of presentation to our users, the permanence of the information needed, and the traditional selection criteria. None of this sounds very new or different. It isn't. Once again, just like our students, we have allowed technology to create the image in our minds of some major changes in the way we should be doing things. The selection of the materials continues to revolve around the same criteria that we have always used. We can't allow ourselves to confuse format with purpose.

Conclusion

As we enter this age of automation and computerized information, there are several major issues or concerns that greatly affect decision making and the performance of our jobs related to reference service. We have finally enabled our users with the ability to access information through automated sources, which far exceeds what they have previously been able or willing to access. The patrons must be taught how to analyze the avalanche of information located and select only that which is most appropriate for their specific needs. They must learn to be very specific. Aligned with that concept is the fact that reference departments must figure out ways of instructing the patrons in the differences in the data bases. We are also faced with the question of how we actually deliver the information now that the patron has found it.

Additionally, we are faced with a perceived major change in selection decisions. Fundamentally, we have based our selection criteria on the curriculum, cost, and usability. Now we assume that technology has changed our criteria when in reality it has not. We must resist the urge to test all data-bases that come along and are offered on trial bases, replacing them one after another with different ones.

The most important effect that automation and the electronic library will have on us will be our need to change the current configuration of bibliographic instruction and to create new and different instruction methods to ensure that all students using our libraries become information literate. This should take number one priority. Teaching our patrons the use of information must become paramount in all academic libraries. I do not believe that the two-year, technical, or community college library is very different from any other undergraduate library. All of us must concentrate on ensuring that the student of today can be a smart and critical information user of tomorrow.

As stated in the ALA Presidential Committee on Information Literacy *Final Report*:

> Information literacy is a means of personal empowerment. It allows people to verify or refute expert opinion and to become independent seekers of truth. It not only prepares them for lifelong learning, but by experiencing the excitement of their own successful quests for knowledge, it also creates in young people the motivation for pursuing learning throughout their lives.[8]

References

[1] W. Lee Hisle, "Learning Resource Services in the Community College: On the Road to the Emerald City," *College and Research Libraries* 50:613–625 (November 1989), p. 614.

[2] Carla J. Stoffle, "A New Library for the New Undergraduate," *Library Journal* 115:16:47–51 (October 1, 1990), p. 47.

[3] Rodney M. Hersberger, "Financing and Managing Technology-Based Services in the Undergraduate University Library," pp. 209–223 in Katz, Bill, et al., *Finance, Budget and Management for Reference Service.* New York: Hayworth Press, 1988, p. 210.

[4] Ibid. p. 211.

[5] P. D. Watson, "Cost to Libraries of the Optical Information Revolution," *On-line* 12:45–50 (January 1988), p. 50.

[6] William Miller and Bonnie Gratch, "Making Connections: Computerized Reference Services and People," *Library Trends* 37:387–401 (Spring 1989), p. 397.

[7] Ibid. p. 398.

[8] American Library Association Presidential Committee on Information Literacy. *Final Report.* American Library Association, Chicago, (January 1989), p. 2.

HARNESSING CD-ROMs AND COLLECTION POLICIES

Jennie S. Boyarski

"CD-ROMs (Compact Disk Read-Only Memory) may be the fastest growing of the library computer media as well as the most important computer application after automated systems," according to William A. Wortman in *Collection Management*.[1] Basically a publishing medium, CD-ROM products have found a niche in community college libraries/ learning resources centers. Why the attraction? The set subscription costs, no connect time, no citation charges, no telecommunication costs or problems, the fairly easy search language coupled with the fact that it is an excellent medium for teaching searchers makes CD-ROM electronic information sources valuable. According to *CD-ROMs in Print* there are five types:

1. Data files containing popular, business and finance, and scientific/technical data that can be displayed and, in varying degrees, manipulated.
2. Text files that contain the texts of printed matter that can be accessed, displayed, printed out, and in some cases manipulated.
3. Graphic files ranging from the picture in encyclopedias to charts and graphs displaying information.
4. Indexes and bibliographies that in most cases replicate print, but add the virtues of computer access—multiple-access points and Boolean searching.
5. Directories and data files that store information compactly, allow multiple-access searching, or bring together and organize information not otherwise available.[2]

This relatively new technology is revolutionizing information access. With the tremendous potential of CD-ROMs and the financial investment in the software/hardware, it is now time to recognize this influential material type in library collection development policy statements.

An informal survey of community college library directors indicates many libraries/learning resources centers have CD-ROM products available, if only on trial bases; however, none yet have incorporated guidelines for acquiring this laser technology in their collection-development statements. Due to the subscription costs and the expense of the appropriate computer hardware, librarians, up to this point, have cautiously acquired data bases on compact disk. Most of the contracted CD-ROM products have been indexes.

The decision to choose CD-ROM or another electronic format (generic description of optical, digital, and magnetic products, which includes CD-ROM) requires a comparative review of the advantages of the format over the cost of delivery. Factors affecting comparative advantages over print include the following: "initial and ongoing product cost, ease of use in the machine-readable form, flexibility of use (better indexing; downloading capability), ease of wide distribution, need for multiple copies, need to replace paper (space saving or poor condition), and more frequent updates."[3]

Including CD-ROMs and the other electronic formats in collection-development policy statements diminishes the possibility of acquiring new technology without regard for the merit of the content. Could the random selection of CD-ROM products be perceived as progressive and innovative?

Guiding CD-ROM Selection

I believe that the collection-development focus in community colleges should emphasize the broadening range of materials and their role in the collection. The diversity in programs and the varied educational development of community college library/learning resources center patrons dictate a multimedia approach to information. "Scholarly journals, information services, CD-ROM bibliographic files, audiovisuals, microforms, along with books all contribute to the collection and should be recognized in the collection development policies."[4]

The American Library Association's *Guide for Writing Collection Policy Statements* defines collection development as "the process of planning, building, and maintaining a library's information resources in a cost-effective and user-relevant manner; explicitly linked to the parent agency's mission."[5] In an era of shrinking revenues and explosion in information access, heeding these words of wisdom is vital to successful collection management.

Policy statements for CD-ROMs as for other material types perform the following functions:

1. Inform about the nature and scope of the collection.
2. Inform of collecting priorities.
3. Force thinking about organizational goals to be met by the collection.
4. Generate some degree of commitment to meeting organizational goals.
5. Set standards for inclusion and exclusion.
6. Reduce the influence of a single selector and personal biases.
7. Provide a training/orientation tool for new staff.
8. Help ensure a degree of consistency over time and despite staff turnover.
9. Guide staff in handling complaints.
10. Aid in weeding and evaluating the collection.
11. Aid in rationalizing budget allocations.
12. Provide a public relations document.
13. Provide a means of assessing overall performance of the collection development program.
14. Provide outsiders with information about the purpose of collection development (an accountability tool).[6]

One of the elements of collection development policies identifies each type of material to be acquired and establishes selection criteria. For CD-ROMs, I find that the format and the content must be equally evaluated to determine the appropriateness of this laser technology. One must also be concerned with the computer components and systems. Will they be compatible with future upgrades? Another concern is the reliability of the producer.

To answer the question of how beneficial a CD-ROM title is to the library collection, consider the following criteria:

1. *Accuracy and Documentation.* Compare a sample search with the results of a manual or on-line search using the same subjects. Compare the results and content descriptions. Read the user documentation that is available and test the producer's claims with sample searches. A toll-free hot line and/or other support services also should be available.

2. *Appropriateness.* Is the arrangement, content, and approach to the subject material relevant and useful to your patrons? What is appropriate for professionals often is unsuitable for students. The same analysis can be made between freshmen and upper division students.

3. *Ease of use/comprehension of software.* Is the CD-ROM product easy to use and understand? Do the commands make sense? Are the abbreviations understandable? Do the screen layouts follow a logical progression? Are the on-line help screens clear? Is there an on-line thesaurus? Is Boolean searching an option, or can menu-driven search strategies be bypassed by experienced searchers? Can one search multiple fields at the same time? Does the product offer print and/or download capabilities? How about the response time? Would a patron who is not computer literate find the system user friendly?

4. *Coverage and Credibility.* Today many of the CD-ROM titles are subsets of on-line services or reference services in print. Information on these products can be analyzed and compared. Those that are new sources must be closely reviewed to determine the qualifications of the contributors and the accuracy of the content. What is the scope of the coverage? How thorough is the indexing? What other sources available in the library provide the same information? How frequently will the disks be updated? What courses in the curriculum would find the source beneficial? What

titles would this product replace? How do the costs compare? If an index, what journal titles are available to patrons? How comprehensive is the coverage of issues, dates, significant people, places, or companies? Finally, what is the reputation of the producer?

5. *Comparisons to similar products.* Read the reviews of the discussions of the products in the literature. Compare the searching commands and protocols with other owned software. Look at the strengths and weaknesses of both. Is there a commitment by the producer to make the software compatible with all editions of the product including the archival disks?

6. *Hardware considerations.* Will the software run on currently owned equipment? If not, what additional hardware is needed and what is the cost? If hardware is compatible, is the operating system compatible with those already loaded? Are the present number of workstations adequate? Estimate the number of expected users per day or week to determine the impact on current hardware usage. If usage will require additional hardware, what hardware will be needed and what is the approximate cost? How many disks will be received annually? How many will be in the permanent collection? Wil! the present disk storage space accommodate the additional disks? If not, what expansion is required and what is the cost? If the CD-ROM title is full-text, the number of disks is particularly critical.

7. *Staffing and service needs.* Though most patrons prefer the rapid, thorough accessing capabilities of CD-ROM products, many need instruction and assistance in successfully completing the search process. The software must be loaded and the hardware maintained. Someone must be available to troubleshoot. Is staff available to address these needs? What impact will the purchase of CD-ROM products have on staff time?

8. *Acquisitions considerations.* Who owns the data if the CD-ROM subscription is canceled? Will the producer require the software and data disks to be returned? What are the costs for the current year's subscription and the archival disks? What are the licensing require-

ments on-site and hardware restrictions, limit on access, and use of data? What are the regulations for networking the product? Is there an additional charge if the software is networked?[7]

Establishing the Collection Policy

The acquisition of compact disk data bases affects many aspects of the library/learning resources center. CD-ROMs require specialized hardware and software, which necessitates a certain amount of technical support and user instruction and support. No one division of the library organization has all of the skills or knowledge required to sort out the complex implications of introducing new formats. Gone are the days when the collection development librarian dealt only with paper reviews of paper resources. Today technical and public services personnel must determine jointly the new formats of information to be incorporated in the growing number of material types. Policy groups on CD-ROM and other computer media should include key staff members from throughout the library organization. The charge of the committee should be to:

1. Set and update collection policies;
2. Gauge the potential impact of new formats on each department;
3. Recommend policy and procedural changes needed to integrate the handling of electronic media into the day-to-day operations.[8]

Selectors should be competent users of microcomputer hardware and software and be able to evaluate the printed documentation accompanying the electronic formats.

The library computer media formats will continue to increase in number. From the 1990 to 1991 edition of *CD-ROMs in Print,* the number of listings increased 500 percent. With the advent of multiple disk storage and retrieval systems, CD-ROMs are an even more attractive reference source. The constraints of diminishing financial resources for collection development encourage library/ learning resources center directors to plan carefully. Teamwork from all divisions of the organization is fundamental to cost-effective decision making in selecting electronic formats. Above all else, a methodical approach to the decision to purchase or subscribe to electronic sources is crucial.

I agree completely with Ross Atkinson's statement, "The challenge facing collection development is to calibrate its operation more precisely, to define its rationale more persuasively, and to apply its methods more rigorously in preparation for the unprecedented economic and technical changes which we have only begun to experience."[9]

References
[1] William A. Wortman, *Collection Management: Background and Principles* (Chicago: American Library Association, 1989), p. 35.
[2] Ibid.
[3] Linda Stewart, Katherine S. Chiang, and Bill Coons, eds. *Public Access CD-ROMs in Libraries: Case Studies* (Westport: Meckler, 1990), p. 295.
[4] Wortman, op. cit. p. 129.
[5] Bonita Bryant, ed., *Guide for Written Collection Policy Statements* (Chicago: American Library Association, 1989), pp. 21–22.
[6] G. Edward Evans, *Developing Library and Information Center Collections* (Littleton: Libraries Unlimited, 1987), p. 67.
[7] Nancy K. Herther, "The Silver Disk," *On line,* 12:107–108 (March 1988).
[8] Sam Demas, "Mainstreaming Electronic Formats," *Library Acquisitions: Practice & Theory,* 13:231.
[9] Ross Atkinson, "Old Forms, New Forms: The Challenge of Collection Development," *College & Research Libraries,* 50:518 (September 1989).

ON-LINE SEARCH SERVICES

Wanda K. Johnston

In 1977, the American Library Association passed a resolution promoting equal access to information. This resolution states, in part, that "it shall be the policy of the American Library Association to seek to make it possible for library and information science agencies, which receive their major support from public funds, to provide service to all people without additional fees and to utilize the latest technological developments to ensure the best possible access to information."[1]

Academic libraries in the United States are suffering from severe economic pressure due to tightened budgets coupled with rapidly increasing costs. Tuition revenue is declining as enrollments decline. State and federal assistance has lessened. Local tax referenda are increasingly difficult to pass. Some costs, such as those for facilities and tenured faculty, are relatively fixed compared with enrollment, necessitating budget cuts in other areas, such as libraries. Academic library budgets are rising more slowly than the overall university budgets and definitely more slowly than information costs.[2]

How are academic libraries, specifically community college libraries, responding to the ALA policy of equal access to information during this period of economic decline? A review of the literature combined with a survey of the membership of the Northern Illinois Learning Resources Cooperative provides more information.

Among published individual case studies, three describe successful free on-line services. The library at California State College considers on-line services an integral part of the total reference service; consequently, on-line search services are not treated any differently from any other reference tool.[3] At the University of Pennsylvania, end-user searching for free is offered successfully, resulting in improved library image coupled with pressures for expanding the services.[4] Governors State University considers the book budget as an information budget and, consequently, provides free on-line search services. Twice as many patrons are being served with more effective results. Subsequent interlibrary loan requests increased with document delivery as the only weak link.[5]

Among academic libraries that do charge fees for on-line services, the fee structure varies. SUNY at Albany had offered free on-line searches for five years but finally had to impose charges for off-line printing. By sharing the costs, the services could be expanded to serve more patrons.[6] At the University of Delaware, a student search program is introduced as a "half-priced" search. On the whole, "students and librarians alike have found on-line searching to be an important new reference tool and student exposure to it an important part of college research experience."[7]

To gain a broader view of how academic libraries are responding to the equal access policy, two published surveys have been reviewed. In 1981, ALA distributed a survey to publicly supported libraries providing on-line search services. Nine hundred eighty-five libraries, including 610 academic libraries, responded. Seventy-two percent of the respondents charged fees for at least some users of the service. Of those charging fees, 75 percent charged only the direct costs of service. The report concluded that "these findings support a current trend of thought that public funds may be used to finance the costs of making a service available to all (i.e., for start-up and general operating expenses or overhead), but that private funds should be used to cover those "direct costs" related to a service from which one person benefits (i.e., communication charges, connect time, and off-line printing for a specific search).[8] The report also found that the "level of funding available" had the most impact on the decision of whether or not to charge a fee.[9]

In 1982, the Association of College and Research Libraries conducted a survey to determine the extent to which college libraries were involved in on-line bibliographic searching.

Two hundred twenty-three public and private colleges with enrollments between 1,000 and 5,000 responded. Of these, 65 percent offered on-line search services. Of those that did not, expense, insufficient anticipated use, and insufficient personnel were cited as the primary reasons. Seventy-three percent indicated that they charged faculty and students for the services. DIALOG was the vendor most frequently used and the average direct cost per search was $10 to $15, with the average range from $5 to $25.[10]

Because little information discussing on-line search services in community colleges is available, I surveyed the membership of the Northern Illinois Learning Resources Cooperative (NILRC). NILRC, a cooperative of two- and four-year institutions in Illinois, Iowa, and Missouri, was established to improve cost effectiveness, to share and exchange resources and information, and to strengthen the skills and knowledge of its membership. Of the thirty-five member community colleges surveyed, thirty-one responded. Of these, eighteen (58 percent) provide on-line reference search services. This is slightly less than the ACRL survey cited earlier. Similar to the ACRL respondents, DIALOG is the most-used vendor.

Of the respondents providing on-line search services, 100 percent provide services to faculty and administration/staff, 83 percent provide services to students, and 72 percent provide services to other patrons. When asked, "Do you charge a fee for reference data base services?," 89 percent did not charge faculty and administration/staff, 61 percent did not charge students, and 1 percent did not charge other patrons. Among colleges charging fees, the fee structures varied, but most charged only direct expenses on a cost-recovery basis similar to the ALA survey findings. These statistics support the stated mission of the community college and the role of its learning resources center (LRC). The LRC provides the resources necessary to support the instructional programs of the college. LRC services then extend beyond the traditional college community into the community at large.

The NILRC survey did not address the issue of why LRCs did not provide on-line search services; however, if the reasons paralleled the ACRL survey, helpful data was gained.

In response to "expense," Jean Koch discusses in-depth the costs involved when a library adds on-line bibliographic search services.[11] The capital outlay necessary to initiate on-line search services totals approximately $2,000 for purchase of a microcomputer system with telephone modem and printer. Within Illinois, the College of Lake County coordinates group discounts to DIALOG for libraries who place $1,000 "on account" each October. NILRC survey respondents estimated the annual direct on-line search costs ranging from $200 to $6,000 per year. Sixty-four percent had annual costs less than $900. The average direct cost per search was $7.77.

In response to "insufficient anticipated use," the NILRC survey showed the number of searches per college ranged from 29 to 1,022 per year, with 71 percent conducting fewer than 100 searches per year. Among the colleges reporting searches by patron category, 30 percent of searches were for faculty, 13 percent were for administration/staff, 39 percent for students, and 18 percent for other patrons. Although use of on-line search services is low, access to the information resources is provided.

Finally, in response to "insufficient personnel," the survey showed the amount of staff time required for on-line searching was low. Seventy-two percent estimated staff time devoted to on-line search services during the academic year to be five hours per week or less.

In conclusion, academic libraries, especially community colleges, consider on-line search services as a part of their overall library service in support of the college's instructional program and institutional mission. Funding availability and philosophy determine the interpretation of equal access to information within budgetary constraints. Fee structures can range from simple to complex, from free to the patron to cost recovery. Structures consider the patron status (student, staff, external), the search category (basic or specialized), and pricing goal (token, discount, or cost-recovery). Community colleges tend to provide free on-line services to faculty, administration/staff, and students more frequently than other academic institutions. On-line search services need not be prohibitively expensive to initiate or maintain, and they will not only provide enhanced reference service but also will improve the image of the library.

References

[1] Sara D. Knapp and C. James Schmidt, "Budgeting to Provide Computer-Based Reference Services: A Case Study," *The Journal of Academic Librarianship,* 5:9 (March 1979).

[2] Donald W. King, "Pricing Policies in Academic Libraries," *Library Trends,* 28:47–62 (Summer 1979).

[3] Paula Crawford and Judith A. Thompson, "Free Online Searches Are Feasible," *Library Journal,* 104:793–795 (April 1, 1979).

[4] Michael Halperin and Ruth A. Pagell, "Free Do-It-Yourself Online Searching . . . What to Expect," *Online,* 9:82–83 (March 1985).

[5] Virgil Diodato, "Eliminating Fees for Online Search Services in a University Library," *Online,* 10:44–50 (November 1986).

[6] Knapp and Schmidt, op. cit. p. 9–13.

[7] Pamela Kobelski and Jean Trumbore, "Student Use of Online Bibliographic Services," *The Journal of Academic Librarianship,* 4:14–18 (March 1978).

[8] Mary Jo Lynch, "Libraries Embrace Online Search Fees," *American Libraries,* 13:174 (March 1982).

[9] ———, "Financing Online Services," *RQ,* 21:226 (Spring 1982).

[10] David Carlson and P. Grady Morein, *Online Bibliographic Searching in College Libraries, Clip Note #4-83,* (Chicago: American Library Association, 1983.)

[11] Jean E. Koch, "A Review of the Costs and Cost-Effectiveness of Online Bibliographic Services," *RSR,* 10:59–64 (Spring 1982).

ON-LINE COMPUTERIZED BIBLIOGRAPHIC SEARCHING

Patricia Twilde

The mission of a community college is to function within the total educational community, in those areas assigned to it to ensure that all individuals in a geographic area are given an opportunity for the continuing development and extension of their skills and knowledge.[1] This is accomplished through career programs, collegiate courses, community offerings, and remedial education.

The library in the community college is part of a learning resource center as are an audiovisual department and a learning laboratory. The library offers basic reference services and instruction in the use of its resources. The collections do not contain advanced research and reference materials that would be found in a four-year college. The library provides materials to support course work, research, and recreational interests of the faculty, staff, and students attending the college. Residents of the community also have access to the library materials.

A recent addition to traditional reference services is the implementation of the use of on-line computerized bibliographic searching, whether it be executed by a librarian or a student receiving on-line instruction.

Professional librarians attend training sessions sponsored by various vendors such as DIALOG and BRS. With these learned skills and the use of a microcomputer, modem, printer, and appropriate software, librarians are able to perform searches and instruct students in the art of searching. Acquiring and using thesauri of the most used data bases is instrumental in obtaining citations relevant to the topic searched. Commonly used data bases for community college use are ERIC, PSYCHINFO, MEDLINE, ABI INFORM, and CINHAL (Cumulative Index to Nursing and Allied Health). If the library has no thesaurus, the terms used can be free text. If this doesn't produce relevant citations, a toll-free call to the vendor or to a particular data base can be made to learn the correct form of the necessary terms.

Examples of searches performed at a community college include student retention, administering a multicampus community college, teaching critical thinking skills, symptoms of depression in children, nursing role of patient education with asthmatic children, terrorism, and surrogate parenting.

Many vendors offer reduced charges if searching is done at a particular time such as evenings and weekends. BRS has its After-Dark Service and DIALOG has Knowledge Index. These are considerably cheaper to use, and thus the savings can be passed on to the patron if one charges for the service. If there is an on-line fund, more searches could be performed with the savings. Funding for searching may come from the library budget, donations from groups at the college, fund-raisers, or search costs charged to the patron.

Data-base Types

DIALOG has several Ontap files. These are shortened versions of regular data bases. Because there is no charge except for telecommunications, it is useful to use these for practice. DIALOG will supply passwords for its Ontap files.

Another feature of DIALOG is CIP (Classroom Instruction Program). It has been used with increasing popularity for formal, supervised programs of classroom instruction about information retrieval. DIALOG provides up to 10 passwords per institution for almost all of its data bases at the reduced rate of $15 per connect hour, including telecommunication charges. CIP can be used for general library orientation, specialized class projects, and training individuals to conduct on-line searches. It is quite successful in demonstrating the benefits of on-line searching to students and in providing them with an alternative access to information. A special form for record keeping should be provided. (See Figure 1.)

```
            DIALOG CLASSROOM     INSTRUCTION PROGRAM (CIP)


Librarian _____      Date _____

Time--From_____       To   _____

No. of students _____

Databases Used  _____

                _____

Cost_____      Time_____


Brief Description




Follow-up
```

Figure 1. DIALOG Classroom Instruction Program (CIP)

Teaching on-line searching can be done in many ways and to diversified groups at a community college.

Informally it can be demonstrated during bibliographic instruction to classes receiving library orientation. Many classes require on-line instruction for class projects on a wide range of topics. English, chemistry, speech, business, and nursing and allied health curricula are a few courses that lend themselves to this computer technology. Students can receive an hour or two of classroom instruction from a librarian. This could cover the purposes and advantages of on-line searching, Boolean logic, search terms and strategies, truncation, data bases, and vendors. (See Figures 2, 3, 4.) Following the lecture, participants can be divided into groups. A librarian can help them clarify their research topics, select appropriate data bases, and plan effective search strategies. To complete the course, students have hands-on experience, and with the aid of a librarian and appropriate search commands perform a search on a microcomputer. (See Figure 5.)

Community college libraries can teach a research skills course for credit. Within the syllabus, a class devoted to on-line searching may be incorporated. A 20-minute video-tape, "Going Online" by Learned Information, Inc., can be viewed by students for an easy, but thorough approach to the basics of on-line searching.

Promoting on-line searching in professional development workshops for faculty and staff is yet another way the community college library can use on-line searching and train end users. Funds from professional development grants can be applied for and utilized to conduct these workshops, thus allowing faculty and staff to keep abreast of current technology and conduct research in their special areas.

To make a successful search and avoid miscommunication a standardized form should be answered by the student or requesting patron and then reviewed with a librarian. (See Figure 6.)

Computer Literates

Many classes in a community college require students to be computer literate. Nursing programs have a formal computer

LOGICAL OPERATORS

OR – puts the retrieval of all search terms into one set, eliminating duplicate records.

AND – retrieves the intersection, or overlap, of the search terms: all terms must be in each record retrieved.

NOT – eliminates search term (or group of search terms) following it from other search term(s).

A OR B   **A AND B**   **A NOT B**

Note: Always enter a space on either side of a logical operator.

Figure 2. Elements of possible instruction—the basic concepts of Boolean logic.

WHAT IS DIALOG?

1. Includes over 280 data bases.

2. Many kinds of data bases:

   Bibliographical: Ex.: ERIC AND MEDLINE

   Financial: Ex.: PTS Annual Report Abstracts

   Directory: Ex.: Amer. Men and Women of Science

   Full-text: Academic American Encyclopedia

3. Cost: $30.00 to $150.00 an hour plus
   telecommunications and per citation charges

4. Some competing services:

   BRS and BRS/After Dark
   WILSONLINE
   THE SOURCE
   COMPUSERVE

STEP 1:   CHOOSE YOUR DATA BASES

EACH DATA BASE HAS A FILE NUMBER.

DIFFERENCE BETWEEN DATA BASES:

1. SUBJECT
2. TIME PERIOD COVERED
3. TYPE OF MATERIAL INDEXED:
   BOOKS, ARTICLES, REPORTS, ETC.
4. TYPE OF SUBJECT HEADINGS
5. ABSTRACTS - SHORT, LONG, OR NONE
6. LANGUAGES
7. SPECIAL SEARCH TECHNIQUES

DIALINDEX (FILE 411) CAN BE USED AS AN
   INDEX TO GROUPS OF DATA BASES

USE BLUE SHEETS FOR SPECIFIC INFORMATION
ABOUT DATA BASES.

MORE SEARCH TECHNIQUES

1. PARENTHESES MAY BE USED. EXAMPLE:
   DROPOUTS AND (ECONOMIC STATUS OR INCOME)

2. (W) OR () IS USED TO CONNECT WORDS IN A
   PHRASE. EXAMPLE: HIGH()TECHNOLOGY

3. ? IS USED FOR TRUNCATION: EXAMPLE:
   BUDGET? FOR BUDGET, BUDGETS, BUDGETING

4. /ti SPECIFIES THAT A WORD MUST OCCUR IN
   THE TITLE.

BASIC DIALOG COMMANDS

B   TO SELECT A DATA BASE. EX.: B

SS   TO ENTER SEARCH TERMS

T   TO TYPE OUT CITATIONS OR
          INFORMATION ON-LINE

PR   FOR OFF-LINE PRINTS

LOGOFF   TO END SEARCH

STEP 2:   ENTER SEARCH TERMS

1. YOU MAY SEARCH BY SUBJECT, WORDS IN
   TITLE, AUTHOR, ETC.

2. COMBINE TERMS USING "OR," "AND," OR
   "NOT."

EXAMPLES:

SS   COMMUNITY COLLEGES OR TWO-YEAR
     COLLEGE

SS   COMMUNITY COLLEGES AND GRADE
     INFLATION

SS   COMMUNITY COLLEGES NOT CALIFORNIA

SS   S1 AND GRADE INFLATION

VIEWING RESULTS

T 4/3/1-10

4=set 4
3=format - bibliographic citation
1-10 first ten citations

Common formats:
3 Bibliographic citation
5 Full record
8 Title and indexing

PR 4/5/1-100

Results will be printed off=line.
Cost: 14¢ to 60¢ or more per item

**Figure 3. Elements of possible instruction—step-by-step in-
struction about search terms and techniques.**

BASIC DIALOG COMMANDS

B   To select a database   Ex. B 218 (NAHL)
SS   To enter search terms   Ex. SS computers and nursing
T   To type out citations or information online
PR   For offline prints
LOGOFF   To end search

HOW TO ENTER SEARCH TERMS

1.   You may search by subject, words in title, author or
        etc.
2.   Combine terms using "or", "and", or "not"
                        EXAMPLES
        SS Patient education or patient compliance
        SS Alcoholism and nursing care

MORE SEARCH TECHNIQUES

1.   Parentheses may be used Ex. Parkinson disease and
        (patient compliance or patient care)
2.   (W) or () is used to connect words in a phrase
        Ex. Nursing (w) care
3.   ? is used for truncation Ex. Nurs? -Nursing,
        Nurse, nurses

VIEWING RESULTS

T   4/3/1-10
        4= set 4
        3= format - bibliographic citation
    1-10= first ten citations
Common formats
        3   Bibliographic citation
        5   Full record
        8   Title and indexing

**Figure 4. Example of Commands, Search Terms, Search
Techniques, and Viewing Results for DIALOG.**

USING THE COLUMBIA MICROCOMPUTER FOR ONLINE SEARCHING

1. Turn on computer, modem, and printer.

2. Put MS-DOS PL disk in Drive A of computer.

3. Boot computer. When a prompt A⟩ appears type PL and hit
    return.

4. Type ATDT 9, 435-1800 or ATDT 9, followed by whatever
    telephone number you are calling. Two alternate numbers for
    telenet are 429-7896 and 429-7800. (Dialnet is 359-2500 or
    359-2564)

5. Wait for high pitch tone. When "Connect" appears on screen,
    hit return key twice (for Telenet) For terminal identification
    question just hit return. (For Dialnet enter: a)

6. Hit function key F4 to toggle on printer.

7. When @ appears type C 41548d. (for Dialnet type: dialog.)

8. Librarian will type passwords.

9. At end of search, log off, and hit F10 to exit program.

10. When A⟩ appears remove disk from computer; turn off computer,
    printer, and modem.

**Figure 5. Students may complete the course with a "hands-
on" experience, using appropriate search commands (such
as those illustrated above) to conduct an online search on a
computer.**

REQUEST FOR ONLINE SEARCHING   NVCC - ANNANDALE CAMPUS LIBRARY

Fill out this form as completely as possible and discuss it with a reference
librarian. Requests will not be scheduled for searching until they have been
approved by a reference librarian.

NAME _____   DATE _____

ADDRESS (or Department and Extension if faculty or staff)

_____

PHONE NUMBER _____

STATUS (Check one)   Student _____   Faculty or Staff _____

Describe the subject, problem, or question to be searched. Be as specific as
possible. List "key words" related to your topic.

_____

_____

_____

_____

If a student, give name of course and instructor of class for which this search
is being done and describe assignment. If faculty or staff, describe research
project, professional development activity, or other assignment to which this
search relates.

_____

What sources have you already checked? (Examples: NVCC COM catalog, printed
indexes, reference books, other libraries)

_____

What type of search do you want? (See information sheet for description.)

Short, exploratory search (free)_____ Standard search _____ I will pay up to _____

_____

LIBRARY USE ONLY
Approved by Reference Librarian   Name _____ Date _____ Time _____

Scheduled for: Date _____ Time _____ Searcher _____

Amount of Donation _____ Reference Librarian's comments _____

_____

Searched by: Name _____ Date _____ Time_____

Searcher's comments _____

_____

Figure 6. Example of Request Form for Online Searching.

requirement in some colleges. A text, *Essentials of Computers for Nurses* by Virginia Saba, is commonly used. This is supplemented by tapes, films, and software. The library can be part of this course by teaching a lesson on on-line searching. This lesson will introduce general computer concepts and their application in health care as they relate to nursing education, nursing administration, and clinical practice. This lesson is best if presented in two parts: a two-hour group presentation, and individual hands-on searching sessions. During the formal classroom instruction the aforementioned video "Going Online" can be shown. Following a discussion of this, the class can be divided into groups to discuss search strategies for the topics selected by the students. At a subsequent time, individual half-hour on-line search sessions can be scheduled for each student. With the assistance of a librarian, the student can perform his or her own search and thus gain hands-on experience. This teaching format can be used for any course taught at the community college. After students have used traditional reference materials such as printed indexes for newspapers and magazines and Infotrac, on-line bibliographic searching can be used to obtain current and more refined information.

By offering formal classroom instruction in on-line searching or a demonstration search as part of a general orientation or a professional development workshop, faculty, staff, and students enhance their ability to use the latest technology to better locate information.

Reference
[1]Northern Virginia Community College, 1989–90 Catalog, p. 15.

PART IV: PERSONNEL

PART-TIME FACULTY: IMPLICATIONS FOR REFERENCE SERVICES

Pamela A. Price

Community colleges are faced with many societal and economic challenges. These include: increased competition for students and finances, rising costs for infrastructure maintenance and repairs, and faculty and staff retrenchments. The use of part-time faculty has become a primary means for maintaining academic standards and realizing a cost savings for the institution. Part-time faculty now constitutes the majority of community college faculty members.

In complement to the maintenance of academic standards is the library and its resources; in many cases the library has been described as forming the heart of the college. If librarians are to provide services that complement classroom instructional practices, the sheer numbers of part-time faculty alone have bearing on the actual practices and approaches librarians must exercise in order to provide balanced and equitable services. Librarians, particularly reference librarians, face challenges equal to those facing their institutions. Employment of part-time faculty requires academic reference librarians to assume roles above and beyond their traditional roles.

Traditional academic library services in community colleges have long since been augmented with programs and practices designed to meet the needs of an increasingly diverse student population. The literature and many conferences have dealt with issues such as the older student; minority students; disabled students, and other unique student populations who are enrolling in increasing numbers. Yet there seems to be very little literature that specifically addresses the issue of part-time faculty library use. The guiding role that part-time faculty assumes in the instructional and professional preparation of students is vital to achieving the academic mission of community colleges. Moreover, for many students, a part-time faculty member is their only link to a college and its academic support systems. Reference librarians must extend services and collaborate with part-time faculty to accomplish individual efforts to achieve institutional success.

Part-time Faculty

The use of part-time faculty has increased significantly during the 1980s. Samuel (1989) points out that part-time faculty were approximately 36 percent of the total instructional staff in higher education in 1986. It is possible that by the year 2000 part-time faculty at two-year colleges could reach an all-time high. A number of factors have contributed to this:

- increased competition for a declining pool of traditionally aged college students
- a smaller funding base coupled with burgeoning operating costs
- the introduction of new courses/programs that require additional faculty for whom the institution is not able, or yet willing, to fully fund, and
- a need to supplement departmental vacancies created by temporary leaves (sabbatical, maternity, personal), retirements, or resignations.

Given that community colleges are generally community-based and student-oriented in their missions, this trend will no doubt continue but at a slower pace. At many community colleges, part-timers constitute more than 50 percent of the faculty. Furthermore, part-time students frequently select evening, weekend, or off-campus classes that are usually assigned to part-time faculty. Depending on class size, the total number of students taught by part-time faculty can match or exceed 50 percent of the student body.

Since a sizable percentage of the community college student body may have contact only with a part-timer, reference librarians should know something about those who provide this vital link between the college and the student. Tuckman describes part-time faculty as a group with diverse backgrounds and qualifications who are either:

- full-mooners: those with full-time jobs
- students: those enrolled at another institution
- hopeful full-mooners: those who want full-time work
- part-mooners: those with multiple part-time jobs
- part-unknowners: those whose motives are unknown
- homeworkers
- semi-retirees (Tuckman 1978)

According to Leslie, Kellams, and Gunne (1982), their study of a large eastern community college revealed that ". . . day part-timers tend to be younger and less experienced than evening part-timers. Housewives and retirees are more attracted to daytime teaching. Otherwise, fully employed professionals dominate the ranks of evening adjuncts. . . . However, full-timers are, by contrast, professional teachers with substantial commitment and experience. . . ." In terms of part-time faculty development, these authors found that less than 10 percent of all colleges provide meaningful assistance beyond "token access" to laboratories and library services. Figures cited by Wallace (1984) from a report conducted by Yang and Zak show that the humanities, social sciences, and business fields combined constitute 42.7 percent of part-time faculty. For some, finding ways to balance a myriad of demands on their time, both professionally and personally, is difficult at best. For others, the fact that they teach off-campus or at off-peak hours only compounds this problem.

The literature cites many reasons for a person to elect to teach on a part-time basis. Some state they like the challenge and stimulation gained from being in an intellectual environment, others feel it is a privilege to contribute to the next generation entering their fields, and still others teach simply because they need the money.

These descriptions aside, part-time faculty are nonetheless

entitled to the same support services provided to full-time faculty. Reference librarians, who are usually the initial contact people for faculty seeking library assistance, should be a part of college-wide efforts to address part-time faculty issues. Visibility is important if the support services available are to be utilized. Therefore, the reference librarian should work closely with division chairpersons and discipline coordinators who may have more contact with part-time faculty.

Biles and Tuckman (1986) state, "Only after an institution has grappled with who its part-timers are, what their needs are, and what its needs are can it begin to formulate meaningful policies." This principle must serve as the basis for formulating reference services that meet the needs of part-time faculty. Additionally, a reference librarian should consider just what a part-timer is expected to do at their institution.

Biles and Tuckman (p. 83) have proposed a generic job description and statement of part-time teaching responsibilities. It states in part:

> Job description:
> • "Use appropriate instructional media for all courses taught.
> • Prepare thoroughly for all courses taught.
> • Foster a climate of inquiry through free expression and class interaction.
> • Be prepared to act as a teaching unit resource in shaping departmental goals, developing curricula, and ensuring course coordination."
>
> Teaching responsibilities:
>   Standards of teaching that are worthy of accreditation must be maintained.
>   Means of improving instruction should be sought out through professional meetings, societies, workshops, and the current literature of the field. Aid and assistance in these matters may be obtained from colleagues, department chairpersons, program coordinators, academic supervisors, and learning resource personnel. (p. 86)

Each statement outlines institutional expectations of part-time faculty. Reference librarians should use these statements to develop responsive services—services that are philosophically based and in tune with the realities of the challenges faced by part-time faculty.

Instructional Practices

Most discussions in the literature on part-time faculty instructional practices concentrate on issues such as quality, equality, and parity of pedagogical styles, and academic qualifications compared with those of full-time faculty. Community college practices of providing little or no incentives to part-timers for activities outside of the classroom seem to be commonplace. Many sources on this topic mention that institutions realize cost savings by not paying part-timers for class preparation, office hours, attendance at departmental meetings, faculty committee meetings, and professional development activities. Furthermore, as stated by Biles and Tuckman (pp. 80–81), part-timers seldom receive equal access to support services. Friedlander explains that if ". . . certain factors (academic degree attainment, teaching experience, continuity of employment, knowledge of one's educational environment, use of instructional technologies, involvement in educational policy decisions, maintenance of office hours, interaction with colleagues, and participation in professional development activities) contribute to program effectiveness, then one could conclude that the quality of instruction provided by a college is likely to be adversely affected as the proportion of part-time to full-time faculty increases." (Friedlander 1980, p. 35) When comparing the two groups in terms of the number of pages assigned for class readings, use of instructional media, and support services, Friedlander (pp. 30–31) discovered some interesting results. First, full-time faculty required an average of 551 pages per course while part-time faculty required 402 pages. Second, instructional media showed a higher percentage of use by full-timers for the following formats:

Type of media	Full-timers	Part-timers
Films	60%	46%
Overhead trans-		
parencies	45%	30%
Scientific instru-		
ments	42%	28%
Slides	39%	30%
Filmstrips	29%	19%
Videotapes	26%	15%

(Friedlander 1980, p. 31)

The fundamental cause for this disparity, stated by 43 percent of the responding part-timers, was that they did not have access to facilities or assistance with these services. Additionally, according to Friedlander Seitz states, "Three additional factors . . . serve to discourage part-time faculty from using instructional media . . . : (1) lack of awareness of what resources are available; (2) lack of familiarity with procedures on how to acquire desired materials; and (3) lack of sufficient lead time . . . to obtain materials which need to be ordered in advance." (Friedlander 1980, p. 31)

To this I will add a fourth discouragement. Given that there tends to be uncertainty regarding whether or not a course taught solely by a part-timer will be repeated, budget administrators are hesistant to commit funds for resources that may have only short-term value. Consequently, requests for resources by part-time faculty may be denied, thus establishing a precedent that discourages future requests from being submitted.

Finally, instructional-support services are available to faculty at most colleges. In terms of the library, however, only 34 percent of the part-time faculty indicated that they used its services. On the other hand, full-time use was 43 percent (p. 32)

Few would argue that student academic success is a vital part of an institution's mission. McCabe (1988) states that some of the most important skills for students to gain from the college experience are ". . . competence in learning and basic-information skills—the ability to find, read, analyze, interpret, communicate, and the ability to formulate new ideas and to make decisions."

Reference librarians must demonstrate that their efforts, combined with those who reach a sizable percentage of students, namely part-time faculty, can help students achieve these competencies. Most classes are taught primarily by lectures supplemented by textbook readings. If, as is the case in New Jersey, discussions are undertaken to measure educational outcomes and test general intellectual skills, reference librarians will have to reassess their services, resources, and programs.

Implications for Reference Librarians

Reference services in community college libraries include: supporting the overall mission of the college; serving as the intermediary between users and the resources and services provided; selecting appropriate resources; and providing user education. Although these are not all of the specific service functions reference librarians perform, these functions explain why reference librarians are usually the first persons approached by users.

It has so far been presented that part-time faculty as a group do not utilize instructional-support services at the same rate as full-time faculty. This author conducted a brief survey of part-time faculty library use at Mercer County (NJ) Community College. My findings showed that of those who responded (22 out of 199) the majority: are female; are between the ages of thirty-one and forty; hold a Master's degree; have served equally for zero to two or five-plus years; and are mainly in the humanities and instructional resources divisions of the college. Even though the response rate was too low to make statistically reliable judgments, one confirming observation could be made. That is, part-time faculty felt that they knew very little about the library and its services and would like to know more. One respondent indicated that payment for preparation time would be an incentive to utilize library services, and others felt that they did not have adequate class time for library assignments. Still, others felt that their classes were not structured for library use.

The reference librarian should review institutional information on divisional part-time employment. This information can be helpful for planning services. Advance knowledge can be helpful in anticipating areas where there will be high demand for resources. If necessary, librarians may arrange to meet with classes during a lecture to emphasize the role the library can have in helping them to meet class requirements. By consulting with these faculty members, a reference librarian can determine if new services need to be developed to meet anticipated user demand. In general, sound reference services mean not only meeting a multiplicity of informational needs that are obvious in an academic setting, but identifying and addressing the needs of the not so obvious user population. Part-time faculty, by virtue of their status, need innovative and creative services. In this case, the reference librarian must develop ways to market the library. For instance, a reference librarian could provide resources at a remote location. By arranging to place selected titles at a remote facility, users could have access to needed information. This service could also enhance access to library services and resources by providing a mail-in or telephone-reference request service. In short, to the extent that personnel and resources allow, a part-time faculty member who cannot get to the library during regular hours should be accommodated by improvising current services. Part-time and full-time faculty can share in collection assessments. Because many part-time faculty members are "full-mooners," their expertise can be useful in this area. Likewise, listings of new acquisitions should be distributed to part-timers along with encouragements to submit requests. The promotion of reference services, moreover, should include a strong user education component. These and other recommendations will be discussed next.

Recommendations

An educated library user benefits both the reference librarian and the user. A thorough library orientation will provide part-time faculty with the knowledge needed to direct students to specific resources and services that aid in developing critical thinking skills. Also, part-time faculty should be introduced to those subject resources that will best support their classroom needs. The primary function of the orientation should be to highlight the library's support service role and demonstrate creative methods for integrating library resources in the classroom. Keeping in mind that scheduling an orientation for part-time faculty may be difficult, the first consideration for a reference librarian should be determining the times when as many people as possible can attend.

More than one time slot is best, as well as varying the days of the week and extending the orientation to weekends. In addition, it may be difficult to have library staff from other key service areas on hand, but whatever arrangements can be made for these people to be present should be attempted. Scheduling the orientation early in the term will allow faculty members to plan for the use of resources as their classes progress. Because some part-time faculty learn of class assignments late, the first two to four weeks in the term is a good time to conduct an orientation session. This will allow time for a reference librarian to identify part-timers and consult with those assigned to remote sites about their availability.

The orientation should include: a tour of service areas, as well as a brief description of the library's collection; photo-copier access procedures; lead time necessary to deliver on a requested service; circulation procedures; library technology (what is available and how to use it); a display with user guides for selected reference materials that are less than five years old; and information on cooperative agreements with local libraries. In addition, an explanation of how services can be requested; how resources can be ordered for acquisition or preview; ways to place resources on reserve; and how resources are arranged on the shelf should be given. Hand-books describing these and other areas of interest in detail should be distributed. This should include: reproducible request forms for those who cannot frequent the library in person; telephone numbers for each service area; the name of the people responsible for these service areas along with the hours they work; and, telefacsimile numbers if a machine is available. If library cards are used, this would be the time to register part-time faculty to receive them.

Orientations should be provided each term, including summers, for new part-time faculty members. Returning part-timers should be invited so that they can learn of any new resources or services. It may also help to seek the assistance of the department chairperson or part-time faculty coordinator to encourage attendance.

Services

There are a number of basic reference services that are commonly provided to any user. But, if access to the library during service hours is a problem for the part-time faculty member, alternative delivery sources should be available. Most security offices are open when other college offices are closed. Information could be left with the security office for pickup at a more convenient time for the part-timer. Telefacsimile machines can also be used to send information that is needed in a short period of time.

Answering machines can be used to leave requests during nonservice hours. The first librarian on reference duty the next business day would be responsible for retrieving requests.

A current awareness service can be provided to keep part-timers abreast of new developments in their field. A file listing journals of interest by the name of the faculty member could be maintained. When the current issue of the journal is received, the contents page is photocopied and sent to the faculty member for review. The same procedure can be utilized for conducting on-line searches at regular intervals.

Guides and Instructional Handouts

Most reference departments have collection and service guides on hand. These resources can be of use to part-time faculty when they compile course bibliographies. In addition to printed handouts, basic reference information can be provided on computer disks or on videotapes. If resources are available on campus, attempts should be made to produce handouts in machine-readable format.

These recommendations are by no means exhaustive. In fact, given the nature of reference librarianship and local college circumstances, only a few may actually be feasible in any one library. Yet, the needs of part-time faculty are a reality that reference librarians, particularly those in community colleges, have to address on a broad spectrum.

References

Biles, George E., and Howard P. Tuckman, *Part-time Faculty Personnel Management Policies,* New York: American Council on Education, Macmillan Publishing Co., 1986.

Friedlander, Jack. "Instructional Practices of Part-time and Full-time Faculty." *Community College Review,* 6 (Winter 1979); pp. 65–72.

————. "Instructional Practices of Part-time Faculty." *New Directions for Community Colleges,* 30 (1980); pp. 27–36.

Leslie, David W., Samuel E. Kellams, and G. Manny Gunne. *Part-time Faculty in American Higher Education,* New York: Praeger Publishers, 1982.

McCabe, Robert H. "The Educational Program of the American Community College: A Transition," In *Colleges of Choice: The Enabling Impact of the Community College,* ed. Judith S. Eaton. New York: American Council on Education, Macmillan Publishing Co., 1988.

Samuel, Fayez M. "A Strategy to Eliminate Inequality of Higher Education Opportunities by Improving Adjunct Faculty Performance." *Community College Review,* 17 (Fall 1989); pp. 41–47.

Tuckman, Howard P. "Who is Part-time in Academe?" *AAUP Bulletin,* 64 (December 1978); pp. 305–314.

Wallace, M. Elizabeth, ed. *Part-time Academic Employment in the Humanities,* New York: Modern Language Association, 1984.

PARAPROFESSIONALS AT THE REFERENCE DESK

Kate Donnelly Hickey

> The objective of a library is not merely to warehouse information, but to help patrons find the information they desire. Though all aspects of librarianship are concerned with this goal, it is at the reference desk that the process of determining the patron's need, formulating a research strategy to fill that need, and providing accurate and complete information to the patron is finally tested.[1]

The use of paraprofessionals at the reference desk has been the subject of a spirited, long-standing debate in academic librarianship. For most libraries the issue has been de facto decided. The question no longer is *whether* to use paraprofessionals but *how* to utilize them most effectively. Theories aside, most community college reference service would grind slowly to a halt if we eliminated paraprofessionals, clerical employees, and/or student workers. In small and medium-sized libraries, often there are only one or two administrators, who with a small number of librarians are responsible for reference, planning, bibliographic instruction, collection development and management, the preparation and implementation of surveys and subsequent new services, research and publication, college committee work, and so one—it is no wonder paraprofessionals are holding down the fort at the reference desk!

Given this reality, it is imperative that we understand the advantages and disadvantages of this staffing pattern so we can utilize paraprofessionals effectively. Well-trained and motivated workers bring immense benefits to the library, to themselves, and to the profession.

In this essay, the term "paraprofessional" generally refers to an employee with a position at the library technician level, usually requiring some library experience and/or education below that of a Master of Library Science. Yet the principles expressed here hold true for any nonlibrarians working at reference, including clerical staff and student workers. The term "reference desk" implies any workstation where patron questions beyond the directional are answered.

Dumont has surveyed community college library directors to determine what qualities are desired when hiring librarians. He lists as most important: 1) a basic understanding of academic librarianship, 2) demonstration of professional development and growth, 3) a strong student service orientation, 4) familiarity with computer technology, 5) attitudes consistent with being a team player, 6) an outgoing personality, with the flexibility and creativity to handle multiple tasks, 7) effective teaching and motivating skills for student learning, 8) the ability to work independently, 9) organizational skills, and 10) the ability to react sensibly under pressure.[2] Not all of these skills are exclusive to MLS graduates! Obviously we cannot expect paraprofessionals to have broad academic knowledge or well-honed pedagogic skills, but nonlibrarians often possess the other desired qualities.

More than half of the community college student population is new each year. Most commute; many are part-time; many are busy adults with myriad responsibilities. Community college students tend to be novice (and often fearful) library users with relatively unsophisticated demands. "Paraprofessionals can play an important role in the total library program by assisting the many uncertain and insecure patrons with services . . . by handling the many 'where is it?' and 'how to' questions, by relating well to the patrons, by providing basic and friendly explanations, and by creating a relaxed climate in the library conducive to good learning."[3] Paraprofessionals often can bridge the gap between the student and librarian, whose depth and breadth of knowledge may tend to overwhelm confused undergraduates.

Recent studies show that paraprofessionals perform many reference desk duties. Courtois and Goetsch report that 61 percent of academic libraries surveyed in Illinois use parapro-

fessionals at the reference desk and that of these 51 percent
are using this staff in increasing numbers. Thirty-nine percent
of these libraries schedule paraprofessionals for more than
half the time the desks are staffed. Significantly, the survey
determined that in 73 percent of the libraries, paraprofessionals at the information desk frequently work alone, without a
librarian as backup. Paraprofessionals often are scheduled for
the early morning, late evening, and weekend hours, when
referral help is at a minimum. "Results indicate that it is
almost always the nonprofessional who must judge when a
question is beyond his or her capabilities and that the
nonprofessional must make this decision in the absence of
detailed guidelines and without a chance to consult a professional."[4] Standard wisdom is that paraprofessionals on the
reference desk are no detriment to service because they
always can refer difficult questions to the librarians; the
findings above call into question this assumption. We must
look closely at staffing patterns and referral policies.

Paraprofessional: Advantages and Disadvantages

Rettig, in a study of reference desk activity at the University of Illinois at Chicago Main Library, determined that
nearly two-thirds of all questions asked fell into the directional and known-item category. He notes, "At an academic
library a large part of the patron pool renews itself every four
years [every two years for community colleges]. In short, no
matter how much libraries want their services to be proactive
rather than passive, no matter how much they want to serve
unexpressed needs, no matter how much libraries want to
develop service programs tailored to the needs of sophisticated users, there is no escaping the perennial need to
establish and maintain service mechanisms to respond to
clearly expressed and recurring needs of a fundamental
nature."[5]

At the time of this study, the University of Illinois at
Chicago's reference desks were staffed entirely by librarians,
who were experiencing increased problems with the volume
of questions asked and the queuing of patrons waiting for

help. Librarians were frustrated by the "subtle pressure to abbreviate the service given to patrons with search strategy and reference questions in order to get back to the desk quickly to answer the questions of the queuing patrons. It was disheartening to have to leave a patron to his own devices after, for example, a very hurried explanation of the use of the hard copy Dissertation Abstracts, only to rush back to the desk where the next patron needed to know only the location of the pencil sharpener. . . . This was far less than optimum use of librarians and far less than optimum service to patrons. In fact, it translated into poor service for the patrons."[6] The library administration's first response to this problem was a pilot program scheduling a technical assistant and a reference librarian together at the desk. While reducing patron waiting time, this arrangement did not serve to direct reference and search strategy questions to the librarian. In time-honored fashion, students asked whatever questions they had to whichever staff member was available, and interactions between the two staff members usually involved awkward interruptions. In this case, it was clear that the librarian could not be stationed in a public area, and the system was redesigned to place the on-duty librarian in a nearby office, connected by telephone to the technical assistant at the reference desk. Patron queuing lessened, and librarians unanimously agreed that they now spend more time with patrons and deliver better reference services.

Woodard reports similar findings in a study of an information desk functioning separately from a reference desk in a major research library. While few community college libraries have the staffing necessary for this luxury, the study results are instructive. Woodard used unobtrusive testing to ask information desk paraprofessionals directional, procedural, bibliographic, subject-oriented, and ready-reference questions. "Correct" responses included not only answering the question accurately but also referring it correctly to the librarian stationed at the nearby reference desk. Using this measurement, a total of 70.7 percent of the inquiries were handled correctly by the paraprofessional staff. "However, the study indicates that adequate staffing levels and professional backup are needed in order for the information desk staff to perform at an optimum level. Their success or accuracy in answering questions increases when a reference librarian is present at the reference desk, when the information desk is double staffed, or if the staff member asked a question of the patron to clarify his or her request."[7]

This is not to say that staffing with non-librarians presents no problems. Many studies show that paraprofessionals, although excellent at answering directional and known-item questions, have trouble with reference interviews and vague and/or complex questions. A sobering study by Murfin and Bunge, surveying 20 academic libraries of more than 100,000 volumes in a size, reveals that in 80 percent of the libraries patrons were less satisfied with the help they received from paraprofessionals than from librarians. There is strong evidence that "paraprofessionals have more communication difficulty with patrons and more difficulty in negotiating reference questions than do professional librarians. . . . Significantly more often, patrons of paraprofessionals reported that they felt that their questions had not been understood than did patrons of professionals."[8]

These findings should not be surprising—what would we say if paraprofessionals and librarians scored the same? The difference in success rate alone is not disturbing, but the further finding that paraprofessionals consulted with others only 7.9 percent of the time is. For reasons not explored in the study, often the expected referrals did not occur. The survey showed that lower-scoring paraprofessionals attempted to answerer a significantly larger percentage of complex questions than did the higher-scoring group. Conversely, the higher-scoring group consulted with others 16.39 percent of the time, significantly more so than the average. Another thought-provoking finding is that often when the patron perceived problems, the paraprofessional did not.[9] This evidence of communication difficulty by paraprofessionals again validates the need for the *ready availability* of referral help as a crucial factor in the effective delivery of a reference service.

This fact is brought home dramatically in a recent study by Christensen and others of reference service at the Brigham Young University Library, where a decision was made to staff reference desks entirely with paraprofessionals and students, who were to summon subject specialists from their offices when help was needed. Using unobtrusive testing with basic reference questions (not directional or known item), the study revealed major problems: "1) the student and department assistants feel isolated from the subject specialists; 2) the referral system works poorly; 3) the training program is inconsistent and often ineffective; and most seriously 4) the student assistants answered only 36 percent of the unobtrusive test questions correctly."[10] What a disaster!

Details of the Christensen findings are instructive. Assistants were judged on their ability to conduct the four components of the reference interview:

1. Question negotiation
2. Search strategies in answering or attempting to fulfill patron requests
3. Correctness of the answer provided
4. Referral, when required, to another more appropriate source to obtain a satisfactory answer.

Many problems stemmed from the assistants' inability to complete this process satisfactorily. "Although the student references assistants recognized and responded well to explicit requests for negotiation, they did not perform as well on the implicit. This suggests that the problem may not be an inability to negotiate with patrons, but either a failure to recognize more subtle requests or an unwillingness to question patrons who seem knowledgeable and informed and state their requests in such specific, positive terms."[11]

Christensen correctly states, "Providing professional-quality reference service is a complex process, requiring extensive subject expertise, knowledge of library collections and systems, and years of practical experience."[12] Student workers always will lack this experience, one reason why this study cannot be extrapolated fully to include all paraprofessionals. Additionally, this study reveals as many problems with the librarians as with the assistants. At Brigham Young, direct reference service no longer was considered one of a librarian's main responsibilities, replaced no doubt by bibliographic instruction, collection

development, research, and committee work. Fortunately, this
same study surveyed the librarians and found they too were
unhappy with the situation. "The subject specialists over-
whelmingly felt that having professional librarians work assigned hours at the desk would have direct and substantial
impact on improved overall reference service. The data also
show that monitoring patron demands, keeping abreast of new
reference tools, training and monitoring reference assistants,
strengthening esprit de corps, and receiving more referrals
from the desk would also be improved with professionals
working assigned desk hours."[13]

Many would echo this need for professional librarians to take
ultimate responsibility for improving reference service both
directly and indirectly, to be readily accessible to patrons when
needed, and to regularly and thoughtfully evaluate priorities.
Vavrek deplores what he sees as the decline of traditional
reference librarianship and the abrogating of responsibilities to
others. He sees the professional librarian as more than an
answerer of questions but as the key to all communication with
the public.[14] Peele, although acknowledging that paraprofessionals answer many types of requests successfully, feels that
the complexity of the reference interview suggests that a
patron's first contact should always be a librarian.[15]

How do we resolve these viewpoints? Most would agree
that neither the librarians nor the paraprofessionals can do it
alone. In community college libraries, expanding hours,
lengthening semesters and summer sessions, stable or shrinking staffs, and increased demands on professional librarians all
necessitate creative solutions to the reference desk dilemma.
The studies make clear that at least three factors are crucial
for the successful integration of various staff in reference
service: 1) adequate orientation and training of paraprofessional staff; 2) clear guidelines for referral; and 3) a team
approach.

Orientation and Training

Education pedagogy lists the four basis steps to successful
teaching: 1) tell the student what you are going to teach

(orientation); 2) teach what you have promised (the training process itself); 3) restate what you have taught (reinforcement); and 4) test on what you have taught (assessment). The elimination of any of these steps weakens a training program.

Orientation for reference desk duty should be comprehensive. First the paraprofessional should be fully oriented to the library's physical layout, because, for better or worse, students ask more questions about bathrooms and pencil sharpeners than about Current Biography. Next, trainees should become familiar with the library staff and its duties so they know to whom to ask what. Socialization is extremely important; the more quickly new employees feel welcome and valued, the more quickly they will learn. Finally, recognizing that many questions will be nonlibrary-related (i.e., Where is my classroom? Who is the dean of students?), strong efforts should be made to provide as much college-wide orientation as possible. Be sure at least that the paraprofessional has had an in-depth college tour and an explanation of college organization and knows the location of campus directories and maps.

Once general orientation is complete, the learning should become job specific. This is the time for careful analysis of the job description, including specific competencies. The trainer should describe a typical desk session and the behavior expected by the paraprofessional. The library's service policies should be explained, using specific examples. While the importance of a service attitude will be emphasized throughout all levels of training, the initial introduction should present the library's philosophy in depth. If the library director is not handling the training, it may be appropriate to ask him or her to speak on this issue in order to emphasize its importance.

Through the orientation it is vital to empower the paraprofessional to provide feedback, questions, and suggestions at any time during the process. No training program is perfect, and a new employee may bring a welcome perspective. The paraprofessional should be asked to help the teacher avoid covering too much too fast. Particularly in small, understaffed libraries there is a natural tendency to be in a hurry to get the new employee up to speed as quickly as possible—to train and be done with it. Both trainer and trainee must resist this behavior. A step-by-step written orientation and training plan will help, but asking the paraprofessional for constant feedback is crucial.

When orientation is complete, training can begin. Teaching, reinforcement, and assessment are separate steps, none of which can be ignored, but in practice all three are intertwined. It is necessary for the trainer carefully to determine how, and especially when, reinforcement and assessment will occur for a specific competency. Some, like being able to change the microfilm lens, will need immediate hands-on practice; others, like conducting an effective reference interview, will require several steps and levels of assessment.

Training for particular elements of reference desk duty may take many forms—computerized, interactive, written assignments, show-and-tell, observation, and so on. Some will be more appropriate than others, depending on the tasks to be learned and the number of trainees. What is important is that careful thought be given to process and sequence. Benson recommends several successful strategies: 1) provide "release time" to librarians to encourage their active participation in the training process; 2) be sure the policy and procedures manual is as complete and current as possible; and 3) assign one person (perhaps the director, perhaps a reference librarian) the clear responsibility for an integrated training program.[16] Content is more important than format.

Whatever the method, it is essential that demonstration be followed both by hands-on experience and by knowledge of where to get help; this may be a manual, the front pages of an index, or an experienced person, but it is critical that paraprofessionals know what to do when they forget how to perform a particular task, particularly when backup personnel are not available. The wonderful variety of reference work assures that it may be days, if not weeks, before a particular question or situation reoccurs.

In an interesting article on the training of MLS graduate students for reference work, Woodard and Van Der Laan suggest that the key to successful training is motivation, which is heavily influenced by the socialization process. One-on-one

training establishes collegial relationships between paraprofessionals and librarians, facilitating learning and allowing
librarians to impart the reference desk philosophy of "consci-
entiousness and accountability."[17]

As in all education, no one absorbs everything at once.
Aspects of both orientation and training must be repeated on
a regular basis. While much of this process can be individualized, some formal reinforcement should occur, if only to
insure that this important aspect not be forgotten. Particularly
helpful is the supervisor's careful observation of the paraprofessional's attitude and behavior at the desk, and the immediate offering of both constructive criticism and praise (don't
forget the praise!). It often is difficult to provide effective
follow-up to the learning that occurs when a librarian helps a
paraprofessional with direct patron service—where is the
time for discussion of search strategy or a resource, when one
or both employees must continue in the public eye? Woodard
and Van Der Laan suggest the use of a "question log" in which
new employees write down all the questions they have, no
matter how trivial, to be discussed later with a supervisor.[18]
Such a log also might be useful for the librarian, who could jot
down suggestions for the paraprofessional. This method will
be effective, however, only if scheduled, regular time is set
aside for consultation.

New employees should know that learning in a reference
department never stops. The director must see that staff
development plans are provided for all levels of employees
and are considered critical for experienced librarians as well
as novice paraprofessionals. In-house mini-lectures detailing
the use of a particular source are an easy way to add a touch of
training to a staff meeting and are especially effective if
paraprofessionals are included among the presenters. Many
workshops, particularly those sponsored by regional groups
and state agencies, are appropriate for paraprofessionals.
Their paid attendance at these workshops not only reinforces
skills but also demonstrates the library's faith in the new
employee.

The fourth phase of an effective training program is
assessment. Here the burden of proof is on the supervisor.
Did the desired learning actually occur? While favorable

trainee reaction to the program is essential, a happy employee is not always a knowledgeable one. "Just because a movie, book, or lecture is accepted by a group or is enjoyable or entertaining does not mean that anyone in the group understood, absorbed, or acquired the principles, facts, or techniques presented."[19] It is easy to overlook the wheel that does not squeak in a busy library. Absolute disasters always come to a supervisor's attention; low-level difficulties may not. No news is not always good news. In a library where supervision is minimal and independence is prized, we must be sure our assessment mechanisms, whether formal or informal, are firmly in place.

Assessment should never be a surprise. Its object is to encourage staff, not to punish them. Testing procedures, observations, even an unobtrusive reference survey should be thoroughly explained in advance. Employees need to know how, when, and by whom they will be evaluated. Conversely, supervisors need to know the value and effects of assessment techniques and must seek ongoing feedback from their staff.

Methods of assessment vary widely and may be formal or informal. Pre- and post-tests bracketing a training session provide immediate results but do nothing to measure long-term retention or practical application. Yet formal tests and worksheets, carefully evaluated and discussed, can be valuable tools, particularly for new employees who can measure their progress in a concrete way. Formal tests also force the trainer to decide what is important and to convey that effectively. Tests may be written or may be practical; simulation of actual reference desk situations may help assess both practical knowledge and communication skills.

While it is relatively easy to assess knowledge of reference sources, ability to use microform equipment, and effective searching techniques for CD-ROM data bases, it is difficult to transmit and measure the more intangible reference interviewing skills. Librarians themselves frequently receive no formal communication training. Somehow all reference desk staff must learn that there is more to reference work than just answering the specific question asked. At this point the value of having our most skilled and experienced reference librarians directly involved in the training process is clear. Assessment of the ability to understand what a patron is *really* asking can occur first through role-playing and, when the paraprofessional has gained confidence, through observation of actual patron interaction. The supervisor should get as much feedback on employee performance as possible, from co-workers and librarians, from patrons and the employees themselves.

Assessment, as with training and reinforcement, never ends. The most time-consuming method is also the most valuable—direct communication. Library directors or other supervisors frequently feel such time-management pressure that they shortchange informal discussion with staff members. A relaxed, unhurried, nonjudgmental conversation frequently unearths employee fears and concerns and also gives the supervisor a chance to reinforce philosophies and policies. This communication is especially useful after employees have completed initial training and are attempting to put their knowledge to work. The need for these regular conferences may diminish slightly with time but never disappears. Face-to-face, open-ended communication never loses its value.

Referral

Referral is a crucial form of communication, one that must be included in all reference planning. Studies cited earlier in this chapter suggest that referral policies may be the most influential factor in the successful use of paraprofessionals at the reference desk. This research presents various modes of referral in varying circumstances.

Regazzi and Hersberger analyze several models for reference desk service at peak periods of a busy mid-sized academic library. They consider various staffing patterns: #1— one librarian; #2—an assistant and a librarian in tandem; #3—a librarian and a student in tandem; #4—two librarians in parallel; and #5—an assistant and a librarian in parallel. The authors' analysis of levels of effectiveness echoes that of earlier studies. Number 1 results in too many long lines, and #3 is great but very expensive. That leaves deciding how best to utilize assistants. Number 3 proves unworkable; the librarian, as the first responder, spends too much time on directional questions. Number 5 is fairly satisfactory but, as noted previously, patrons are indiscriminate as to whom they ask what, and the two staff members constantly have to interrupt each other. Number 2, where the assistant fields the initial inquiry and passes on to the librarian complex reference and search strategy questions, proves most effective, both in lessening patron waiting time and in providing needed service.[20] Clearly, studies consistently demonstrate that scheduling two people, an assistant at the public desk and a librarian on duty in a nearby office, is an ideal situation.

Yet the ideal is not always practical. How many community college libraries have enough staff to commit two people at one time to reference duty? Can we give our paraprofessionals enough skills so they can function fairly independently, but at the same time encourage them to seek professional help when needed? This is not easy!

Our training programs should make it clear to paraprofessionals what we expect them to know. If they have, or acquire, additional expertise, they should be encouraged to use it, but they must not feel guilty when help is needed. The problem is that while our policies encourage, maybe even require, referral, our behavior frequently has the opposite effect. For example, we may tell assistants to refer questions that are beyond them, thus subtly suggesting some kind of failure. Librarians, busy with other responsibilities, may resent being interrupted for "just a reference question" and may show that resentment through body language or inattention. Librarians may make themselves physically and/or psychologically inaccessible, by, for example, pounding frantically on the computer keyboard, clearly much too busy to be bothered. These are natural behaviors. Even if the professional staff manages to overcome these tendencies, and truly believes in the primacy of reference service, it is still prone to a willingness to let sleeping dogs lie. If a paraprofessional rarely refers, we simply assume he or she is doing a great job; we value independence, especially in a busy, understaffed library, and are reluctant to probe beneath the surface to see if service is truly at the level we desire.

Referral is further complicated by the fact that, as stated earlier by Courtois and Goetsch, 73 percent of the libraries that use paraprofessionals at the reference desk frequently schedule them alone, usually in the evenings and on weekends.[21] This reality throws the theoretical models out the window. When paraprofessionals are scheduled alone, they must be carefully trained in procedures to use when they are unable to provide full assistance to a patron. Several options are possible.

First, paraprofessionals should never apologize for their own lack of knowledge—this is not the problem—but may apologize that more staff is not on duty. If patrons become upset or angry, the assistant may suggest that they voice their concerns to an appropriate dean (some libraries even have complaint forms ready). The library director can use such comments as justification for seeking funds for increased staffing. Secondly, the paraprofessional should use reference interview techniques to determine the urgency and level of the patron's question. Perhaps it will be possible at least to get the research started. If more help continues to be needed, several referral techniques are possible.

If the request seems truly urgent and important, the paraprofessional needs to investigate all alternatives. First, the paraprofessional should scour the library offices for any possible assistance. Even though the librarians aren't present, another assistant may be able to help. In many libraries, the director expects to be called upon when needed, especially if he/she advocates a strong service ethic. Failing this, the patron can be referred to another nearby library that may be more fully staffed; the paraprofessional can phone ahead on behalf of the patron if appropriate. Some referral policies encourage the telephoning of librarians at home.

On the other hand, if the question does not appear urgent, paraprofessionals can do both themselves and their patrons a service by deferring the problem to a later time. The patron can be asked to return when the appropriate librarian is present, with a formal appointment if feasible. Even more straightforward would be to refer the question itself to the librarians and have them telephone the patron when the answer is found.

Clearly, referral does not work well if the library staff has a hierarchical attitude that discourages communication and implies failure. Librarians can lead by example by showing their own willingness to refer quickly; pride in being able always to answer the question is unrealistic and leads to poor patron service. The important point is not who finds the answer, but that it gets found.

Team Building

In a superb, thought-provoking article, McCarthy articulates what many of us have tried to put into practice. She decries the "myth, based on outmoded principles of scientific management, which says questions can simply be divided between librarians and assistants according to level of difficulty, thereby increasing our efficiency while allowing us to remain responsive to client needs."[22] Instead, she suggests we use Japanese management techniques to create a team, with unspoken coordination and no organization chart. She uses terminology from Ouchi's Theory Z[23] to call this team a clan.

> In Ouchi's kind of clan, there is intentional ambiguity as to who in the group is responsible for any given task or activity; the clan is responsible. Everything important is a result of teamwork. People work together in an atmosphere of trust and commitment. Rigidly defined separate duties for supervisors and workers, with the feelings of inferiority and superiority they produce, are kept to a minimum. Above all, the clan tries to bring out the best in people by setting expectations high and by showing them in all possible ways that they are important to the success of the whole group.[24]

McCarthy sums up the primary concerns in using nonlibrarians at the reference desk as, first, that they will not recognize the often hidden question behind the one asked, and secondly, that they will not ask for help when needed. Our other cited studies bear out these concerns. Our professional attention has not sufficiently focused on "getting everyone to refer questions clearly not within their competence, and to ask for help whenever there is the slightest doubt as to whether a question has been adequately answered."[25] She feels we must concentrate, not on the questions asked, but on the people who answer them. "To provide the best possible service we must have the best possible staff, interested in their jobs and constantly challenged to learn more."[26]

The rigid assignment of "routine" tasks to paraprofessionals and "challenging" work to librarians has many negative aspects. Intelligent, motivated paraprofessionals become broad and resentful, resulting in, at best, high staff turnover, and, at worst, a staff that does not take pride in its work and that may even consciously or unconsciously sabotage operations from within. Librarians also benefit from a variety of tasks, including at least some routine ones. How can professionals provide leadership if they don't know what others are doing? Some routine work even can be restful, providing a sense of completion in a job that often seems never-ending.

McCarthy recommends we treat our assistants as apprentices, working directly with librarians and learning as they work. This practice, while not clearly defined, probably is common in many community college libraries, where informal training of one new employee at a time is the norm. We, however, may not have viewed this system as a valid management technique; more frequently we apologize for not being better organized! Japanese theory suggests that what many of us practice is not only practical but highly effective as well. Many traditional ideas of efficiency are based on classical organization theory, historically used in corporate bureaucracies and factories and "particularly unsuitable for reference departments, where the work is characterized by the unexpected and unpredictable and the 'production line' consists of people!"[27]

McCarthy suggests a reference clan would exhibit such behavioral characteristics as: 1) a shift in emphasis from the efficient performance of duties to finding the best answer no matter who must be interrupted; 2) a desire by all levels of staff to learn more about library research; 3) the valuing of team behavior, rather than independence, with people scheduled to work together whenever possible; 4) referral, now called collaboration, as the norm, not the exception; and 5) the holding of regular staff meetings, which would include all clan members.[28] Many will note that this pattern often is occurring now in small libraries where the luxury of a hierarchy does not exist. I submit that, no matter how large the library, the care and nourishment of a reference clan, although perhaps "inefficient" and chaotic, will result in the patron service we desire.

Summary

If we could assign only librarians to the reference desk, would we? The regular, systematic use of trained paraprofessionals in reference brings benefits to the employee, to the library, and to the profession as a whole.

Paraprofessionals, to be successful, need adequate training, interesting work, an environment that values and rewards their efforts, and a career ladder that includes some way to move into professional status if desired. Welsh, herself a paraprofessional in a small academic library, describes her role:

> The essence of the role is flexibility—the flexibility needed to perform an assigned group of tasks, while responding to the pressures exerted by the professional ranks above and the nonprofessional below. This could result in being interrupted while processing an ILL request on OCLC to provide in-depth reference service and later to shelve books because the workstudy is sick.
>
> Having to be flexible and yet responsible for a set number of duties creates a role in which the individual could be described as a jack-of-all-trades and master of some or perhaps a generalist with specific duties. The jobs which develop from such flexibility can be interesting, diversified, and very satisfying to perform. . . . Who would not enjoy a job which has been shaped in part by one's own unique abilities and interests?[29]

People given challenging work, for which they receive appropriate training and support, discover their own abilities and, best of all, often fall in love with the profession. Paraprofessionals often enter their first position with no clear idea of librarianship. Many later decide to pursue a Master's degree in the field; in the author's library, for example, four out of five librarians, including the director, began their careers as paraprofessionals.

In a recent editorial in *American Libraries*, editor Tom Gaughan addresses the issue of recruitment for the library profession. He feels intensive efforts to recruit undergraduates will be a poor use of our energies. Instead, "We're better off recruiting thirty-year-olds who have already learned that no career is perfect; who have raised families; who are prepared to make an informed career choice and apply their experience to that career; who have learned that the intrinsic reward of work worth doing is more valuable than a country club."[30]

Why should we encourage and nurture our paraprofessionals, and why, above all, should we give them interesting, challenging things to do? Because from their ranks will come many of the best of our future librarians.

References

[1]John O. Christensen and others, "An Evaluation of Reference Desk Service," *College & Research Libraries* 50 (July 1989), p. 468.

[2]Paul E. Dumont, "Library Education and Employer Expectations: the Two-Year Perspective," *Journal of Library Administration* 11(3) (1989), pp. 59–77.

[3]Theresa C. Goss, "The Status of Paraprofessionals as Perceived by Community/Junior College Library Directors and Librarians," *Community & Junior College Libraries* 3 (Spring 1985), pp. 47–48.

[4]Martin P. Courtois and Lori A. Goetsch, "Use of Nonprofessionals at Reference Desks," *College & Research Libraries* 45 (September 1984), p. 389.

[5]James Rettig, "Users and Services," in *The Academic Library in Transition: Planning for the 1990s,* ed. by Beverly P. Lynch (New York: Neal-Schuman, 1989), p. 100.

[6]Rettig, p. 101.

[7]Beth S. Woodard, "The Effectiveness of an Information Desk Staffed by Graduate Students and Nonprofessionals," *College & Research Libraries* 50 (July 1989), p. 463.

[8]Marjorie E. Murfin and Charles A. Bunge, "Paraprofessionals at the Reference Desk," *The Journal of Academic Librarianship* 14 (March 1988) p. 12.

[9]Murfin and Bunge, pp. 10–14.

[10] Christensen and others, p. 468.

[11] Christensen and others, p. 470.

[12] Christensen and others, p. 468.

[13] Christensen and others, p. 480.

[14] Bernard Vavrek, "When Reference Librarianship Died: It Began in Detroit," *RQ* 17 (Summer 1978), pp. 301–305.

[15] David Peele, "Staffing the Reference Desk," *Library Journal* 105 (September 1980), pp. 1706–1711.

[16] Larry D. Benson, "Reference Assistant Training: an Integrated Approach," in *Enter, Save, Delete . . . : Libraries Pioneering into the Next Century*, ed. by Douglas G. Birdsall (Emporia, KA: Emporia State University, 1989), pp. 16–43.

[17] Beth S. Woodard and Sharon J. Van Der Laan, "Training Preprofessionals for Reference Service," *The Reference Librarian* 16 (Winter 1986), p. 239.

[18] Woodard and Van Der Laan, p. 248.

[19] Woodard and Van Der Laan, p. 249.

[20] John J. Regazzi and Rodney M. Hersberger, "Queens and Reference Service: Some Implications for Staffing," *College & Research Libraries* 39 (July 1978), pp. 293–298.

[21] Courtois and Goetsch, p. 388.

[22] Constance McCarthy, "Paraprofessionals, Student Assistants, and the Reference Clan: an Application of Contemporary Management Theory," in *Academic Libraries: Myths and Realities*, ed. by Suzanne C. Dodson and Gary L. Menges (Chicago: Association of College and Research Libraries, American Library Association, 1984), p. 382.

[23] William G. Ouchi, *Theory Z: How American Business Can Meet the Japanese Challenge* (New York: Avon Books, 1982).

[24] McCarthy, p. 384.

[25] McCarthy, p. 383.

[26] McCarthy, p. 383.

[27] McCarthy, p. 384.

[28] McCarthy, p. 384.

[29] Janet Welsh, "The Key Is Flexibility: the Role of the Paralibrarian in a Small Academic Library," *Colorado Libraries* 13 (June 1987), p. 17.

[30] Tom Gaughan, "In Praise of Older Recruits," *American Libraries* 21 (November 1990), p. 932.

REFERENCE WORK AND THE CLERICAL STAFF

Stanley N. Ruckman

The small community college library with only one professional librarian has many challenges—among them, the ability
to provide expert reference assistance to library users during
times the librarian is not available. Often the expectations of
library users are that small libraries will provide the same
range of services as that of larger multistaffed libraries.

Adequate reference service to the library user is perhaps
the most outward public indication of how well the library is
doing its job. Without some sort of training program for the
nonprofessional clerical staff the reference assistance provided is frequently inadequate.

The library at New Mexico State University at Alamogordo
serves a two year-community college branch campus. During
the past few years this problem has been addressed by development and implementation of a reference services training
program for the nonprofessional clerical staff of five persons.

Such a reference services training program for nonprofessional staff was possible without a great deal of time or effort
being expended. But it didn't happen overnight, and a good
plan, prepared by the librarian, was necessary.

The plan included these three elements: 1) providing the
staff with a rationale and understanding for the reference
service training; 2) equipping them with reference interview
and communication skills; and 3) teaching them about reference titles that are available in their library.

Reference Service Training

Initially it is important to discuss with the clerical staff the
reasons for improving their skills in answering reference

queries. As this is discussed, be certain that you do not convey to the staff that they have been doing a bad job in the past. Rather approach them with the concept that you understand their limitations in answering reference questions and wish to improve their ability to respond to the questions asked.

The initial discussion must also include an understanding of the kind of college the library serves, the level of comprehension of most of the users, and the kinds of recurring reference assignments to be expected. No doubt the staff already has this sort of understanding, but reinforcement is always useful.

Much has been written in library literature about reference interviews. But for clerical staff it is a new idea. Therefore, initially one or two sessions are spent in discussing reference interviews, along with some practice in conducting them. In these discussions two basic concepts must be included.

The first is an understanding of the kinds of questions most frequently asked. Three kinds are asked in libraries: 1) directional (Where is the pencil sharpener?); 2) simple single fact (What is the population of Albuquerque?); 3) research (I need to find information about anorexia for my term paper and I don't find any books in the card catalog). The staff can discuss these in relation to actual queries they have received.

The second is understanding how to find out what information the library user really wants. Frequently a library user will ask for help in such a manner that makes it seem as if extensive research information is needed. A few questions about the specific information sought will provide the understanding that what is really wanted is just a few facts or statistics. It therefore becomes important that the library staff member ask about the topic in such a way that the "real question" can be determined. Discuss with clerical staff how to actually conduct the reference interview. Again, using real questions asked by library users will be the most meaningful.[1]

Following the introduction of these basic concepts each staff member participates in role-playing using predetermined questions. As part of the discussion following the role-playing the initial question is examined and a list is prepared of all the topics that might generate such a question. An example of a topic that has been used with success is the query for "information about china." Other topics with dual meanings and just as general are easily prepared with a little thought. There are also several books available that list typical reference questions, along with the sources of their answers.

Time is also spent discussing the team approach to finding information for the library user. Asking for assistance from the other staff can be accomplished more easily when all have had some reference skills training. Every staff member has different special interests and background with the result that each person's approach to finding the information differs.

Reference Materials

Once the "real question" has been determined the answer must be sought. The next level of training relates to the examination of specific reference sources in the library. This has become an ongoing activity in our library.

Begin this area of training by examining titles that relate to the kinds of questions most frequently asked. Then follow with discussions of general titles, such as: encyclopedias, indexes, dictionaries, statistical sources, and handbooks. This is followed by examining titles available in other specific subject areas.

Two activities that have been used with great success are those that we call show-and-tell, and treasure hunt.

For show-and-tell, each person is asked to report to the group about two or three titles. They are to examine the titles in depth before the meeting and then report to the entire staff about their findings. Their examination is to include: the purpose of the publication; the kinds of information included; the physical format; ease of use; special features that make it different from other similar titles; in what situations will it be most useful. Even with a staff of only two or three this kind of activity can prove useful.

Treasure hunt is the traditional method of teaching about reference books used with students of all ages. But it does work because the books are physically located and handled. A series of questions is prepared in which the answers can only be found in the specific reference titles being examined. For the clerical staff training, each staff member takes turns being the teacher who prepares the questions. The questions are distributed to the other staff members and they seek the answers. Upon completion, the titles in which the answers were found are discussed using the criteria outlined in the show-and-tell examination.[2]

Both of these activities call for staff involvement. The librarian participates along with the clerical staff, but does not always lead the sessions. Each staff member has the opportunity to prepare the learning activity, as well as leading the discussion. One of the services that can be provided as information is sought is referral to another agency in the community that may be able to provide information and assistance in addition to that found in the library. At least once a year the staff discusses these other community information sources.

Also, as part of the continuing program, reference questions that have been posed to staff are recorded. At least once each month the staff reviews them and talks about the logical sources for the information sought.

In addition to these activities, the staff regularly looks at the new titles added. These include reference and circulating books, magazines, state documents, and audiovisual programs. Discussion about them relates to why they were purchased for the library and how they compare with titles already owned.

Training Results

The results of the training activities have all been positive. As expected, staff has much greater confidence in dealing with reference questions. An unexpected result is the confidence the staff has exhibited in their ability to assist library users in all their requests, not just those related to reference.

The people using the library's resources have benefited through immediate access to the information sought, rather than having to wait until the librarian is available.

The clerical staff has also assisted the librarian in other "professional" areas as a result of this training. These include such things as the staff suggesting the purchase of books on topics for which we have few titles, or for which there was nothing found in the library. All music sound recordings that are now purchased are selected by one of the library clerical staff.

And the clerical staff has assisted in preparing topical "pathfinders" that are made available to library users. These single subject pathfinders provide the library user with a way to begin doing research about the subject covered. Included are subject headings to use when searching the card catalog and magazine indexes. Also listed are some of the basic reference and periodical resources available in the library for the topic covered. The organization and preparation of several of these have been completed by the clerical staff.

As resignations occur, and new staff are added, the introductory and reference interview information is repeated, though in somewhat abbreviated form. The entire staff assists with this new staff orientation and training. At the same time, it provides them with a review and reinforcement of the information presented.

Conclusion: The training ideas presented above will never offer the in-depth background that is provided the professional librarian. But the clerical staff now has the information and the background to better meet the needs of the library users. And the staff has developed positive feelings about the performance of their job, in part due to their ability to better respond to the reference needs of the library users.

References

[1] An excellent source for tips on reference interview training is the book by Catherine Sheldrick Ross and Patricia Dewdney entitled *Communicating professionally; a how-to-do-it manual for library applications.* New York: Neal-Schuman Publ., 1989. 88–35713. OCLC # 18986868 pp. 101 to 112.

[2] Should questions be difficult to prepare for the treasure hunt, you may find a book by Thomas P. Slavens useful. Entitled *Informational interviews and questions* Metuchen, NJ: Scarecrow Press; 1978. 77–18502. OCLC # 3516622, it has lists of reference questions along with the most logical sources for finding them.

Another title containing "case studies" of approaches to reference questions and their sources is *Personnel needs and changing reference service,* by Rosemarie Riechel. Hamden, CT: Library Professional Publ., 1989. 89–8091. OCLC # 19627321, pp. 55–93.

PART V: BIBLIOGRAPHIC INSTRUCTION

BIBLIOGRAPHIC INSTRUCTION AND INFORMATION TECHNOLOGIES

Wanda K. Johnston and Joan S. Clarke

Bibliographic instruction (BI) is becoming an increasingly frequent discussion topic among academic librarians. Contributing to this popularity are the realizations that students need instructional assistance using information resources, information availability is growing exponentially, the technology necessary to access this information is increasingly complex, and the role of librarians is changing in the information world. In addition, accrediting agencies, such as the Middle States Commission on Higher Education, now are requiring colleges to have a bibliographic instruction program and that its effectiveness be clearly demonstrated.[1]

Academic bibliographic instruction is defined as "reference services that teach patrons how to use the LRC in particular and libraries in general—the who, what, when, where, why, and how of library use."[2] Its role "is not only to provide students with the specific skills needed to complete assignments, but to prepare individuals to make effective lifelong use of information, information sources, and information systems."[3]

Most recently, bibliographic instruction has been considered a facet of the broader information literacy concept. "Information literacy is meant to prepare people for lifelong self-education in a global, electronic environment; it extends beyond the library by preparing people to handle information effectively in any given situation."[4]

Lutzker provides some specific questions to consider when developing or reviewing a bibliographic instruction program:

- Is there a formal statement of objectives for the program? To what extent are those objectives being met?

- How does the program fit with the teaching/learning environment of the institution? Is the program teaching what students need to know?
- Is the program a coherent, incremental one with instruction available for all levels of students, freshman through graduate?
- Is there internal evidence of quality and caring? Are instructional materials appropriate and produced attractively?
- Is there recognition of different learning styles?
- Are students taught the type of research strategies necessary for them to become independent learners?[5]

This chapter briefly describes the community college, summarizes trends in bibliographic instruction, reviews the impact of the information technologies, and introduces the comprehensive bibliographic instruction program at St. Louis Community College at Florissant Valley. The goal is to provide a pragmatic overview of bibliographic instruction with an emphasis on outreach and promotion, group and individualized instruction, and program evaluation.

The Community College

Since its conception in 1896, the community college movement has grown from infancy to its current strength. "Community colleges enroll approximately 43 percent of all undergraduates and 51 percent of all first-time entering freshmen, forming the largest single sector of higher education in the United States."[6]

"The public institutions, because of community control, are generally more responsive to local needs. Moderate costs and open-access allows greater flexibility to students who would not otherwise be able to attend college. Emphases on vocational and adult programs and continuing education provide employable skills to many adult students through responsiveness to changing vocational needs. At the same time, while allowing for remedial work to remove deficiencies, academic programs in private and community college parallel education in the arts and sciences in four-year institutions."[7]

As part of their responsiveness to local needs, community colleges serve increasing numbers of nontraditional students. Community college instruction may be extended to employees in the workplace and to students still in high school. The college serves single parents, women seeking reentry into the workforce, individuals planning to change careers, and older students. The college's open access draws increasing numbers of educationally disadvantaged students. Students' curricular programs may include liberal arts transfer, vocational, developmental studies, and community interest courses. Many community college students have never used a library and do not understand how its use can benefit them.

"Thus, given the community college's mission, curricula, and diverse student body, various approaches to bibliographic instruction should be offered. Ideally, the program would incorporate the following key elements of adult education: 1) several starting levels; 2) several profitable points of termination; 3) several rates and directions of advancement."[8]

Breivik cites "six additional elements that must be part of any good learning experience: It imitates reality; is active, not passive; is individualized; makes provision for a variety of learning styles; is up-to-date; and finally, is essential to lifelong learning."[9]

National Bibliographic Instruction

Four recent surveys of academic libraries, which include community college learning resources centers, provide data on national trends in bibliographic instruction. In 1985, Janney surveyed community college librarians in North Carolina to determine how they addressed BI in practical terms. Most of the 48 libraries responding promote their BI program through informal discussions with faculty or printed handouts. The most prevalent teaching method is the orientation tour, followed by individualized instruction/reference service. In addition to the points summarized later, she notes that the subject of BI "warrants additional study, particularly in the areas of bibliographic instruction for vocational/ technical students, faculty involvement, and the coordination of efforts with library and public schools."[10]

Beristain surveyed 38 Canadian academic libraries, including 20 community colleges, in 1985. She concluded that because BI instruction is part of the public services librarian's position description and the materials used for BI are part of the library's operating budget, BI is considered a standard part of academic library service.[11] Course-related instruction is the most frequently used method of group instruction because it has been found the most effective. Traditional printed teaching aids, which could be updated and printed economically, are most frequently used. Forecasts for the future include a greater reliance on audiovisual and computer-related instructional aids, content instruction for computer-assisted literature searching, and the importance of continued staff development in BI, possibly through required BI methodology courses in library school.

The LOEX Clearinghouse conducted a national survey of 1,826 academic libraries in the United States in 1987. Of the respondents, 22 percent were two-year colleges. "The largest reported increases in use were for point-of-use programs (such as videotaped instruction at the OPAC terminals or printed guides accompanying the CD-ROM indexes) and individualized instruction."[12] "Methods and materials that have declined in popularity or use since 1979 include; credit courses, term paper clinics, audiotape use (in general), printed handbooks for students, and instruction or orientation for groups other than faculty and students."[13]

In 1988, Niemeyer and Lawson surveyed 56 Missouri academic libraries, including 12 community colleges. Survey results indicate the library tour, which exposes students to the library, its contents, and library staff, is the most frequently used form of bibliographic instruction because it reaches the most library users. Neimeyer and Lawson note that only slightly more than half the respondents keep statistical data on bibliographic instruction and caution that only by evaluating current BI programs "can we truly know if our time is being used to properly educate our patrons."[14]

Summarizing the four surveys, the trend toward expanding existing BI programs or instituting new ones is apparent in both the United States and Canada. Orientation tours, course-related lectures, individualized instruction at the reference desk, and print/nonprint point-of-use programs are the most prevalent modes of instruction. Instructional content consists of three levels of complexity: general procedural and location orientation; introduction to basic library tools including the card catalog, indexes, and general reference books; and instruction in the use of specialized reference tools. Economic factors have encouraged the trend toward the lecture method of instruction followed by reference exercises and brief printed user aids. Audiocassette tours and expensive printed handbooks have declined in use. Respondents anticipate the instructional challenge of teaching the use of the newer information technologies, such as the CD-ROM and OPAC. Informal comments from discipline faculty and students combined with observation of user performance are the most prevalent evaluative techniques.

Information Technologies' Impact

The information technologies have impacted bibliographic instruction by improving the librarian's productivity, introducing new options for methods of instruction, and expanding the content of library instruction. Dunn notes that "10 years ago, the instruction librarian needed a place to teach, some chalk, an overhead projector, a supply of blank transparency sheets, a typewriter, and access to a photocopier. Now we need all of these tools plus enough personal computers for data base management, word processing, on-line searching, CAI presentations, and desktop publishing; special software to enhance graphics capabilities and create tutorials; and a liquid crystal display screen, or an even more sophisticated and expensive alternative, to permit demonstration of on-line searching."[15] She then describes how librarians are becoming more productive through the use of relational data bases to create regular reminders for faculty, template programs for producing handouts, desktop publishing for creating flyers and point-of-use aids, and data-base management programs for program evaluation.

Sample articles promoting the use of the newer technologies as alternative instructional tools cite CAI (computer-assisted instruction) at Purdue[16] and at University of Wisconsin–Stout,[17] interactive video at University of Minnesota–St. Paul,[18,19] and hypercard at Apple Library[20] and at St. Paul Public Library.[21]

Summarizing the experiences of these programs, further research comparing instructional benefits between traditional and technological instructional modes are encouraged. Generally, student and librarian attitudes promote use of the technological tools. Self-paced instruction, active participation in learning, and focus on individual needs are benefits listed by students. Librarians note the time savings, the reduction in repetitious basic instruction, and the lowered risk of librarian burnout as benefits. Limitations for implementing these tools include developmental time and hardware cost. Software copyright, hardware incompatibility, and the unique aspects of every library discourage the creation of generic programs or the sharing of locally created ones. The authors consistently encourage merging BI instruction into the student's broader educational goals and permitting him or her to select from a variety of instructional media.

Nowakowski surveyed 23 major Canadian libraries using OPACs in 1985 to determine the types of instruction used for teaching the OPAC user. She found that generally "libraries will have a combination of the three methods of instruction: printed, verbal/audiovisual, and on-line. A new user might be uncomfortable using a terminal and would prefer to get instruction from a person or a printed source. Others might be too shy to approach a staff member and would prefer to learn on their own. Still others will have no fear of the terminal and will want to get started right away without having to read a manual to do so."[22] The most frequently used methods are printed manuals, brochures, and quick reference sheets; verbal instruction via one-on-one interactions and group seminars; and on-line instruction using help screens, command prompts, and error messages.

Baker and Nielsen describe their experiences teaching the

OPAC user at Northwestern University. Instructional techniques include a series of on-line introductory and help screens, single-sheet printed handouts, one-on-one interaction and informal instruction, and the LUIS Workshop. LUIS, library user information service, is the on-line public access user component of NOTIS. During the LUIS Workshop, a reference librarian uses a chalkboard, printed handouts, and three video monitors attached to a single CRT terminal to teach general concepts relating the on-line catalog to the card catalog and to introduce the specific features of the LUIS system. Informal comments, a LUIS worksheet, and a transaction log providing a record of every input at every public terminal provide evaluative data.[23]

The newer information technologies also impact the scope and content of bibliographic instruction. In 1985, the Reference and Adult Services Division of ALA developed objectives intended to guide BI in libraries where patrons directly use on-line catalogs, on-line circulation systems, or other bibliographic and nonbibliographic data bases. The four primary objectives cited include: to know which on-line systems are available and what each system represents; to analyze each information need and to develop a search strategy appropriate to the need and the system; to operate the system in an efficient manner; and to understand how to interpret the search results and how to obtain the needed information.[24]

Through these objectives, BI content would be expanded to teach a person to become information literate, to "be able to recognize when information is needed and have the ability to locate, evaluate, and use effectively the needed information."[25] BI content would be expanded to include a conceptual foundation of information generation, organization, and retrieval followed by "the critical evaluation of any information: how it was gathered, its currency, the principles by which it was selected, its intended audience, its implicit or explicit biases. Students would be encouraged to work in an orderly way, first considering the various aspects of a topic, then honing in on a single one for research, and next identifying key issues, terms, and tools for accomplishing their research."[26] Bodi further expands upon the critical evaluation aspect of BI to include critical thinking in which students are "encouraged to think critically about the search process in order to 1) refine and narrow a topic, and 2) use the results to develop their own positions on an issue."[27]

In addition to conceptual instruction in information storage and retrieval and critical thinking, procedural instruction also would be included to introduce each system's unique file structure, command language, and other idiosyncrasies, as well as techniques for subject searching, multidata-base access, and more.

St. Louis Community College

St. Louis Community College is a public, coeducational community college offering more than 90 career and college transfer programs as well as developmental and continuing education courses through three campuses and other extension sites. The college "recognizes the dignity and worth of all human beings and believes that postsecondary education should be available to all who can benefit from it. The college further believes that education should be a rewarding experienced offered in an environment that fosters the growth and well-being of all members of the community it serves."[28] Current district enrollment totals more than 30,000 students.

Florissant Valley is one of three campuses in the district. It serves a student population of approximately 11,000. College transfer students total 45 percent of this population, occupational students total 49 percent, and developmental and other students comprise the remainder. The average age is twenty-eight. Females comprise 57 percent of the student population. Seventy-seven percent of the population are part-time students.[29]

The David L. Underwood Library provides a combination of resources, facilities, and services to meet the instructional needs of the entire college community. It houses a collection of more than 85,000 books and subscriptions to more than 600 periodical titles. Holdings also include popular and classical records, compact discs, tape cassettes, slide/tape programs, filmstrips, videocassettes, and microcomputer software.

Resources are accessed through a combination of traditional as well as on-line data-base and electronic tools. LUIS, the OPAC component of NOTIS, provides a complete listing of all books, periodicals, and nonprint materials owned by the district's three campus libraries and college center. Because LUIS does not index periodical or newspaper articles, both general and specialized paper indexes as well as electronic indexes are available in the reference area. In addition, the district participates in resource-sharing agreements through the St. Louis Regional Library Network and the Higher Education Center.

Library facilities include a number of special areas in addition to the print and nonprint collections, the circulation/reserve desk, college archives, and study areas. The CAVE (Computer and Audiovisual Equipment area) provides public access to IBM, Apple and Macintosh microcomputers with printers, VHS videocassette players, compact disc players, and other audiovisual equipment. The data-base office houses a microcomputer with terminal emulator, a modem, a CD-ROM reader, and a line printer as well as appropriate guides and thesauri. The BI classroom is equipped with an IBM XT with terminal emulator and monitor, a modem, a Sony VPH-1 color video projector, Sony PC 701 interface, and laser pointer. With this equipment, up to 30 people can participate in instructional activities combining lecture and discussion, demonstration of LUIS and on-line searches, and viewing of video programs.

Each reference workstation includes a microcomputer with a terminal emulator, a modem, a CD-ROM reader, a laser printer, and a microfiche reader. This equipment permits easy on-line access to the NOTIS data base, electronic mail, or neighboring library catalogs; CD-ROM access to BIP+, the Missouri Union Catalog, or other bibliographic resources; computer software program access for word processing, data-base management, and desktop publishing; and microfiche access to the Missouri Union List of Serials.

Eight librarians provide reference services with general reference, collection development, promotion of library services and resources, and bibliographic instruction as their primary responsibilities. The reference staff works together

Each reference workstation includes a microcomputer with terminal emulator, modem, CD-ROM reader, laser printer, and microfiche reader. (Photo courtesy of Len Kroesen)

cooperatively through informal oral communication, written notes in the reference notebook, and formal reference meetings.

Library staff have taken a proactive role in making bibliographic instruction part of the college's teaching/learning process. Consequently, a comprehensive bibliographic instruction program has been developed to accommodate a variety of learning styles and needs. Use of the newer information technologies has been integrated into this ongoing bibliographic instruction program. Formal group, point-of-use, and individualized instructional methods have been implemented.

BI Promotion

"Rather than trying to market a general program to an unidentified group, find an opportunity to use library instruction as an appropriate way to meet the specific needs of a group of users. The idea is to do the job so well for them that other groups will recognize that they would benefit from similar instruction."[30] This philosophy is exhibited as librarians promote bibliographic instruction through both informal interaction and a formal liaison program with discipline faculty. Informal interaction is facilitated through the faculty status held by reference librarians and their subsequent service on campus and district committees with discipline faculty. They participate in college activities and sponsor campus organizations with their peers. Recently, one librarian represented library services through the Positive Peer Group Program, which promoted support and interaction among participating faculty from a variety of disciplines and culminated in the observation and critique of each participant's classroom instruction. Group participants observed the librarian teaching a BI lesson.

Through the liaison program, each reference librarian is assigned to one or more instructional programs on campus. The librarian participates in formal department meetings, informal conversation, and other activities to determine ways the library can augment the educational process. Results of BI promotion include increased numbers of classes participating in group instruction, the development of the library workbook, requests for specialized bibliographies and study guides, creation of library-related assignments, and references to library resources in course syllabi.

Instructional Program

Library instruction has become an integral part of the curriculum for many courses, including Reading, English Composition, Career English, Technical Writing, and the introductory course for many vocational programs such as Dietetics, Fashion Merchandising, Human Services, and Nursing. Reference librarians have created goals and instructional plans for each course to ensure consistency in inclusiveness and presentation. (See the Appendix, page 253, for an

Reference librarians highlight relevant resources during formal library instruction tours, which fall into four categories: basic orientation, workbook tour, advanced research tour, and subject-specific orientation. (Photo courtesy of Len Kroesen)

example of an instructional plan.) In addition, the course instructor is asked if there are any special assignments or materials to include in the presentation.

Although group instruction follows standard instructional plans, instructional pace and techniques are varied to accommodate the students participating. For example, honors sections receive the same information but at a more rapid pace; summer classes include more students from other colleges and require greater emphasis on local procedures and transferability of skills; evening students are frequently older and more motivated and require more pragmatic examples. As feasible, instruction is limited to 20 students per group to encourage more personal interaction. The method of instruction includes lecture, visual, and print resources. Electronic tools are integrated into the instruction program and are presented as additional tools for locating relevant information. The concepts of search strategy and selection of appropriate reference sources are presented along with the mechanics of using library resources at the college and other libraries.

Types of tours generally fall into four categories: basic orientation to library services and facilities, workbook introduction to basic resources, instruction for more advanced research, and subject-specific orientations. The basic orientation tour is developed to provide an introduction to library resources, facilities, and staff. For example, the goals for the Developmental Reading tour state: "Students should feel comfortable in the library, be able to use the catalog, find a book and current magazine on the shelf, be aware of the variety of library resources, view the library as a source of information and recreational reading, and know that staff members are here to help." Following a librarian's classroom demonstration of LUIS, distribution of the *Pocket Guide to Library Resources,* and a walking tour of the library, the reading instructor distributes an assignment requiring each student to find call numbers for books in LUIS, to use an encyclopedia, and to answer questions about library services. Not only does this assignment require active participation in learning, but it also demonstrates that the instructor believes the tour is an important part of the curriculum.

The *Library Workbook* lesson is part of the English Composition I and Career English curriculum. Students are given a workbook, which they are encouraged to use for reference during the lesson. The workbook introduces author, title, and subject searching in LUIS, Library of Congress subject headings, locating books on the shelf, the reference collection, *Readers' Guide to Periodical Literature, New York Times Index,* vertical file, and the reserve collection. Then, following an introductory lecture, a demonstration of resources, and a tour of the library, they are given related worksheets to complete for correction by reference staff. Students are required to return at a later date to discuss their work with a librarian. The classroom instructor sets the due date, collects the worksheets from the library, and grades them.

Because either English Composition I or Career English is required of all degree candidates, basic library instruction is an integral part of each student's education. The *Library Workbook* was developed in conjunction with English Department faculty.[31] (See the Appendix, pages 248–252, for samples of a *Workbook's* contents.) It is updated annually by reference librarians and is professionally designed and printed. It provides a resource for future reference and reduces the repetitive basic instruction provided by librarians. Twenty-two different related worksheets of 20 questions each were created so nearly every student can have a different set of questions. Because each worksheet follows the same format, students may work collaboratively without copying. The exercises on each worksheet follow one subject through various resources simulating the research process, and the required review ensures feedback and greater retention.

Advanced library instruction is usually given to classes in English Composition II and Technical Writing. Students enrolled in these courses should have had English Composition I or Career English and, consequently, should have a foundation in library skills. For example, the goals for English Composition II state: "Students should reinforce library skills already acquired and develop advanced reference skills, advanced catalog searching skills, and learn about a variety of reference sources; develop into independent library users and understand how these skills will transfer to other libraries;

and know that library staff members are here to help." The lesson concentrates on special subject indexes and reference resources most relevant to the class assignment, which usually is a research paper. During the lesson, students are given printed study guides listing relevant resources and subject headings, such as "Horror & Supernatural Literature." Because either Composition II or Technical Writing is required of all degree candidates, all degree graduates receive advanced library instruction.

Subject specific orientations include a brief introduction to library services, facilities, and staff and then focus on resources relevant to that specific subject. Careers for Homemakers, Information Systems for Business, Mass Communications, Engineering Mechanics, and more participate in these specialized orientations. As an example, reference librarians concentrate on resources relevant to specific professions for introductory courses in vocational programs. The emphasis is that as future professionals, students should be aware of the literature in their field. Printed study guides are distributed during the presentation to augment the presentation. These study guides, such as "Fashion Merchandising" or "Dietetic Technology," include a selective bibliography of reference resources, suggested subject headings for LUIS and periodical indexes, a list of related periodicals that contain pertinent information, and encouragement to ask a reference librarian for further assistance. For each subject-specific orientation, the class content is developed jointly between the librarian and the discipline instructor. (See the Appendix, pages 253–257.)

Not all library users are enrolled in classes that include bibliographic instruction. Some are uncomfortable asking a reference librarian for help. Others just want to use the resources immediately. For these library users, point-of-use instructional aids have been created. Near the entrance to the library is a threefold brochure, *Pocket Guide to Library Resources,* which lists library hours, loan periods, and services. Also near the entrance are floor plans showing the location of library services and resources.

Beside the LUIS terminals are threefold brochures, *LUIS: Library User Information Services,* describing the on-line public

Point-of-use aids, including brochures, help screens, and keyboard guides, assist OPAC users at the LUIS terminals. (Photo courtesy of Len Kroesen)

access catalog for St. Louis Community College Libraries and how to use it. In addition, LUIS provides a variety of on-line introductory and help screens as well as command prompts. Clear, enter, and reset keys on the terminals are clearly labeled.

Specialized "how-to's" have been created for every paper and electronic index as well as for each public-access computer and audiovisual station in the library. Index how-to's include a statement of purpose for the index and a sample entry with explanatory labels. For example, the *St. Louis Post-Dispatch Index* is described as "a subject index to significant articles in the *St. Louis Post-Dispatch* newspaper. It includes a short summary of the article followed by the date, section number, page, and column where the original article may be found." (See the Appendix page 258.) Electronic index how-to's also include a brief statement of purpose and explanation of entry to augment introductory and help screens and command prompts. For public-access computer and audiovisual stations, the how-to's include basic operational information, such as how to turn on the machine and reach the A>. All how-to's have been placed in clear acrylic stands for ease in modification and aesthetic purposes. Their content is updated regularly to reflect new equipment or to respond to frequently asked questions.

General study guides responding to discipline faculty or

Each public-access computer and audiovisual station includes basic operational information. Popular computer programs are loaded into the hard drive and can be accessed via menu to assist users. (Photo courtesy of Len Kroesen)

Study guides responding to course assignments or specific requests are readily available to assist library users. (Photograph courtesy of Len Kroesen)

library user assignments and requests have been created and displayed with course-related study guides in a rack for library users to take as desired. For example, in response to an Introduction to American Politics assignment requiring students to write a critical book review, "How to Find Book Reviews," was created. Sample guides responding to general requests include "Researching an Employer" (See the Appendix, pages 259–263, for an example) and "Locating St. Louis Material."

In addition to group and point-of-use instruction, reference librarians are readily available to provide individualized reference assistance. Minimally, two librarians are on reference duty during library hours to ensure better service. Because this is a teaching library, staff members concentrate on helping students find and evaluate the information they need so they will learn to become independent library users. Through the liaison program, discipline faculty are encouraged to send copies of their course syllabi to the library. These syllabi are filed by instructor in the reference desk so librarians can more readily understand the topic the student is working with. Reference librarians will help students choose a topic, narrow or broaden a topic, find materials to support a thesis statement, locate specific facts or statistics, and research resources for specific class assignments. If the needed resources are not available at Florissant Valley, librarians will help library users access them through intercampus loan, interlibrary loan, Infopass to a neighboring library, or referral to a relevant agency.

BI Evaluation

Evaluation of the bibliographic instruction program is conducted through statistical analysis, observation of user performance, and discipline faculty input. A comparison of annual service statistics indicates that while enrollments have remained fairly constant, library service statistics have increased, indicating a successful BI program. For example, the number of reference questions increased 20 percent over the past two fiscal years. Transaction log statistics, recording the input at each LUIS terminal, noted 3 percent improvement in search success during the past two years. On-line data-base searching and interlibrary resource sharing also increased statistically.

The number of BI classes increased from 217 serving 3,507 students in fiscal year 1988 to 265 serving 4,466 students in fiscal year 1990. Of these classes, 60 percent represented English and 9 percent Reading while 24 percent were from 15 other programs. Seven percent of the classes were for high-school English students or participants in the Two-Day College, a program introducing the college to area high-school students.

Librarians also observe patterns of library use as an evaluative technique. For example, if the number of instructors in a program requesting BI classes declines, the liaison attempts to determine what caused the decline and how the library can provide better service. If certain questions are frequently missed in a library worksheet, the questions and instructional content are reviewed for improvement. The creation of point-of-use instructional aids for the public-access computers and specialized indexes demonstrate responsiveness to frequently asked questions.

Discipline faculty provide informal evaluation through comments and suggestions. Their participation in the development of the BI class goals and instructional plans provided necessary evaluation of BI efforts. Specialized study guides and bibliographies have been created in response to their requests.

Future plans for improving the BI program include adopting the designated "expert" plan, revising the instructional content in light of forthcoming electronic tools, expanding the scope of the BI program, and developing additional instructional aids. Through the designated "expert" plan, a different reference librarian is assigned responsibility for each new electronic reference source—"for becoming familiar with the resource, identifying minimum competencies for other librarians (including such fundamental skills as logging on and off, finding on-line help, searching, printing, and downloading), writing appropriate documentation, and offering training to both staff and the public."[32]

The addition of more electronic indexes and the forthcoming expansion of multiple data-base access through the OPAC increase the necessity of revising BI content to expand instruction in concepts of keyword and Boolean searching. Instructional content would begin to guide students on when specific resources are most appropriate, and how to use them in an efficient manner.

Potentials for expanding the scope of the program follow the mission of the college and its responsiveness to community needs. Ideas under discussion include workshops for college secretaries and administrators, introducing appropriate resources and services,[33] and for workers recently laid off from employment, introducing job hunting resources and St. Louis employer information. A librarian is participating on the task force to develop a program assisting the educationally underprepared student. Another is participating in discussions for a proposed new student orientation program. Still another will be taking a sabbatical to work with local high-school librarians to promote and instruct students in the use of the college library.

Developing improved or alternate instructional aids is also an ongoing consideration. A small flip chart on an easel is being developed for point-of-use LUIS instruction to supplement the existing threefold brochure. A commercial video introducing the concepts of WILSONDISC is being incorporated into the instructional program both for group and individual use. Creation of two single-concept videos introducing Library of Congress subject headings and the shelf arrangement of books is in progress. The feasibility of interactive video, hypercard, or CAI for individualized instruction is being reviewed.

In conclusion, academic bibliographic instruction is not an end in itself nor is its goal to teach students how to complete assignments. Instead, its goal is to prepare individuals for effective lifelong use of information, information sources, and information systems. To be successful, however, a bibliographic instruction program must be relevant to the student, either through his or her personal interests or through coursework.

The mission of the community college combined with its

diverse student population and curricula present greater challenge for bibliographic instruction librarians. The comprehensive BI program borrows techniques of adult education to incorporate library skills into the total academic process and lifelong learning. Such a program accommodates a diversity of learning styles and interests by providing a variety of instructional options, several starting and termination points, and individualized rates of advancement.

The newer instructional technologies are improving librarians' productivity, introducing more varied methodologies for instruction, and expanding the scope and content of instruction in the age of information literacy. Although economic factors, including budget for hardware and software as well as for staff time to learn the technologies and develop instructional aids, may limit BI programs, existing ones are expanding and new ones are being developed. Program content is growing to include the broader concepts of information generation, organization, and retrieval combined with critical evaluation skills and the narrower procedural skills for accessing specific resources. The successful BI program prepares people for lifelong learning by teaching them the ability to determine the information they need and the skills to locate, evaluate, and use effectively the needed information.

References

[1] Marilyn Lutzker, "Bibliographic Instruction and Accreditation in Higher Education," *College & Research Libraries News,* 51 (Jan. 1990), p. 14.

[2] Susan Janney, "Bibliographic Instruction at Learning Resources Centers in North Carolina," *North Carolina Libraries,* 44 (Spring 1986), p. 16.

[3] "Model Statement of Objectives for Academic Bibliographic Instruction: Draft Revision," *College & Research Libraries News,* 48 (May 1987), p. 257.

[4] Trish Ridgeway, "Information Literacy: An Introductory Reading List," *College & Research Libraries News,* 51 (July/August 1990), p. 647.

[5] Lutzker, "Bibliographic Instruction and Accreditation in Higher Education," pp. 16–17.

[6] W. Lee Hisle, "Learning Resource Services in the Community

College: On the Road to the Emerald City," *College & Research Libraries,* 50 (Nov. 1989), pp. 614–615.

[7]"Standards for Two-Year Community, Junior and Technical College Learning Resources Programs: A Draft," *College & Research Libraries News,* 50 (June 1989), p. 496.

[8]Janney, "Bibliographic Instruction at Learning Resources Centers in North Carolina," p. 16.

[9]Robert B. Ford, Jr., "Bibliographic Instruction for the Nontraditional College Student: The Medgar Evers Experience," *The Bookmark,* 46 (Fall 1987), p. 33.

[10]Janney, "Bibliographic Instruction at Learning Resources Centers in North Carolina," p. 21.

[11]Maureen F. Beristain, "Bibliographic Instruction Methods and Aids Currently Used in Canadian Academic Libraries: A Survey," in *A Place to Stand: User Education in Canadian Libraries,* (Ottawa: Canadian Library Association, 1988), p. 73.

[12]Teresa B. Mensching, "Trends in Bibliographic Instruction in the 1980's; A Comparison of Data from Two Surveys," *Research Strategies,* 7 (Winter 1989), p. 8.

[13]Ibid., p. 10.

[14]Mollie Niemeyer and V. Lonnie Lawson, "Bibliographic Instruction: A Brief History with an Analysis of Methods Used in Missouri Academic Libraries," *Show-Me Libraries,* 40 (Fall 1988), p. 10.

[15]Elizabeth Bramm Dunn, "The Challenges of Automation and the Library Instruction Program: Content, Management, Budget," *North Carolina Libraries,* 46 (Winter 1988), p. 222.

[16]Judith M. Pask, "Computer-Assisted Instruction for Basic Library Skills," *Library Software Review,* 7 (Jan./Feb. 1988), pp. 6–11.

[17]Denise Madland and Marian A. Smith, "Computer-Assisted Instruction for Teaching Conceptual Library Skills to Remedial Students," *Research Strategies,* 6 (Spring 1988), pp. 52–64.

[18]Barbara A. Kautz et al., "The Evolution of a New Library Instruction Concept: Interactive Video," *Research Strategies,* 6 (Summer 1988), pp. 109–117.

[19]Patricia M. Rodkewich and Barbara A. Kautz, "The Dissolution of a New Library Instruction Concept: Interactive Video," *Research Stategies,* 7 (Summer 1989), pp. 114–118.

[20]Monica Ertel and Jane Oros, "A Tour of the Stacks: Hypercard for Libraries," *Online,* 13 (Jan. 1989), pp. 45–53.

[21]Bill Vaccaro, "Hypercard Applications," *Computers in Libraries,* 9 (Jan. 1989), pp. 28–31.

[22]Fran Nowakowski, "User Education for Online Public Access

Catalogues in Canada," in *A Place to Stand: User Education in Canadian Libraries,* (Ottawa: Canadian Library Association, 1988), p. 32.

[23] Betsey Baker and Brian Nielson, "Educating the Online Catalog User: Experiences and Plans at Northwestern University Library," *Research Strategies* 1 (Fall 1983), pp. 160–164.

[24] Dennis Hamilton, "Library Users and Online Systems: Suggested Objectives for Library Instruction," *RQ,* 25 (Winter 1985), pp. 195–196.

[25] Ridgeway, "Information Literacy," p. 645.

[26] Dunn, "The Challenges of Automation and the Library Instruction Program," p. 220.

[27] Sonia Bodi, "Critical Thinking and Bibliographic Instruction: the Relationship," *Journal of Academic Librarianship,* 14 (July 1988), p. 150.

[28] *1990–91 General Information and Programs Catalog: St. Louis Community College at Florissant Valley,* (St. Louis: SLCC, 1989), p. 5.

[29] Richard Tichenor, *Student Body Profile: Spring 1990,* (St. Louis: SLCC, 1990), pp. 25–27.

[30] Anne F. Roberts and Susan G. Blandy, *Library Instruction for Librarians,* 2d rev. ed., (Englewood, CO.: Libraries Unlimited, 1989), p. 37.

[31] Joan S. Holt and Steven Falk, "Evaluation of Library Workbooks in a Community College Setting," *Reference Librarian,* 44 (Fall/Winter 1984), pp. 321–334.

[32] Linda J. Wilson, "Education for the Electronic Reference Environment," *Journal of Academic Librarianship,* 15 (May 1989), p. 96c.

[33] Joan Getaz, "Library Orientation for College Secretarial Staff," *College & Research Libraries News,* 51 (May 1990), pp. 427–428.

Appendix 1. Sample of *Library Workbook*.

TABLE OF CONTENTS

Appendix 1. Sample of *Library Workbook* (continued).

INTRODUCTION

This workbook is designed to introduce you to the library of St. Louis Community College at Florissant Valley. By following the explanations and exercises, you will learn how the library is arranged and what services and resources are available to you.

There are five basic ways to find information in the library.

LUIS, *the Online Catalog*	is a listing of all books and nonprint material owned by the library. When you can find a book on a specific topic, it will usually be your most complete source of information.
The Reference Collection	consists of books designed for easy access to facts and basic information. This is the best place to find a broad overview of a topic or a quick answer to a question.
Periodical Indexes	are used to find periodical articles. These articles are published more quickly than books and therefore may contain more current information. They also may be about more specific subjects than books.
Newspaper Indexes	are used to find newspaper articles. These articles are your best source of factual information on current events.
The Vertical File	consists of pamphlets and clippings contained in folders arranged by subject. This is a good source of concise information on contemporary topics.

The exercises with this workbook will help you develop some skill in using these resources. Once you know the basic skills, you will be able to do much on your own, and the library will be a place where you can feel comfortable and confident. These skills will also help in other libraries—either your local public library, which you may use for your personal pleasure, or a different college library if you continue your education at another school.

Appendix 1. Sample of *Library Workbook* (continued).

LUIS*, *The Online Catalog*
*Library User Information Service

General Information

LUIS, *the online catalog,* is a complete listing of all books, periodicals and nonprint material owned by the St. Louis Community College Libraries at Florissant Valley, Forest Park, Meramec, and the College Center. It does not include periodical articles, newspaper articles, or pamphlets. **LUIS** gives complete bibliographic information, location, call number, and circulation status for each item. Access is by author, title, and subject.

Press the CLEAR key to bring up the introductory screen.

To search **LUIS,** type your command (**a=, t=, s=**) and your search term. Press ENTER to send your message to the computer. You may start a new search from any screen. If you make a mistake, backspace and type over.

If, after you press ENTER, the computer does not respond, check the status line at the bottom of the screen. You may need to press RESET or wait for the computer to process your request.

Every screen in **LUIS** gives directions on how to continue your search and how to get help online. The following pages give detailed directions for using **LUIS.** Be sure to ask a reference staff member if you need additional help.

When you are finished searching, press CLEAR to return to the introductory screen. You do not need to turn off the terminal.

Appendix 1. Sample of *Library Workbook* (continued).

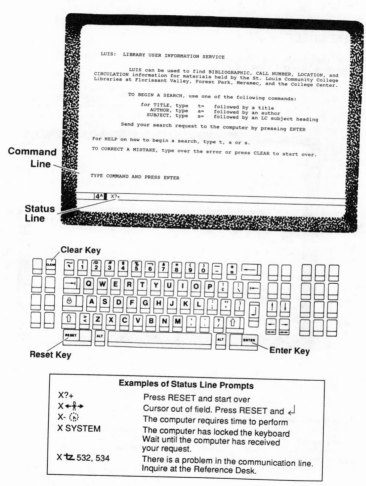

LUIS: LIBRARY USER INFORMATION SERVICE

LUIS can be used to find BIBLIOGRAPHIC, CALL NUMBER, LOCATION, and CIRCULATION information for materials held by the St. Louis Community College Libraries at Florissant Valley, Forest Park, Meramec, and the College Center.

TO BEGIN A SEARCH, use one of the following commands:

for TITLE, type   t=   followed by a title
AUTHOR, type   a=   followed by an author
SUBJECT, type   s=   followed by an LC subject heading

Send your search request to the computer by pressing ENTER

For HELP on how to begin a search, type t, a or s.

TO CORRECT A MISTAKE, type over the error or press CLEAR to start over.

TYPE COMMAND AND PRESS ENTER

Command Line

Status Line

4A   X?+

Clear Key

Reset Key

Enter Key

Examples of Status Line Prompts	
X?+	Press RESET and start over
X←↟→	Cursor out of field. Press RESET and ↵
X- ⬡	The computer requires time to perform
X SYSTEM	The computer has locked the keyboard Wait until the computer has received your request.
X ↧ 532, 534	There is a problem in the communication line. Inquire at the Reference Desk.

7

Appendix 1. Sample of *Library Workbook* (continued).

LOCATING BOOKS AND NONPRINT MATERIAL ON THE SHELF

The bibliographic record in **LUIS** gives you the location, sublocation if there is one, call number, and circulation status for each item.

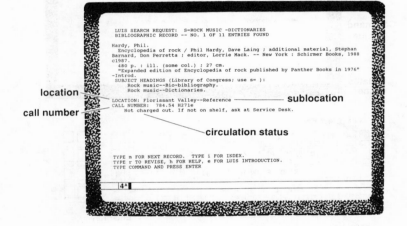

Campus Location and Sublocation

The location tells you which campus(es) own a particular item. Material owned by Forest Park, Meramec, and the College Center may be borrowed on intercampus loan and will arrive 24-48 hours after requested. You may initiate your request at the Circulation Desk or the Reference Desk.

18

Appendix 1. Sample of *Library Workbook* (continued).

SPECIAL SUBJECT INTRODUCTORY TOUR

GOALS: Students should develop an understanding of and basic skill in using the catalog, a periodical index, LCSH, reference sources pertinent to their subject area, a newspaper index, special collections, and library services. Students should understand that the skills they learn will transfer, that the library is for curricular and recreational use, and that the staff members are here to help.

To Be Covered:

1. LUIS -- author, title, subject
2. LCSH
3. Circulation Desk; how to get a library card, intercampus loan
4. Best Sellers
5. Videotapes
6. Public access computers
7. Copy machines
8. Periodical indexes applicable to field
9. Newspaper index
10. Services available in reference
11. Appropriate special files (probably not occupation)
12. Reference sources
13. Reference sources pertinent to subject area and helpful in completing any special assignments
14. MULSP
15. Resources available at other libraries; Applied Science Library at St. Louis Public, Education Library at UMSL, etc.
16. InfoPass

Presentation:

1. Impress upon students that as a professional, they should be aware of professional literature in their field--newsletters, journals, reference books, etc.
2. When demonstrating the catalog, use examples related to the field.

Instructional Materials:

     LUIS demonstration
     LCSH
     Periodical Index
     Study Guide for subject area

Appendix 2. Special Subject Introductory Tour.

Fashion Merchandising
A Study Guide

Introduction

This study guide was prepared to help you use the library to find information on topics related to fashion merchandising. The study guide covers different tools and resources you can use to systematically and thoroughly research your topic.

Reference Collection

In the reference area are handbooks and dictionaries on textiles, fashion, retailing, designers and costumes. The major Dewey Classification numbers for these subjects are: 391 for <u>costumes/fashion history</u>; 658 for <u>retailing/marketing</u>; 677 for <u>textiles</u>; 687.014 for <u>production terminology</u>; 746.92 for <u>fashion/fashion designers</u>.

Following are representative reference titles in these areas:

Costume/Fashion History

R 391.003 O36e	O'Hara, Georgiana. <u>The Encyclopaedia of Fashion</u>. N.Y.: Abrams, 1986.
R 391.009 G618o	Gold, Annalee. <u>One World of Fashion</u>. 4th ed. N.Y.: Fairchild, 1987.
R 391.009 W929a	Worrell, Estelle Ansley. <u>American Costume, 1840–1920</u>. Harrisburg: Stackpole Books, 1979.
R 917.303 T583t	<u>This Fabulous Century</u>. N.Y.: Time-Life, 1970.

Fashion/Fashion Designers

R 746.92 H835f	Houck, Catherine. <u>The Fashion Encyclopedia</u>. N.Y.: St. Martin's Press, 1982.
R 746.92 M139m	McDowell, Colin. <u>McDowell's Directory of Twentieth Century Fashion</u>. Englewood Cliffs: Prentice-Hall, 1985.
R 746.92 M638c	Milbank, Caroline Rennolds. <u>Couture: The Great Designers</u>. N.Y.: Stewart, Tabori & Chang, Inc., 1985.

Appendix 3. Sample of Fashion Merchandising Study Guide.

R 920.02   Current Biography. New York: H.W. Wilson, 1940-.
  C976
(This set contains brief articles about a wide range of people,
including fashion designers).

Textiles

R 677.028   Montgomery, Florence M. Textiles in America,
  M787t   1650-1870: A Dictionary... . N.Y.:
                   W.W.Norton, 1984.

Fashion Production

R 687.014   Gioello, Debbie Ann. Fashion Production.
  G494f   Terms. N.Y.: Fairchild, 1979.

Retailing/Marketing

R 658.8   Beacham, Martin M. Beacham's Marketing Reference
  B365b   Washington, D.C.: Research Pub., 1986.

R 659.157   Pegler, Martin M. Language of Store Planning
  P376L   and Display. New York: Fairchild, 1982.

LUIS, The Online Catalog

        LUIS is a listing of all books, audio visual materials, and
periodical titles owned by the St. Louis Community College District.
Information on Fashion Merchandising can be found under the following
subject headings:

        Business Mathematics--   Fashion Shows
            Retail Trade   Men's Clothing
        Clothing and Dress   Merchandising
        Clothing Trade   Purchasing
        Clothing Trade--History   Retail Trade
        Color in Clothing   Show-windows
        Costume   Textile Design
        Costume Design   Textile Fabrics
        Costume Designers--Biography   Textile Fibers
        Display of Merchandise   Textile Industry
        Fashion   Textile Printing

Periodicals and Periodical Indexes

        Periodical articles will give you the most current information on
Fashion Merchandising/Fashion Designers. The periodical indexes listed
below index pertinent articles. A designer may be searched by last
name. Other relevant subject headings are listed below following each
index.

(BE SURE TO NOTE THE "SEE ALSO" REFERENCES FOR LEADS ON RELATED OR MORE
SPECIFIC SUBJECT HEADINGS)

**Appendix 3. Sample of Fashion Merchandising Study Guide
(continued).**

GENERAL PERIODICAL INDEXES:

1. Magazine Index:

Clothing and Dress	Men's Clothing
Clothing Trade	Show Windows
Color in clothing	Textile Design
Costume	Textile Designers
Display of Merchandise	Textile Fabrics
Fashion	Textile Fibers
Fashion Merchandising	Textile Industry
Fashion Shows	

2. Readers' Guide to Periodical Literature:

Clothing and Dress	Dress Accessories
Clothing Industry	Fashion
Clothing Stores	Fashion Designers
Color in Fashion	Fashion Shows
Computers--Fashion Use	Show Windows
Costume	Textile Fabrics
Costume Designers	Textile Fibers
Display of Merchandise	Textile Industry

SPECIALIZED INDEXES:

1. Business Periodicals Index:

Clothing and dress	Fashion Merchandising
Clothing Industry	Merchandising
Clothing Stores	Purchasing
Color in the Textile Industry	Show Windows
Display of Merchandise	Textile Fabrics
Fashion	Textile Fibers
Fashion Designers	Textile Industry

2. Biography Index

Biography Index cites magazine articles about people. This is an excellent source for finding articles on fashion designers. Searching by the last name of a designer will get results. Another approach, if a designer has not yet been selected, is to use the "Index to Professions and Occupations" in the back of each volume. By looking under Fashion Designers, a list is provided of the designers covered in that specific volume.

PERIODICALS OWNED BY THE LIBRARY WHICH CONTAIN PERTINENT INFORMATION

Advertising Age	Harper's Bazaar	Stores
Esquire	Mademoiselle	Vogue
Essence	New York Times Magazine	Women's Wear Daily
Gentlemen's Quarterly	Seventeen	Working Woman
Glamour		

Appendix 3. Sample of Fashion Merchandising Study Guide (continued).

Newspapers and Newspaper Indexes

Newspapers are another excellent source of current information on fashion and fashion designers. The library has indexes to the New York Times and the St. Louis Post-Dispatch.

In addition, the index to Newsbank leads the researcher to a set of reprinted newspaper articles from across the United States. The most pertinent subject headings in Newsbank are CLOTHING and TEXTILES AND FABRICS.

A complimentary index to Newsbank is Names in the News. This comes in conjunction with reprinted articles on microfiche, but concentrates solely on articles about people. Searching under the last name of the designer, or searching by the profession, in this case, FASHION DESIGNERS, yields results.

Vertical File

The Vertical File contains many pamphlets and clippings. Look under the headings FASHION DESIGN--ACCESSORIES and FASHION DESIGNERS.

Reference Staff

If you have any questions be sure to stop at the Reference Desk. Our staff will be glad to help you.

St. Louis Community College/Florissant
Valley Reference Bibliography 26
May, 1988
Shelle Witten

Appendix 3. Sample of Fashion Merchandising Study Guide (continued).

ST. LOUIS POST-DISPATCH INDEX

This is a subject index to significant articles in the St. Louis Post-Dispatch newspaper. It includes a short summary of the article followed by the date, section number, page and column where the original article may be found.

SAMPLE INDEX ENTRY_____

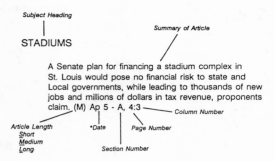

The year of the article corresponds to the year of the index

The St. Louis Post-Dispatch is available on microfilm here at Florissant Valley.

FOR ASSISTANCE, ASK A REFERENCE LIBRARIAN

Appendix 4. Sample Index Entry, *St. Louis Post Dispatch Index.*

Researching an Employer
A Study Guide

<u>Why Research an Employer</u>:

- to determine what companies hire in your field.
- to consider whether you would like to work for a particular company.
- to prepare for a job interview (a good way to impress a prospective employer).
- to feel confident and knowledgable during an interview.

This bibliography is designed to help you find information about an employer. Reference books will provide basic information: address, telephone number, product or services, number of employees, subsidiaries and branches, corporate rosters, financial reports, SIC numbers and the like. Periodical articles may give you a feeling for a company's policies, practices, and general work environment. The Career Information Center houses annual reports, news releases and other data from various employers.

All of the following books and other resources may be found on the second floor, Instructional Resources. Reference librarians are available to help you locate materials.

<u>A Word about SIC numbers</u>

Many reference books refer to a Standard Industrial Classification (SIC) number. Each number represents a type of industry or business activity (eg: 209 = tuna fish canning). Under the name of a company you may find a SIC number or numbers. In a cross index you may look up a SIC number and find a listing of all companies involved in that particular industry.

Appendix 5. "Researching an Employer" Study Guide.

Missouri Sources

R 361.609   Community Service Directory. St. Louis, Missouri:
C7345   United Way of Greater St. Louis, 1985.
1985

             Lists primarily not-for-profit health, social
             welfare, recreation, and education agencies in the
             bi-state Greater St. Louis area. Each entry
             provides address, telephone number, name of
             director, office hours, and description of services.
             Classified index included.

R 338.097   Microcosm, St. Louis. Mountain Lakes, New Jersey:
M626   Dun's Marketing Services. Annual. Microfiches.

             Lists businesses in Greater St. Louis area on
             microfiche. 3 sections: Alphabetical by company
             name; SIC number; geographic, including zip code.

R 338.097   Missouri Directory of Manufacturing and Mining.
M6782   St. Louis: Informative Data Co. Annual

             Basic information about Missouri mining and
             manufacturing firms. Listed in several sections:
             alphabetic, geographic and SIC code.

R 382.097   St. Louis International Trade Directory.
S146   St. Louis: Regional Commerce and Growth
1981   Association, 1981.

             Information on St. Louis importers and exporters.

R 338.74   The Sibbald Guide. Chicago: John Sibbald
S563   Associates. Annual

             Profiles public and private corporations in
             Missouri. Includes income statements for five
             years; a current condensed balance sheet; stocks
             traded; auditiors; transfer agents; and registrars.

R 338.097   Sorkins' Directory of Business and Government.
S714   St. Louis Edition.
             Chesterfield, MO: Town Publications. Annual.

             Information on business, non-profit organizations
             and federal, state, and local governments of the
             11-county St. Louis area. Indexed by type of
             industry, geographical location and personal name.

R 338.097   The Who's Who of St. Louis Business. St. Louis:
W628   Town Publications, Inc., 1983.

             Basic information on companies in a wide variety of
             fields including business, arts and entertainment,
             colleges and universities, and hospitals and health
             care. Personal name index included.

-2-

Appendix 5. "Researching an Employer" Study Guide (continued).

National Sources

R 338.097   America's Corporate Families. Parsipanny, NJ:
B5982   Dun's Marketing Services. Annual.

             Indexes more than 8,000 U.S. parent companies and
             their 44,000 subsidiaries. Companies also listed
             geographically by state and SIC number. Indexed by
             parent company and by subsidiary.

R 338.888   Directory of American Firms Operating in Foreign
A581d   ,bu Countries. New York: Uniworld Business
             Publications, Inc. 1979. 3 volumes.

             Interested in working in a foreign country? This
             reference directs you to thousands of foreign
             businesses controlled by U.S. firms. Listing by
             firm and by country.

R 338.767   Directory of Foreign Manufacturers in the United
A772d   States. 2d ed. Atlanta: Georgia State
             University, 1979.

             Shell Oil and Nestle's Chocolates are just two
             foreign-owned U.S. companies listed. Includes
             foreign and domestic addresses, type of product and
             SIC number.

R 658.87   Franchise Opportunities Handbook. Washington, D.C.:
F816   U.S. Department of Commerce. Annual.

             Information on franchisors (McDonald's, Radio Shack)
             number of franchises, the equity capital needed,
             training provided, etc. Also, general information
             on investing in a franchise.

R 338.097   Million Dollar Directory. New York: Dun &
M655   Bradstreet. Annual. 4 volumes.

             Alphabetical list of businesses including their
             address, telephone number, annual sales, number of
             employees, stock exchanges, corporate roster,
             division names, SIC number and import/export data.
             Cross indexed by geographical location and SIC
             number.

R 332.67   Moody's Investors Service Series. New York.
             Annual.

             Separate volumes for Bank and Finance, Industrial,
             Public Utility, and Transportation provide
             information on U.S. companies including corporate
             history, management, finances, stock and bond
             ratings. Companion volumes called News Reports
             update corporate information twice-weekly.

-3-

**Appendix 5. "Researching an Employer" Study Guide (con-
tinued).**

R 332.67   Standard & Poor's Corporation Descriptions. New
S785s   York: Standard & Poor's. Monthly. 6 volumes

              Current data on thousands of U.S. companies
              including corporate background, subsidiaries, stock
              data, earnings and finances.

R 338.097   Standard Directory of Advertisers. Wilmette, Il:
S785   National Register Publishing Co. Annual.

              Lists 17,000 companies with annual appropriations
              for national advertising campaigns. Includes
              address, telephone number, corporate roster,
              subsidiaries, advertising agencies and amount
              appropriated per advertising medium (TV, radio,
              etc.).

R 670.257   Thomas Register of American Manufacturers and Thomas
T454   Register Catalog File. New York: Thomas Publishing
              Co. Annual.

              Use to find products and services and who supplies
              them. U.S. company profiles; and catalog
              information. Brand name index included.

Periodicals & Indexes

Index   Business Periodicals Index. New York:
Tables   H.W. Wilson. Monthly.

              For magazine articles about a particular company or
              industry.

Index   Index to the St. Louis Post-Dispatch. Wooster,
Tables   Ohio: Bell & Howell Company. Quarterly.

              Feature articles about local and national companies
              and industries.

Newpaper   St. Louis Business Journal. Weekly

              Browse through this newspaper for current articles
              on St. Louis business. Also publishes the annual
              Book of St. Louis Businesses with its "top 25 lists"
              (i.e. 25 largest employers, brokerage firms, hotels,
              construction firms, automoble dealers, etc.).

Periodical   St. Louis Commerce. St. Louis, MO:
              Regional Commerce and Growth Association. Monthly.

              Articles on St. Louis business.

-4-

Appendix 5. "Researching an Employer" Study Guide (continued).

For further information.....

<u>LUIS, THE ONLINE CATALOG:</u>

    Using the online catalog, type "s" and the following subject headings to find directories for particular businesses or career fields:

                 HOSPITALS -- DIRECTORIES
                 HOSPITALS -- MISSOURI
                 MUSEUMS -- DIRECTORIES
                 PUBLISHERS AND PUBLISHING -- DIRECTORIES
                 SOCIAL SERVICE -- DIRECTORIES

Career Information Center

    Florissant Valley is fortunate in having an extensive collection of career materials in the Career Information Center located on the second floor, Instructional Resources. When researching an employer, be sure to check the <u>Industry File</u>. It contains annual reports, news releases, personnel data, proxy statements and 10-K forms for most Fortune 500 companies as well as many large St. Louis firms. The staff of the Career Information Center will be glad to help you use these resources.

St. Louis Community College at Florissant Valley
Reference Bibliography 20
April, 1986 - updated August, 1988
C. Reilly & C. Shahriary (FP)
/kav

-5-

Appendix 5. "Researching an Employer" Study Guide (continued).

TEACHING "SKILLS" AND "CONTENT" IN THE LIBRARY

Donald Ray

In education our hopeful rhetoric soars above the day-to-day realities. Education begins with a yearning and ends up as an institution. Idealistically we say that students should be "empowered" as "critical thinkers" and "active, lifelong learners," but we know how fitfully this happens. The words in quotes describe education as transformation, not as training area, and the community college's teachers—let alone its librarians—find that transformation a chancy business.

The community college library may not even be used extensively as a library. The most conspicuous obstacle is created by the students' modest experience with written language and (as both cause and effect) the lack of reading and writing demands in most of the coursework.[1] More fundamental, perhaps, is the problem of student passivity and sheer disbelief in the learning process. The labeling of "remedial" or "nontraditional" students may lull us into regarding them as exceptional, but they are not; the resistances of mainstream community college students often seem to continue the "normal" experience of high-school education.[2] Nor do they have time to get far beyond that experience; only a minority will ever go on to a four-year school, and the blurring of the line between "vocational" and "transfer" programs makes it difficult to identify those students as a group. Some basic writing experts can inspire us with the ways they usher unprepared readers and writers into the realm of academic discourse, but they generally operate in the university, not in the community college.[3] Within two years (or less), what can these students learn in a library?

The answer may depend on the way a community college

steers between two models of education: as academic discipline, and as social service. Although the two frameworks can
be brought into alignment, they rest on very difficult assumptions. Academic traditions emphasize the student's individual
responsibility to a civilization and its broad body of knowledge. The social service approach, with frankly socioeconomic goals, promotes the students' own careerist orientations and may claim a higher esteem for their local community
and family base. Between the supportiveness of "community"
and the more disinterested values of "college," the institution's very name seeks to contain the tension.[4] And the
tension is necessary; each approach may pretend to be more
holistic than the other but cannot work without it. In extreme
cases the academics eventually become as insensitive and
irrelevant as the social service providers can become patroniz-
ing and functionalistic. (Worse, the cost-benefit calculations
of administrators working with limited budgets may vitiate
social *and* intellectual goals.) When community college staff
of every stamp waver uneasily between these two standards,
that is probably the best they can do.

"Library Skills" and Course Content

In a library, the academic model values quiet, individual
study among sizable, college-level collections. The library as
social service takes a more supportive stance, with more
attention to "library skills." And again, neither approach
makes sense without the other. It is clear enough that a library
content to offer the finest collection, without offering proper
avenues into it, will not be used. Nor will it be used if students
are oriented to it without coming to appreciate their stake in
it. How will librarians credibly impart skills to students for
whom the "finest collection" holds so little promise?

Given the recalcitrance of these students, and the increased
interest in outcome assessments for community colleges, it is
tempting to teach and assess minimum library competencies,
reductively and uniformly. The drawbacks of this approach
should be clear from the experience of other areas of the
community college. The standardized tests already common

there generally reduce higher-order thinking to multiple choice items and encourage the herd instincts of mass testing, including the tendency to "teach to the test." And Patricia Cross has indicated a bigger problem:

> Skills training must be integrated into the other college experiences of the student. We have known for years that "transfer of training" does not take place automatically. Bridges must be consciously and carefully built, so that the communications skills learned in remedial English, for example, carry over to the term paper for social studies.[5]

Some library skills—say, the rules of a book catalog or a bibliographic citation—may carry over more successfully. Other skills are harder to abstract from the student's actual ventures into the library collection.

To stop at the lower, descriptive level of "how to use the library" falls short of the student's greater need: to encounter the language of others (in or out of the library) and respond to it in his or her own language. One reason Patricia Breivik's experiment at Brooklyn College Library is still cited, after 15 years, is her assessment of instructional outcomes in terms of student writing.[6] By contrast, a recent article criticizes term paper workshops by showing that they succeed less well than library instruction, but only according to the scores on a standardized library skills test.[7] Is it not more significant to assess term paper workshops according to the quality of the term papers? If "library skills" are not subordinated to the intelligent use of library sources, students are justified in seeing them as arbitrary requirements.

Tutorial approaches like those workshops at least ground library skills in subject matter: ultimately, in the use of language. For all the confusion over the meanings of "literacy," nothing will be clarified by pursuing, as a separate competency, something called "information literacy."[8] This pursuit is a particular danger in the community college, where technical expertise of any kind sounds most prestigious. Even those who probably know better can fall into the giddy rhetoric of the "Information Age":

> Very soon, progressive community colleges will have at
> the center of their instructional process the library,
> which will exist in a new form to provide vast amounts of
> information at students' fingertips. This transformation
> of the library will hinge upon computing and telecom-
> munications. This also *leads to* an important new literacy
> called "information access literacy." All people now
> have information overload. In most fields, professionals
> have a hard time keeping pace. They tend to treat many
> topics superficially and inefficiently because they are
> overwhelmed with this expansion of information.[9]

For the phrase "leads to" (my italics) one may as well write
"collides with." Real students, who seem almost absent from
this prediction, usually look for fewer sources of information,
not more. Their expressed needs lead less often to expanded
data bases than to digested sources such as *SIRS,* or even
Masterplots, or to the use of abstracts *in place of* articles. Any
academic librarian eventually wrestles with the choice between such convenience and the demand that students learn
to screen and synthesize text themselves. If they are able to
do that, it will not be through esoteric skills and technologies.
Whatever "information access literacy" is, its most critical
phase has to be the assessment and use of written materials, as
it was before computers were invented. Otherwise, as Colette
Wagner recently put it, when "asked to find a book or three
articles, the nontraditional student stops as soon as the magic
quota is reached, without regard for the quality or authority of
the articles he has found."[10] The computer can even aggravate
the convenience-store mentality by playing into the common
fantasy of a knowledge machine that produces all required
data on demand.

Apart from its support of the most technical subject areas,
the bibliographic data base could improve pedagogy if the
librarian and student develop a search together and access its
output together. *If* time is made for this consultation, it might
shift the student's focus from a willy-nilly search through
indexes to a more disciplined learning experience. But it
would have to be structured as a collaborative phase of
student research, lest it simply transform the student's research into the librarian's.

It takes such formalized, labor-intensive approaches to involve librarians significantly in the learning process. Most library reference service is still a waiting game, dependent on the student's initiative, which presupposes the student's awareness of his or her needs as well as his or her belief in the possibility that a librarian can meet those needs. To quote again from Wagner,

> Thus, to a great degree, the success of the reference interview is dependent upon the skills and attitudes of the student—i.e., the student who is articulate, at ease in the library environment, and self-confident enough to approach a librarian to ask questions, reveal needs, listen and follow directions is more likely to benefit from the reference encounter. The nontraditional student . . . typically possesses very few of the prerequisites for success if the library research game as played by the traditional rules of reference.[11]

To make the case more critical, she is talking about older, "highly motivated" people, and not the less focused students who often come straight out of high school.

The librarian can take an active role if her interventions are built right into the course work. And that course work should involve an encounter in some depth with subject matter, which poses another question within the community college curriculum. The split between social service and academic styles, described earlier, is in a way reproduced in the split between "skills" and "content" courses. Basic skills students have to work in a narrow compass, as compared with the breadth and depth of a library. Then again, when they finally launch into their major fields, accreditation and other requirements often pace them through standard materials with little outside reading. The switching—sometimes back and forth—from building cognitive skills to covering subject content can widen the distance between the student and her discipline and may leave the library effectively out of the picture.

The lack of integration in the learning process may force us to do the right things in the wrong courses. In a recent *Journal of Basic Writing,* for example, it was most heartening to see a librarian and an English teacher, *together* describing a library instruction program, especially one so well conceived: They set up their own worksheets, team taught the classes, and gave them ample feedback. On the other hand, this was—of necessity—an artificial assignment that did not lead into a paper or other reading. The authors made the students simulate a subject search, out of concern for their survival in other courses:

> One of the difficulties . . . is that while Developmental Writing students are working on their assigned paragraphs (and then, eventually, short essays), they are concurrently being asked to produce lengthy term or research papers in at least one of their courses.[12]

This lament, coming out of a four-year school, will sound at least familiar to anyone who has been in the two-year college in recent years, where as Arthur Cohen and Florence Brawer put it, "few students attended courses in the sequence envisaged by program planners [and] the drop-in and drop-out approach had gained the day."[13] They conclude that, whether we like it or not, "every course must be considered as a self-contained unity, presented as though its student will never consider its concepts in another course."[14] To apply that principle, professors who assign papers would have to collaborate carefully with librarians. But those teachers— whose students could make the most use of the library—often see librarians as intruders in their field. Meanwhile it is often the developmental teachers whose lower status and openness to wider-ranging instruction makes them more approachable to librarians. Politics determines pedagogy.

Library Instruction for Assigned Papers

Term papers, and even shorter "library papers," call for nurturance at all stages. They are predicated on tasks that many community college students cannot begin to handle by themselves. Mina Shaughnessy observed that basic writers have the greatest difficulty bridging one thought to another—

cases to generalizations, concrete observations to abstract ideas, or a series of premises to a conclusion.[15] Even more advanced writers, once they can articulate their own ideas, are challenged when they must relate them to someone else's. A lack of strong feedback from the instructor often leaves the student in a vacuum from the moment the paper is assigned. Stephen Tchudi warns, "Too often the teaching of writing seems to hibernate at this point with instructors passively waiting for papers to come in, at which point they can teach through error correction."[16] In the yawning gap left between the specifications and the product, the student does the paper essentially on his or her own. It is no wonder that so many student writers have plagiarized sources or used them at the cut-and-paste level.

Tchudi and others have suggested some teacher interventions that help—especially the better definition of a paper's objectives and the requirement of multiple drafts.[17] Librarians should also intervene at the source-gathering stage. As an example, Figure 1 shows a simple worksheet that I have used in the past.

Students, with topics ready, fill out this worksheet immediately after brief instructions to the class (about 30 minutes). Because it helps them begin their research with a minimum of fuss, I have found their instructors receptive to this approach in several disciplines. Of course, it only starts the student off in the right direction; if he or she has found an article in one place, the student can probably find more articles in the same place. For the actual paper he or she may not use the titles found now.

What are some of the benefits and limits of this approach? Benefits—

1. On a word processor it is easy to vary the questions to serve a variety of library assignments. The example offers assistance in a required English course. For a Speech class one might replace the book catalog in #2 with the *New York Times Index;* for a Nursing class one can replace #3 and #4 with two citations from the nursing index; and so forth.

2. The worksheet gives the library valuable information about students' miscues as well as their subject interests. A librarian who reviews the worksheet can also give them

FIGURE 1: WORKSHEET

1. What is the topic of your paper? _____

2. Find one book in the catalog that sounds especially relevant; give the *subject heading* where you found it: _____

   Then write a bibliographic citation for the book:

   _____ , _____
   Author (last name, first name)

   _____
   Title

   _____ : _____ , _____
   Place of publication   Publisher   Year

   Now give its call number: _____ Is it on the shelf? ___

3. Next find a useful article in a recent *Readers' Guide,* giving the complete *subject heading* for it: _____

   Then give a bibliographic citation for the article:

   _____ . " _____ "
   Author (last name, first name)   Title of *article*

   _____ (_____ , _____)
   Title of magazine   Date,   Year

4. Select at least one index and subject heading which is *relevant:*

   Humanities Index:

   Subject heading _____ Year of index ___

   Social Sciences Index:

   Subject heading _____ Year of index ___

   Business Periodicals Index:

   Subject heading _____ Year of index ___

   Cumulative Index to Nursing and Allied Health Literature:

   Subject heading _____ Year of index ___

   Education Index:

   Subject heading _____ Year of index ___

feedback about other subject headings, new titles, and so on that they can use.

3. If the librarian's preliminary talk can be focused on the worksheet, the whole exercise can usually be done in 50 minutes, if necessary, thereby competing as little as possible with regular class time. In fact, it helps the teacher by nudging students to start thinking abut their papers.

4. Instead of sitting through a library instruction session he or she may have heard before, the student is starting to research a topic on which (we hope) he or she will not have written before.

Problems—

1. With this hands-on approach, much of the instruction perforce takes place on a one-to-one basis near the catalog and indexes. It is more difficult to accommodate a large class there, but if some students start with the indexes and others with the catalog, the recent index volumes and updates should suffice. It doesn't hurt to have another librarian on hand, as well as the course instructor. Students can also help one another!

2. The "bibliographic citations" shown above will, in many cases, not quite match the real thing. Still, they provide some practice. Students will be completing their bibliographies later and should not get sidetracked beforehand by such details. They need to know that the work of research and writing is more important—in much the same way that the paper's content will be more important than its grammar and punctuation.

3. The habit of interpreting language is so undeveloped in many students that they look for word-for-word correspondences between the topic they seek and the title they find. Subjects may blur into titles even on this simple worksheet— perhaps a sign of carelessness, but more likely of this reification of "subject" into mere words. With more time, students' judgments of subject relevance should be brought out and examined.

4. Once the librarian gets the finished worksheets, many students consider their role finished as well. Perhaps students could be required to see a librarian to pick up the corrected worksheet, to encourage more discussion, before turning it in

to the teacher for full credit. It is hard even to enforce such a modest requirement, which still leaves a dearth of follow-up and feedback. Ideally, students would truly *select* the sources for the paper, a process that would finally involve the "critical thinking" so often promoted in recent library and education literature. Unfortunately, librarians and teaching faculty work out of two separate domains, and the student's evaluation of sources often gets lost in the border zone between them. The more interdisciplinary and "holistic" the skill, the more it requires interdisciplinary cooperation. Again, students may overcome their cognitive fragmentation as we overcome our political divisions.

Exploratory Students, Tutorial Librarians

The full-dress paper, of course, is only the most time-honored of library-based assignments. Many faculty simply ask students to compare two articles on a topic, or to produce a brief annotated bibliography, or to find a few corroborative sources for the findings from an interview or other fieldwork. Still other assignments confine themselves to a part of the reference collection or do not require any subject access at all. For example, a student may be asked to look up her birthday in the old microfilm of a newspaper and say something about the news of that date. Another may be asked to write on an article he or she picks arbitrarily from a recent psychology research journal. These assignments commonly disappoint the research strategist in us, but they may offer more than meets the eye—if, for example, the psychology research must be analyzed for mode of observation, sample size, and so on, or if the newspaper search leads into a history lesson.[18]

A wide range of assignments, in fact, succeed or fail according to their degrees of freedom. They may fail by being too open-ended—as when students are left on their own with a term paper; or by being too "closed" and prescriptive—when students are asked questions that have only one answer. It is most difficult to design an assignment falling between the extremes of "open" or "closed," offering students responsibility as well as security. It is always easier either to leave everything, or nothing, up to them. The library, in these terms, is an "open" environment—indeed, to most students an uncharted sea—while the classroom experience tends to be "closed." For a meaningful experience of the library, then, either it must be imported into the classroom or, more feasibly, the classroom must be brought to it.

Most librarians would probably agree with this goal already, yet its attainment does imply a formal redefinition of the "librarian." It might require a convergence of the reference service with the community college's tutorial services to make the library a seminar area, almost a laboratory for readers, rather than a study hall lined with books. Then, for example, a librarian who is asked to verify suspected plagiarism might instead help students head off the problem when they are starting to use their sources. A librarian asked for a book on "how I can write a paper" might be able to help the student as a beginning writer and not just as a book requester. A librarian who sends a class off to find sources for a paper might have them report back with the results. Or that librarian, in collaboration with the course instructor, might have the class locate and retrieve sources on a common topic and then compare those sources as a group; or have the class compare several periodicals in their field to decide which are more scholarly, more useful, and so on.

Some of the scenarios already occur now and then. Others lie closer to the realm of fantasy. Admittedly, they assume a redefinition of courses as well as librarians. The traditional, distant treatment of content as textbook plus lecture notes would have to give way, here and there, to the testing of ideas and perceptions. Cohen and Brawer seem to open up this possibility when they suggest, "Career educators . . . say their students must practice their craft, not merely talk about it. What if the faculty in the liberal arts took similar views?"[19]

The teaching role of librarians, if enlarged, might seem to infringe on that of classroom teachers. Yet students as well as faculty now tutor other students on a regular basis. Why don't most librarians? On occasion, we already show students the forms and purposes of individual books and journals. Mary Ann Ramey describes library discussion classes in which remedial students at a state college were given different books and asked for what audience each title was written, what was "most noticeable" about it, and so on.[20] After all our training in systems and strategies, it may sound naive to finally ask questions about a book. But her students found this discrete but flexible challenge refreshing. And if Ramey was working with remedial students, might more experienced students be able to compare the books within, say, a given call number, in terms of their currency, audience, and general approach; or in terms of their applicability to a given topic?

Such exercises take librarians beyond the mandate to locate "information"—a quantifiable kind of stuff, as it were, contained in books. (And a student operating within that perspective applies the word "book" to anything from *Good Housekeeping* to *War and Peace*.) Students who are used to boiling their reading down to "main ideas" need to recapture a sense of the writer's active appeal to a reader, and the active seeking of meanings by that reader. They cannot get this from a library that is presented as a data bank of facts arrayed under fixed subject terms. But a library that—some day—could be offered as a field of writings that intercommunicate in different voices, with different purposes, might help to liberate students' attitudes toward reading.

As it is, they usually encounter texts outside the library in the somewhat denatured form of text-books. Even a *library* of textbooks does a little better, by demonstrating their relativity. A more varied collection can reveal how a topic is situated in a hierarchy of subjects, even as it cuts across those subject boundaries (and across different forms of material). The immediate interest in expensive "hypertext" is an almost desperate expression of our wish to develop the student's telescopic, relational sense of subject matter. A few homely examples will suggest how the library can already show that "all texts exist in context"[21]: we would like students to see, for instance, how a magazine article or encyclopedia article about the same topic are shaped by different agendas; or how some questions are best answered through books, others through periodicals, audiotapes, and so on; or how various magazines express various political persuasions; or how the face of the law changes as it passes from the political process through legislatures and then into case law; or how "child abuse" becomes a different subject in the hands of a journalist, a policeman, and a psychiatrist. Insights gained from the "library as context" go far beyond "library skills" and give those skills an aim they really don't have otherwise.

Ideally, the intercommunication of texts finds an echo in the intercommunication of students. It may be impossible for the student to engage the complexities of a college library alone. Ramey had her students work in pairs, and even the setting for the worksheet shown earlier encourages some mutual assistance among students. Here is another setting in which students are *asked* to share ideas:

> The session opened with an overview of basic research strategy, followed by a detailed discussion of more specialized indexes, abstracts, encyclopedias, and microfilmed material. Then the librarian divided the class into groups of students with similar topics and gave them materials pertinent to the topic of one group member. Each group worked for about 15 minutes and decided in what order they would use the materials provided. A spokesperson for each group then presented the results and the rationale for the group's decision. Discussion followed.[22]

Community college students would not cover this much ground—the example is a 75-minute class for first-year students at George Washington University—but they need the collaborative strategy at least as much. This convivial approach, oriented to common goals, transforms library instruction into a kind of "group reference," and reference into a form of tutoring. Such practices might preserve academic goals without all the burden of the library's depersonalized academic image.

In the 1970s that burden practically made "library" a pejorative word. A recent article, describing the shift to the "total media concept," sets up an all-too-familiar contrast:

> Much was written about incorporating audiovisual materials into the library. Libraries were renamed "media

centers" or "learning resource centers" and librarian
were often called "media specialists."

But the professional literature also reflected a back-
lash to this concept, many librarians emphatically resist-
ing this approach in their libraries.

On a continuum a decade later, just where is the
two-year college library in embracing this concept? Has
there been any change in the traditional role of the
library as a book depository to a new vital role at the
center of teaching and learning?[23]

This identification of books with a "depository," and of media
with "a new, vital role," may be fair enough *historically,* but is
it true *necessarily?* Media may get a higher profile now, in part
because faculty are ready to lean on someone else's expertise
in that area, and not in the area of written language where
they take pride in their own expertise. In any case, media
specialists know that it takes more than the addition of sound
and light to turn a community college library into a community of learners. Somehow the student, feeling isolated in the
library carrel, must be brought to see the potential community in library instruction and in the collection itself. As
Kenneth Bruffee remarks, "A library . . . is not a repository;
it's a crowd."[24]

If the print library does not find more imaginative uses,
arguments for its obsolescence will become harder to oppose.
My earlier remark that the library could come to the classroom, or the classroom to the library, was not meant
facetiously. Under present conditions I suspect that one could
make a strong case for the presentation of more written
materials within the classroom or in reading labs, rather than
in libraries. To bring book and journal collections back to the
center of the community college (where the PR brochures say
they are already), some basic changes would be needed—
changes that would make library skills, subject knowledge,
and reading and writing skills part of the same continuum of
learning.

References
[1]See Richard C. Richardson, Jr.; Elizabeth C. Fisk; and Morris A.
Okun. *Literacy in the Open-Access College* (San Francisco: Jossey-

Bass, 1983) and Alison Bernstein, "Urban Community Colleges and a Collegiate Education: Restoring the Connection," in *Colleges of Choice: The Enabling Impact of the Community College,* ed. Judith S. Eaton (New York: Macmillan, 1987).

[2]For a good picture of the diminished expectations that high school students internalize and externalize, see Michael Sedlak et al., *Selling Students Short: Classroom Bargains and Academic Reform in the American High School* (New York: Columbia Teacher's College, 1986).

[3]See especially Mike Rose, *Lives on the Boundary* (New York: Viking Penguin, 1990) and David Bartholomae, *Facts, Artifacts and Counterfacts: Theory and Method for a Reading and Writing Course* (Upper Montclair, N.J.: Boynton/Cook, 1986). Rose and Bartholomae are at UCLA and the University of Pittsburgh, respectively.

[4]An interesting advocacy for the social resources of "field- dependent" students can be found in K. Patricia Cross, *Accent on Learning: Improving Instruction and Reshaping the Curriculum* (San Francisco: Jossey-Bass, 1976). Lois Weis, in *Between Two Worlds: Black Students in an Urban Community College* (Boston: Routledge and Kegan Paul, 1985), tells how the students in her study clung to communitarian values even at the cost of the individualizing educational demands made by their professors.

[5]Cross, *Accent on Learning,* p. 42.

[6]Patricia Senn Breivik, *Open Admissions and the Academic Library* (Chicago: ALA, 1977).

[7]Patricia Morris Donegan, Ralph E. Domas, and John R. Deosdade, "The Comparable Effects of Term Paper Counseling and Group Instruction Sessions," *College and Research Libraries,* 50 (March 1989), pp. 195–205.

[8]Admittedly, Breivik herself recently published a book, which takes this phrase as its title, but in it she is careful to distinguish information from knowledge, and to place "information literacy" within an expanding concept of literacy. See Patricia Senn Breivik and E. Gordon Gee, *Information Literacy: Revolution in the Library* (New York: Macmillan, 1989), pp. 18–24.

[9]Ronald Bleed, "Innovative Management Through the Use of Communications Technology," in Terry O'Banion, *Innovation in the Community College* (New York: Macmillan, 1989), pp. 132–133.

[10]Colette Wagner and Augusta Kappner, "The Academic Library and the Non-Traditional Student," in *Libraries and the Search for*

Academic Excellence, ed. Patricia Senn Breivik and Robert Wedgeworth (Metuchen, NJ: Scarecrow, 1988), p. 46.

[11]Ibid., pp. 47–48.

[12]Boyd Koehler and Kathryn Swanson, "Basic Writers and the Library: A Plan for Providing Meaningful Bibliographic Instruction," *Journal of Basic Writing,* 9 (Spring, 1990), p. 57.

[13]Arthur M. Cohen and Florence B. Brawer, *The American Community College,* 2nd ed. (San Francisco: Jossey-Bass, 1989), p. 60.

[14]Ibid., p. 328.

[15]Mina P. Shaughnessy, *Errors and Expectations* (New York: Oxford, 1977), pp. 227 and 243.

[16]Stephen N. Tchudi, *Teaching Writing in the Content Areas: College Level* (National Education Association, 1986), p. 35.

[17]Bruce Tone, "Guiding Students Through Research Papers," *Journal of Reading* 32 (October 1988), pp. 76–79 gives a useful review of the literature.

[18]Even raw comparisons between current news items and the news 20 years ago can be worked up into a quasi-paper. See Charles R. Duke, "Re: Search Writing," *Teaching English in the Two-Year College,* 13 (February 1986), pp. 35–41.

[19]Cohen and Brawer, p. 302.

[20]Mary Ann Ramey, "Learning to Think About Libraries: Focussing on Attitudinal Change for Remedial Studies Students," *Research Strategies,* 3 (Summer 1985), pp. 125–130.

[21]Jay L. Robinson, "Literacy in Society: Readers and Writers in the Worlds of Discourse," in *Literacy and Schooling,* ed. David Bloome (Norwood, NJ: Ablex, 1987), p. 332. Any number of philosophers and literary critics have made the same observation; Robinson's article is noteworthy for his insistence on social understandings between reader and writer, even where a text seems most "stable" and "depersonalized."

[22]Marsha C. Markman and Gordon B. Leighton, "Exploring Freshman Composition Student Attitudes About Library Instruction Sessions and Workbooks: Two Studies," *Research Strategies,* 5 (Summer 1987), pp. 126–134.

[23]B. E. Pitts and A. C. Thomas, "How Library Directors and Academic Deans in the Southeastern United States Perceive the Future Role of Two-Year Libraries," *Community and Junior College Libraries,* 5 (1988), pp. 65 and 67–68.

[24]Kenneth A. Bruffee, "On Not Listening in Order to Hear: Collaborative Learning and the Rewards of Classroom Research," *Journal of Basic Writing,* 7 (Spring 1988), pp. 3–12.

LIBRARY INSTRUCTION IN AN AUTOMATED LIBRARY

Tisa M. Houck

Chattanooga State Technical Community College (CSTCC) is the largest community college in Tennessee. Enrollment for the 1990–1991 year was a record 4,660 FTE with a total enrollment of 7,800. The college grants certificates in vocational programs, associate degrees in applied sciences, and associate degrees and transfer credit in general education. The library staff at CSTCC makes every effort to respond to the needs of these programs by acquiring materials, both print and nonprint, that relate directly to course requirements. In addition, the administration has been very supportive of the library's efforts to acquire computerized access to its book and journal holdings. As a result, the library has automated the card catalog using Bibliofile's Intelligent Catalog and installed three Infotracs, three Wilson workstations, and an IBM PC, all of which run a variety of CD-ROM data bases and indexes to magazines. In the midst of this automation, the library staff comes face-to-face with students of varying ages, educational backgrounds, computer familiarity, and library anxiety. Because we have a strong commitment to library instruction, we have devoted a great deal of time to planning, revising, and designing an instruction program tailored to the needs of each instructor and his/her course.

Our daytime staff consists of two full-time librarians, one part-time librarian, three full-time library technicians, one clerk-typist, and one library assistant. Evenings and Saturdays are staffed by four part-time school librarians who work one night a week each (closed Friday night) and one Saturday a month, and one clerk who works two evenings and Saturdays. The small number of staff necessitates cross-training in many areas, one of which is library instruction. During the 1989–1990 school year, our staff taught 242 classes. Because we do schedule so many classes, the librarians, as well as three of the technicians, and the assistant all teach library instruction. After a year that challenged our minds and bodies, we decided to take a close look at our methods and the results we achieved and to once again revise some of our previous strategies. With enrollment increasing in record numbers, it is essential that our instruction time be productive, and it is toward this end that we strive.

Goals

At a retreat for the library staff held before school began this year, we made some observations about our effectiveness and implemented some changes. The results of our meeting and discussion are summarized in these four objectives:

1. To improve the students' retention of what they hear during a session
2. To focus more attention on hands-on instruction at the computers
3. To eliminate unnecessary instruction time spent on routine skills
4. To ease the burden of the daily instruction/preparation/presentation time.

The following is a description of how our library staff is attempting to meet these objectives in a way that is satisfactory for us as well as our students.

One of our main concerns has always been that too often students did not seem to remember what we showed them in an instruction session. We found ourselves doing one-on-one instruction for many students who had already had a library instruction class. After discussing what could be causing this situation, we determined that we were trying to teach them too much information in too short a time. One 45-minute session is not enough time to demonstrate the use of three different computers, to explain the location and use of periodicals, as well as provide routine policy information. In order to accomplish our first goal, we had to pare down and restructure each type of instruction session. To capture interest and increase retention, we decided to more closely tailor the content of the class to follow the topics of the assignments. Many of our students have the opinion that if they have been to one library instruction class, they know all there is to know about the library. In an attempt to change this attitude, we have tried to design library instruction classes that fit each instructor's assignment. We have purposefully tried to provide only that instruction which pertains to the assignments that the student has on the course syllabus. For example, students in the developmental English course, EN 081, are required to do speeches and short reports using periodicals only. Their topics are of a current, controversial nature. Our focus for that course is on how to use the Infotrac Magazine Index and the SIRS (Social Issues Resources Series) reprints. We use photocopies of the Infotrac keyboard (original is in the operator's manual) along with overhead transparencies and handouts to describe the functions of the major keys and to explain the meaning of the information they will see on the computer monitor as they perform a search.

Reserve signs are placed on the three Infotracs prior to the class session so that students using the library will know that the indexes will be in use for a 20-minute period during the hour. When students in the class are brought into the index area, they are divided into three groups (eight to ten in a group) and are given an opportunity to try a search while several of the library staff observe their efforts and offer help when necessary. Although every student may not get hands-on practice, those who don't are able to watch several other students try and succeed or try and fail only to try again. During most of this kind of session, we have observed students helping one another learn how to use the computer—a method that is often more effective than watching the librarian demonstrate the process. Before bringing the students over to use the computers, we use part of the class time to explain how to use the SIRS reprints. These collections always get a positive response from the students and teachers. When we are in the library with the class, we then show them where these notebooks are kept. For this English class, then, we are teaching them one major skill—how to use a computerized index—and showing them one additional source to use when their topics fit those issues covered by the SIRS articles.

Added Resources

Subsequent levels of English require the use of additional resources. Students in the first-level English composition course do a short research paper on topics of their choice, or they select one from a list provided by the instructor. Most of our students enroll in this freshman-level English class during which the standard research paper is taught. Generally, these students are newcomers who have not needed to use the library, and, consequently do not know which computers do what. Their research requires them to use both books and magazines, and their topics are of a general interest nature. It is for this class that we must teach the use of two computer indexes—the Intelligent Catalog and the Infotrac. Our methods now consist of giving each student his or her own copy of a step-by-step search done on each of the computers, complete with reproductions of the computer screens they will see as they perform a search. Because each instructor's topics may be different, we spend a considerable amount of time developing these handouts, but they are more meaningful to the students if the topics they will be searching are the ones used in the example. Part of the class time is spent going over the information on the handouts while referring to the facsimiles of the computer keyboards they will see. By showing them the keys that they push to search, enter, select, and so on, and then showing them the screens they will actually see, we are able to reinforce what they will be seeing when they are taken to the computers themselves. By reserving the computers, we are able to have an entire class work at the six Intelligent Catalogs and the three Infotracs.

Half of the class goes to one area, while the other half goes to the other. Usually, one other staff member circulates among the students while they practice searching some of their own topics. They are able to refer to the handouts as they proceed on their own. If a problem with terminology arises, the librarian is able to help them over the block. Again, we observe students helping one another learn how to find information that they will actually need to use for their papers. Students who have had the developmental English course usually recall some of the instruction they received at that time. This is very helpful to other members of the class who are learning these skills for the first time. In addition, the students who already know how to begin with the Infotrac are able to show off some of their library expertise. They are visibly proud of their abilities and are willing participants when a volunteer is needed to break the ice. After practicing for about 10 minutes, each group swaps places and spends the remaining class time with the other index. Occasionally we have some difficulty getting students to change places. They often want to stay and look for more information, but we assure them that they will be able to return and find the same information just as easily as they did during class. This method has worked very successfully so far. Students who are ready for this English class are, for the most part, ready to learn both of these searching methods in one class period. Of course, there will be those whose topics require a little more in-depth knowledge of the indexing terms, but when these students return, at least they are able to find the correct computer, begin searching on their own, and have some level of success. We try to be aware of those who seem to be having problems and offer assistance when we feel it is necessary.

Most of the time the instructor will send a copy of the assignment to the staff person who will be teaching the class. Our choice of topics to use for our instruction will be similar to those the students will be using or will actually be one of the topics on the list. For example, one instructor has her students research occupations, preferably the ones they are considering for their own careers. Our instruction session would include topics such as computer programming or accounting. We would show them the indexing terms to look for—such as the subheading "vocational guidance"—in the subject headings for both the magazine and book indexes.

This helps them find exactly what they need relatively quickly when they return to do independent research, while at the same time reinforcing the idea that the library actually has the information that they need in a computer they will be able to use themselves.

Specialized Instruction

Specialized courses in English, such as Technical Communications, Afro-American Literature, Composition II, and Popular Fiction require highly specific library instruction. For those courses, we assume that the students are far enough along in their program requirements that they have already had our basic courses. It is for these courses that we teach the use of the Wilson computerized indexes. We do an introductory discussion of which CD-ROM disk is appropriate for their needs and follow the discussion with a hands-on session at the three indexes that have been reserved for part of the hour. We subscribe to *Business Periodicals, Applied Science & Technology, Humanities, Essay & General Literature* indexes, and Readers' Guide Abstracts. Students learn how to check to see of the disk they need is in the computer, as well as how to search some of the topics they will be covering in their courses. Instruction for the Intelligent Catalog is limited to a discussion of the appropriate subject headings they may wish to try. Instruction in how to operate the Intelligent Catalog is not included because they probably had this in a previous English class. If the class is a literature course, an introduction to the appropriate reference works is included.

Library instruction classes are by no means limited to English courses. Special sessions are designed for nursing students to learn how to use the SilverPlatter CINAHL-CD; education majors learn how to do a basic search on the ERIC data base; and computer literacy classes learn how to access the PC-SIG public domain software. For these kinds of classes, which require highly specific instruction, students are also given a handout that includes excerpts from screen displays and directions that take them step-by-step through the search process. When they return to do additional research on their own, the handouts become a kind of programmed instruction.

Once the library staff realized that we could not teach every student how to use every computer in one class period, we were better able to focus on what they really needed to know to complete an assignment successfully. Nursing students are not shown how to use the Intelligent Catalog, because we assume that they will learn that procedure when they take English. Likewise, students in Composition II are taught how to use the *Humanities Index* and reference sources in literature, not the Infotrac or the Intelligent Catalog. Of course, there are always those students who miss a session, take courses out of sequence, or have computer phobias. These people will need extra help learning or relearning how to find information. Our intent, though, of narrowing our focus for an instruction session and providing more instruction time for hands-on experience should enable the students to better remember what it is they really need to know how to do. In addition, most of our faculty stress the importance of the library class time and come with their students to take attendance, answer questions about the assignment, and help the librarian emphasize the need to take notes and remember the information being presented. Faculty support has been extremely helpful in our preparation of materials and in building positive attitudes in students. When the library staff knows ahead of time what an assignment will be, we are better able to prepare an instruction session that will be relevant and thereby important enough to hold the students' attention.

Streamlining the Presentation

A third element in our revision of the instruction program concerned eliminating time spent teaching routine skills such as the use of periodicals on microfiche. In the past we have included a demonstration of how to retrieve periodicals on microfiche, and how to make copies on the reader/printers. Our frustration was caused by the fact that most students did not remember much if anything of this part of the presentation. Groups of eight or 10 students would stand around the machine while a staff member demonstrated how to insert the film, adjust the image, focus, and make the copy. At best, the two students who were standing next to the machine could see well enough to know what was going on. At worst, eight students were gazing around the room or checking their watches to see if it were time to leave. We found ourselves doing the same demonstration again for each student who returned and needed to use these periodicals. Our answer, which has worked exceedingly well, has been to staff this area with well-trained student workers. These assistants are taught to show students how to find the film and make copies, a relatively easy task, but one that requires individual assistance. These same student workers are also able to refile used fiche, to keep the machines filled with paper and toner, and to correct paper jams or report a machine that is not working properly.

Except for a few scattered hours each day, someone is scheduled in this area at all times. No longer do we use class time to demonstrate a skill that is essential to know but quickly forgotten. Instead, we show students in the class where to go when they need to use the microfiche and advise them that a student worker will show them how to find the fiche and how to make copies if needed. This has been an incredibly efficient solution to a simple problem. Prior to this semester, staff or student workers from circulation have had to leave this area numerous times a day to help with this repetitive task. Now we rely on well-trained students who we know will be there to keep the research process running smoothly. All of us feel the beneficial effects of adding this student-manned area. Our regret is that we did not do it sooner.

The final element of change, which we have tried and been fairly successful implementing, relates to the actual scheduling of classes. In order to reduce time spent on duplicate preparation of materials, we decided to evenly distribute the kinds of classes taught by each staff member. Both full-time librarians, three library technicians, and the library assistant teach library instruction classes of various types. At the retreat, we decided among ourselves who would be responsible for which type of class. By dividing the responsibility, we share the work load. For example, two of the five may teach all sections of Composition I, while one of the five will teach all sections of the first-level nursing course. Another person may do any special course requests, such as landscape management, electrical engineering, or dental hygiene, but will not do any Composition II classes. The library assistant teaches all the computer literacy classes that come in to learn how to use the public domain software. Preparation time varies for each kind of course, but we know that we are not all going to be teaching all types of classes. Whenever appropriate, we share materials in order to further reduce the preparation time. As an additional help, we decided to aim for no more than two classes per person per day, and no more than four classes in the library in any one day. After teaching a record number of instruction sessions—242 in 1989–1990—we had to do something. Because part of the instruction is hands-on, the computers would be reserved a significant part of the day if more than four classes were brought in during one day. Moreover, several of us may be involved in the hands-on aspect, because we like to observe the students' efforts and give help when needed. This participation by additional staff provides the students with an opportunity to interact with several of us, thereby lowering their level of library anxiety. When more than one of us helps, the students get to know us and they feel more comfortable asking any of us when they need help. Oftentimes, students will ask to see the person who taught their class, and this may not always be possible. If they are familiar with several staff members, they are more likely to feel comfortable asking any of us for assistance. Because we like to be available as much as possible, and because we have other responsibilities in our own areas, we decided that four classes in one day was the most we could schedule and still effectively serve the rest of the student requests as well as perform our other duties.

Conclusion

Instruction is an important part of Chattanooga State's library program. Like many libraries that have become automated over the last 10 years, we have gone from teaching students how to use the divided card catalog and the multiple volumes of the *Readers' Guide,* to how to locate any book or magazine article by searching a CD-ROM data base. When students at Chattanooga State enter the library, they are confronted with a wide selection of data base options, none of which they have ever seen before. With several thousand new students enrolling each fall, we know that our instruction program will be demanding, challenging, and rewarding, if we design a program that will accommodate faculty and students' needs as well as allow staff time for preparation of materials and participation in the learning process. We encourage students and faculty to do their own searching on computerized data bases, which allow them a high degree of success on their own. We are, however, willing to intervene at any time when we see that a search is not being done successfully or to the greatest benefit of the patron. With regular assessment of our own success and frequent revision of instructional methods, we hope to maintain a library instruction program that is beneficial to all who participate at any level.

PART VI: COLLECTION DEVELOPMENT

EVALUATION: "WHERE'S THE BEEF" IN COLLECTIONS?

Camila A. Alire

Collection evaluation is an important part of the entire collection development process. Inadequate attention has been given to this aspect of collection development particularly in the community college library. It is important to realize that having a collection development policy with all the recommended necessary components is only part of what I call dealing with the integrity of the collection. And the integrity of the collection should include a collection evaluation process that encompasses quantitative and qualitative assessment and analysis.

The reality of many community college libraries is their financial and human resources. One of the driving forces that determines the investment of the time and resources in the collection evaluation process is the constraints on a community college library's budget. With library directors more and more having to tighten their fiscal belts, it is important that they know how, where, and why their learning materials budgets are being spent. This needs to be done systematically to provide for the most objective data that will assist, particularly, in the decision making concerning learning materials budget allocations.

The human resources reality enters in when one is looking at a community college library that has a "one-person show." Throughout this country there are such learning resources programs that have, at the most, one professional librarian, and, if lucky, some paraprofessional staff. Many community college libraries have the professional librarian with the rest of the "staff" comprising student FTE (full-time equivalents). One might ask, "How can anyone expect a library with such limited staff to become involved in a collection evaluation process?" What is more important to ask is, "How can a library continue to invest its limited financial resources in acquiring material when the professional staff is unsure about the quality and utility of the collection it has or needs?" Magrill and Corbin wrote:

> Information on the scope, usefulness, accessibility, and quality of a collection must be accumulated systematically if those in charge of the collection are to assure that its development will be consistent with current and anticipated needs.[1]

Collection evaluation consists of three integral parts: collection description, collection assessment, and collection analysis. Collection description deals with accumulating the necessary data to develop a "quantitative profile of the collection." Collection assessment deals with procedures that aid in judging the quality of the collection. It also assists in determining whether the collection is meeting the stated goals and objectives. Collection analysis takes the first two into consideration as well as other criteria such as looking at institutional and curriculum goals; reviewing the history of the collection; judging quality; formulating policy; and determining procedures for allocation.[2] From this analysis, collection development change can be made.

The purpose of this chapter is to provide community college library personnel with an overview of collection evaluation. Before they can decide how to proceed with collection evaluation, they must understand the concepts involved in this evaluation. And more specifically, this chapter will deal with collection assessment. Various collection assessment techniques will be discussed with the intent to provide the reader with ideas and/or choices. The emphasis, however, will be placed on the collection evaluation planning process and on a model that has been successfully used at the community college level.

For the sake of clarification and brevity, the term community college "library" is used synonymously with the term "learning resources programs." Also, for the sake of brevity, reference to the term "community" college includes those institutions that are junior and technical colleges with similar library/learning resources programs.

Collection Evaluation: Convince Me!

Community college Library A was in a situation where the funding for the entire college had gone through the "golden days" and had succumbed to the days of bread and water. The institution was in a state of financial exigency; and so was the library. Consequently, Library A could not continue to acquire material requested by the faculty at the same rate it used to. Austere times of learning materials budget limitations forced the library to approach its collection development more systematically.

Questions needed to be answered concerning Library A's holdings. How systematically are the learning materials funds being allocated? What does the current collection look like (e.g., size, age, format)? What is the usage of the collection by subject discipline or course offerings? Is the collection meeting the curriculum needs of the institution? What are the strengths of the collection? What are the collection weaknesses? Library A realized that an evaluation of its collection was the only way to determine objectively the answers that would ultimately assist in the possible modification of its collection development process. Library A had to demonstrate "where the beef" was in terms of collection strengths and weaknesses and in terms of budget allocations!

Evans provided internal and external reasons for conducting collection evaluation. Internally, the community college library staff could determine the scope and depth of the collection, the collection use, collection development program problems, data for weeding and deselecting, funds to build up weak subject areas and maintain strong areas.

Data from a collection assessment could be used effectively outside the library (but within the institution) to demonstrate how the library is performing or if its budget request is reasonable. In addition, data could be used for accrediting agencies, funding agencies, or for cooperative efforts within a consortium or network.[3]

In addition to those reasons, Kusnerz mentioned other

advantages to collection evaluation. One included developing an increased awareness of the library collections among the librarians and faculty members involved in the process. The evaluation would also provide relevant information for support of budget requests and a possible review of collection development procedures.[4] All this information is instrumental in assisting community college libraries to develop collection strategies for the future.

Collection Assessment

Library A's staff was first interested in determining how effective it was in spending its materials budget. Were they systematically building their collection in the most appropriate areas? To do this, they needed to acquire more information about the collection. Therefore, the evaluation focused on a "collection-centered assessment." But they realized the shortcomings to doing only this type of assessment. They were also able to use some "client-centered techniques" to determine the usefulness of its collection to the users.

In order to determine collection size, depth, and scope of the collection (strengths and weaknesses), one would use collection-centered techniques. According to Krueger, the collection-centered assessment "focuses on the intellectual breadth and depth of the collection and on its value related to the future needs of the users."[5] Client-centered assessment focuses on the use of the collection: how much and by whom (that is, students and faculty from various subject disciplines). Techniques used for either type of assessment can be quantitative or qualitative.

Magrill distinguished between quantitative and qualitative concerns. If the community college library staff wants to answer questions such as the age of the collection, the percentage of various formats, average cost per item, the amount spent in a particular subject discipline, and so on, then those responses would be determined using quantitative measures. But, if the collection questions at the community college level deal with the quality of the collection, the views of experts, heavily used sections, and so on, then qualitative measures also need to be considered.[6]

There are five basic collection assessment techniques that could be used at the community college level. These include list-checking, quantitative analysis, examination of the collection directly, application of standards, and use studies.[7] These techniques incorporate both collection-centered and client-centered approaches that use quantitative and qualitative assessment. What is important for any community college library considering collection evaluation is the determination of which technique or combination of techniques should be utilized depending on the purpose of the evaluation. The staff first needs to decide which questions they want answered, and then they can decide which techniques will help them in answering those questions.

List-checking is a qualitative, collection-centered technique. This technique commonly makes use of standardized lists of "basic" collections or a variety of lists. At the community college level, the basic collections list would suffice. Some of the more commonly used are ALA's *Books for College Libraries* and *Choice's Opening Day Collection*. The objective of using a list is to find a greater number of matches between the titles on the list and the library's holdings, which, supposedly, reflect a greater quality of holdings.[8]

List-checking can be done using a random sample technique. Those involved in the process need to determine the size of the sample needed and then use a random number table, which can be found in most research methods or statistics books. The titles selected randomly from the list are checked against the titles in the card catalog. The results from using this technique are reported in percentages (that is, what percentage of the titles listed did the library have?) and, according to Hall, will provide information regarding the "quality and adequacy of the collection."[9] That interpretation of the collection, however, has to be based on the community college library's collection development policy objectives; the development level established by the policy; and the types of resources the collection will focus on (e.g., primary, secondary, reference books, indexes).[10] Hall's manual does an excellent job of providing step-by-step procedures for doing this. If any community college library is interested in applying this technique, I would recommend using Hall's manual as a guide. Medina (and others) also cites numerous sources that can be used for list-checking.[11]

Some disadvantages to list-checking, relative to community college libraries, are that manuals may include titles in the list that are irrelevant to the community college library's "community." The lists may not take into account the special types of materials needed to support the vocational/technical curriculum at the community college. Also, there are many specialized areas in the community college curriculum that do not even have basic/core bibliographies; and the lists may be dated. In terms of human resources, list-checking can be very labor intensive.

Katz supported these disadvantages. He stated that list-checking may be too specialized for smaller libraries and that "what is good for a dozen libraries may not be appropriate for your library."[12]

The staff from Library A attended a statewide collection evaluation workshop for all academic libraries in hopes that techniques shared at the workshop could be implemented at their community college library. The purpose of the meeting, however, was to prepare for the implementation of a statewide standard evaluation method using the "RLG Conspectus." It was only after that workshop that Library A staff knew something had to be done that would be more germane to the community college collection level. No community college library in the state would be able to provide the staff and time necessary to do the Conspectus evaluation. It was not relevant to community college libraries.

Although the Conspectus was modeled somewhat after ALA's *Guidelines for Collection Development,* the purpose of the Research Library Group's Conspectus was to support RLG's Cooperative Collection Management Programs, which necessitated "interinstitutional comparisons by demonstrating collection strengths of members and coordinate future collection levels."[13]

This Conspectus is considered another type of collection-centered evaluation technique and is listed here only to warn any overzealous community college library from using it for its purposes. This methodology for collection evaluation is totally inappropriate for community college libraries even if it is presented in terms of statewide collection development purposes or resource-sharing. In fact, it is inappropriate for many small four-year colleges where collection development policies goals do not even mirror those of research libraries. There are other models and/or techniques that can be implemented for "statewide cooperative purposes," particularly those like Krueger's in Illinois or Medina's in Alabama (which included all academic libraries in the state).[14]

Quantitative analysis techniques are collection centered and usually are the most cost-efficient and objective. Most of these techniques incorporate the gathering of statistics. If a community college library already has an automated, integrated library system, much of the work can be done using that system. Even if the library has a stand-alone circulation system, that system should be able to generate the necessary data to assist in the collection assessment. Nonetheless, quantitative analysis should be done even if it has to be done manually. For various reasons, libraries start with some type of quantitative technique and then follow up with a technique(s) that also assess the quality of their collections.

What is important for the community college library staff is knowing that most of the data needed for this type of analysis is readily available in some type of format. The types of data could include, but is not limited to, the size of the community college library's collection. This is determined by the number of volumes and titles in the library; number of periodical subscriptions; and number of volumes added within a certain time period. In addition, statistics could be used to show the amount of funds spent on materials by subject discipline, possibly for a year, and/or the percentage of the library budget that is spent on particular disciplines.[15] Again, remember that the library's purpose for doing collection evaluation (what questions will be answered?) will determine what assessment technique or combination of techniques are most appropriate for the community college library.

Golden at the University of Nebraska at Omaha (UNO) shared the assessment technique used in the library, which was basically the first phase of their collection evaluation.

Their primary purpose in this phase was to answer the question of whether the UNO's library collection supported the curriculum. They wanted to conduct a quantitative analysis before they started a qualitative one.

At UNO they assigned each course listed in the university catalog a Library of Congress (LC) classification number, and one course could have more than one LC number as long as the assignment met the "principle of primary support" rule. Then a count was made of items with this classification number in the shelf list. The data was then charted for interpretation. The chart included the course number, the LC classification number, class enrollment statistics, collection size, and the level of user (lower division, upper division, graduate student). After the interpretation was completed, the results were shared with the appropriate departmental faculty for input. Given the results of the study, decisions on budget allocations could be made to build up weak areas of the collection. The disadvantage of this method was the inability to fit some subject or program areas in limited LC classes. Consequently, it was difficult to draw significant distinctions with those affected areas.[16]

The technique they used could be very applicable at the community college level, particularly in determining how well the library's collection supports the vocational/technical aspects of the college's curriculum. The community college library could also do this evaluation in phases—first determining the collection utility to the curriculum; then determining the quality of its collection using another method.

Shelf list counting is another method of quantitative, collection-centered analysis. This technique involves measuring the shelf list and taking a random sample of the cards within each subject discipline. The information obtained from each random sample includes the subject area, age of the item, and availability (checking the shelves or the automated circulation system).[17]

The advantage of this technique is that it enables one to determine the percentage of the holdings in a particular subject area; the median age of the subject discipline; and the percentage of items available on the shelf. This technique can be done for the entire collection. It can be completed with minimal staff time devoted over a concentrated period of time depending on the size of the collection.

Magrill notes that one of the disadvantages to this technique is the possibility that there may be a high percentage of titles in a given subject area that are not classified in the relevant LC classification area.[18] The advantages, however, outweigh the disadvantages, and this technique could be used at the community college level. I strongly recommend it for the community college library combined with a technique(s) determining the quality of the collection.

Direct examination of the collection is probably the easiest and least time-consuming of most collection-centered techniques. This method deals with the quality of the collection directly on the shelf, which is assessed by "experts" in each subject discipline. Not only does this type of assessment determine the scope, depth, size, age, and physical condition of the collection, but it also determines the collection's relevancy to the curriculum. It is important to employ experts who not only know the subject field but also know "the scope of the specific academic program."[19] That leads to one of this method's disadvantages. It is not that easy to find a person who has expertise in various subject disciplines and who is knowledgeable about the academic programs of the institution. Another disadvantage is not having all the items on the shelf. Consequently, the evaluator must also use the shelf list simultaneously to evaluate those missing items.

For the community college library, this would be the easiest way to assess the strengths and weaknesses of the collection. The reality of this assessment technique is the difficulty in finding the subject expertise of all the disciplines taught at the community college level. Because the faculty at the community college are not required to produce research and/or scholarly publications as part of their faculty status, it is increasingly difficult to find "experts" who know, in depth, the literature in their field. Katz's humor relative to another disadvantage of using expert assessment describes this type of assessment as "so subjective as to frighten the statistician out of his calculator."[20]

In addition, unlike many university libraries, the commu-

nity college personnel who offer community college reference services are usually not subject specialists but general-
ists. So their knowledge in a specific discipline may also be
very limited, which could exclude them as subject experts.

Because the 1990 ACRL *Standards for Community, Junior, and Technical College Learning Resources Programs* have
been approved, it is important to address the use of standards
as another way to do collection assessment. The ACRL
Standards gives the purpose and basis for community college
collections. Yet, the only quantifiable standards provided for
collection goals are the IPEDS definitions and numbers,
which constitute a "minimum" to "excellent" collection.
Full-time student equivalencies are used with minimum
numbers of volumes, current serial subscriptions, video/ film,
other items, and the total collection.[21]

The disadvantage of using the ACRL *Standards* is demonstrated in the numbers, which may be very unrealistic for
many community college libraries. In addition, the *Standards*
do not deal with the integrity of the collection because they
use only numbers and not other more relative, quantifiable,
and/or qualitative data. I do not recommend the use of most
standards as an in-depth collection assessment tool. If a
community college library wants to use the *Standards* for
determining collection goals or to use as leverage for more
funds to achieve those goals, that is fine. The *Standards* will
not help, however, in establishing the relevancy or adequacy
of the community college library's collection; in determining
which sections of the library's collection are weak; in demonstrating who is using the collection; or in providing the
scope and depth of the collection.

Use studies can be considered mostly client-centered. They
also provide more qualitative information because this data
can assist in terms of interpreting how useful the collection is
to the community college users. Evans mentioned two basic
assumptions made when considering usage methods: first, the
"adequacy of the book collection is directly related to its use
by students and faculty"; and secondly, "circulation records
provide a reasonably representative picture of use made of
the library."[22]

More easily, data to gather to ascertain collection usage is circulation statistics and interlibrary statistics. Circulation data helps determine the various classes of statistics that can be collected. They provide information on the class of users (e.g., undergraduate/graduate student, faculty, community); subject areas being utilized or underutilized; date of material used; and type of format used. ILL statistics provide similar information, such as the subject disciplines requested; different classes of users; and format requested.

Although these types of statistics have some disadvantages, especially if the data has not been recorded properly or if some data is not interpretable,[23] they are still very suitable for use as part of the community college library collection evaluation. Yet, the collection evaluation process would only be stronger if use studies were combined with other assessment techniques, particularly those dealing with assessing the quality of the collection.

User opinions, mostly based on surveys, are another use-studies method of determining the value of the collection. One of the advantages of soliciting the opinions of the users is allowing the library to determine, based on the results, what user interests are and if the library is meeting user needs. Another advantage is the capability of this method of assessment to deal directly with the opinions of the users. The disadvantages of these types of studies, however, include being very costly, time-consuming, and, possibly, too subjective. Magrill and Corbin listed the difficulty of this technique and the skill that it takes to design a survey as additional disadvantages.[24]

These disadvantages are significant enough for a small staff of a community college library to consider. Again, those community college libraries considering embarking on a collection evaluation process must weigh the advantages and the disadvantages of each method and then determine which method or combination of methods would best suit their individual purposes. If proper planning is done, then collection evaluation can be implemented and completed within a planning period set by the libraries based on their human and financial resources.

Collection Evaluation Plan

The director of Library A made a commitment to the collection evaluation process. In consultation with a collection development consultant, the director proceeded with developing a plan that guided the library staff in completing this much needed project.

The planning process for collection evaluation is very important. A well-thought out plan is necessary to be successful in this evaluation process. The first step is determining the objectives to be achieved. This in fact may be assessing the entire collection or sections of the collection. The objectives are based on the questions that the community college library is attempting to answer about its collection. Once the objectives are set, selection of the assessment technique(s) to be used can be made. It is also important to estimate the human and financial resources it will take to complete the project and the time frame for the project. Implementing the assessment techniques, collecting and analyzing the data follow.

Once the data analysis has been completed, collection development decisions can be made and implementation plans designed. Figure 1 shows the planning cycle for *Library A*. What is important is the fact that this planning process must be repeated in a cyclical fashion to continue to maintain the integrity of the library's collection. That is, the community college library collection should be evaluated every X number of years. About the time the last phase of collection development has been completed, a new plan must be developed. This is increasingly important because the curriculum at the community college is ever changing to meet the instructional needs of the community.

Any community college library staff can follow the planning cycle in Figure 1 and adapt it to fit their particular needs and process. A word of caution, however: Do not begin any collection evaluation without a well-thought out plan. This is not to say that mistakes during the process will not be made. It is only to stress the need for a plan before the process begins. Time and resources, particularly at the community college library level, are at a premium. A collection evaluation

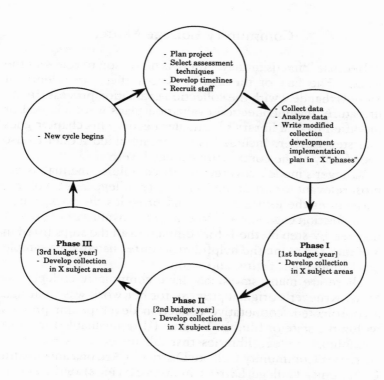

Figure 1. Library A's Planning Cycle.

plan helps in estimating how much of each will be necessary.
It also should prevent wasting either in the process.

*The results of the collection evaluation plan allowed Library A
to determine how future collection development would be handled
and how the allocation of the learning materials budget would be
made. Library A had to consider and set in place a "phase-in"
collection development plan that would allow the strengthening of*

the collection over a period of budget years. By doing this, the Library could consider first those subject areas that, based on the collection analysis, were the weakest but necessary to support the college's academic programs.

Community College Model

Because "time is money," there is no reason to reinvent the wheel. The fact of the matter is that there are plenty of models that deal with the collection evaluation process. In the literature, many collection evaluation plans were adapted or modified to fit a library's particular needs. This chapter goes one step further. Included is a recommended model to use specifically at the community college level.

Krueger's model, covered in a three-volume manual, is the most relevant for use at the community college level. Volume I describes the entire process and provides the background for collection evaluation.[25] Volume II is invaluable in providing step-by-step methods for completing all the steps listed in Volume I. Among the helpful procedures listed are a sample plan, timetables, forms, and so on.[26]

There are many states that have community college districts. Krueger's original purpose for her work was to design a coordinated, cooperative collection development process within the state of Illinois. Volume III is invaluable for those community college libraries that fall under a district (e.g., Maricopa Community College District in Arizona and Austin Community College District in Austin, Texas) or a system/network (e.g., CC Link in Colorado). This volume provides the process to do cooperative collection development among libraries.[27]

Krueger's method follows a three-step process. First, is the collection and analysis of the data; second is the data interpretation and collection development decisions; and third is the written plan for collection development and management. Concentration in this section will be on the first step.

Included in the first step is the collecting of library data. Krueger divides the data collection procedure into three levels. The size of holdings at a community college library would, most likely, determine at which level to conduct the assessment. Level 1 analysis divides the subject areas into 20 broad categories. Level 2 subdivides those 20 into 119 subject areas. Level 3 is designed for libraries with large holdings because this level further divides the subject categories into 507 subject areas. The individual community college library will have to decide which subject level to use. Most typically, it would be at the first or second level.

The quantitative data collection to determine the holdings in each subject area, the percentage of those holdings to the entire collection, the median age and the availability of titles (that is, how many subject area titles were on the shelf) can be completed using a sampling procedure. This is achieved by measuring the shelf list, taking a random sample and recording each item's subject area, age, and availability. If a community college library has an automated, integrated library system or a stand-alone circulation system, the availability of titles on the shelf can be determined using these automation functions. The availability of titles is one procedure to help determine "use" statistics.

Krueger's method further determines usage. By assessing the subject distribution and age of items circulated (including in-house circulation), a community college library could determine the percentage of total circulation a certain subject area would have and the median age of those items used in a specific time. Krueger cautions, however, that doing a sampling technique might be inappropriate for academic libraries because of changing assignments and different courses in a given year.[28] This would be for the individual library to determine. Again, with any type of automated circulation system, this would be less time-consuming. Such a system would provide utility data for certain subject areas (by call number) for a specific time (e.g., last year's circulation data).

Another Krueger method to assess additional client-centered usage is to determine the percentage of all ILL requests that were made in a particular subject area. This would be completed by sampling the previous year's ILL requests.

In addition, Krueger's method includes collection data concerning the subject distribution of the community college library's previous year's acquisitions. By taking a sample from the previous year's acquisitions information in a given subject area, a library can determine what percentage of total acquisitions was made in the subject area.

Many community college libraries' acquisitions processes are automated because they are linked to their college's computer system. If this is the case or if a library has an acquisitions module in its automated library system, then this data would be easy to come by. If not, a manual random sample will do just as well. Krueger also provided the assessment technique for a library that wanted to decide what percentage of total U.S. publishing output for the previous year was done in various subject areas.

What is important for any community college library to realize is that all or any combination of assessment techniques provided by Krueger may be used. Again, which technique(s) to use is determined by the library-set objectives of the collection evaluation process; that is, what questions does the library want to answer? The library may just want to complete a collection-centered quantitative analysis first and, later, a qualitative analysis. I strongly recommend that the community college library select assessment techniques that will provide some of both.

Library A utilized Krueger's model successfully. Two staff members were able to complete shelf list (40,000-plus titles) and ILL sampling in two days. Meanwhile, because Library A had an automated library system (public access catalog and circulation modules available), data was collected on shelf availability and circulation statistics. Acquisitions data was collected from the college's acquisition subsystem and interpreted. Library A chose not to collect data on in-house usage or on the subject distribution by U.S. publishing output.

The library did, however, decide to review the college's catalog to determine if any new programs had been introduced since the last assigning of subject liaison areas to the librarians. Because this process was not, by any means, scientific, the library had to rely on the "historical" knowledge of the professional staff to determine if any programs had been cut.

Data collection (full-time), data interpretation/analysis, and the development of a collection development phase-in plan (part-

time) were completed over a two-week period in the summertime when library activities were somewhat slower. After its three-year phase-in plan, the library is now planning another collection evaluation cycle. Only now it will be able to use its acquisition module operating in its automated library system. In addition, the library will be assessing its periodicals holdings in the new cycle.

Two important points need to be made. Much of the data collecting can be done by library paraprofessional staff and/or well-trained students. Yet, the data interpretation and collection development decisions need to be made by the professional staff. "Professional judgment is necessary to interpret the data collection and then to determine what collection development decisions need to be in place and how that fits into the library's goals and objectives"[29]

Conclusion

Any community college library, no matter its staffing or holdings size, can complete the collection evaluation process. Do not let the process intimidate you. Plan the process and carefully select the assessment techniques most relevant to your library's collection concerns.

Collection development is only as good as the objectives the library is trying to meet. The community college library should periodically review those objectives. It also needs to assess its collection and determine whether it is current enough, particularly for the technical/vocational subject disciplines. It needs to determine if its collection is retrospective enough in the subject areas supporting the liberal arts, academic-transfer programs. And as important, the library needs to ensure that its collection is meeting the needs of the ever-changing curricular programs. All of this demonstrates that the collection evaluation process must be included in the "beef" or in the substance of the overall collection development process.

References
[1]Rose Mary Magrill and John Corbin, *Acquisitions Management and Collection Development in Libraries,* 2nd ed. (Chicago: ALA, 1989) p. 234.

[2]Rose Mary Magrill, "Evaluation by Type of Library," *Library Trends,* 33 (Winter 1988), p. 276.

[3]G. Edward Evans, *Developing Library and Information Center Collections,* 2nd ed. (Littleton, CO: Libraries Unlimited, 1987), p. 313–314.

[4]Peggy Ann Kusnerz, "Collection Evaluation Techniques In the Academic Art Library," *Drexel Library Quarterly,* 19 (Summer 1983), p. 38.

[5]Karen Krueger, *Coordinated Cooperative Collection Development for Illinois Libraries, vol. 1, Description* (Springfield: Illinois State Library, June 1983).

[6]Magrill, pp. 268–269.

[7]Evans, p. 314; *Guidelines for Collection Development,* ed. David L. Perkins (Chicago: ALA, 1979), pp. 12–18.

[8]Kusnerz, p. 39.

[9]Blaine H. Hall, *Collection Assessment Manual* (Provo: Brigham Young University, 1981), 18, ERIC, ED 217852.

[10]Ibid, p. 19.

[11]Sue Medina et al., *Collection Assessment Manual* (Montgomery: Network of Alabama Academic Libraries, September, 1987), pp. 30–31.

[12]William A. Katz, *Collection Development: The Selection of Materials for Libraries* (New York: Holt, Rinehart and Winston, 1980), p. 86.

[13]Frederick J. Stielow and Helen R. Tibbo, "Collection Analysis in Modern Librarianship: A Stratified, Multidimensional Model," *Collection Management,* 11 (Number 3/4, 1989), p. 78.

[14]Karen Krueger, *Coordinated Cooperative Collection Development for Illinois Libraries, vol. 3, A How-to-Manual for Systems* (Springfield: Illinois State Library, June 1983), Medina.

[15]*Guidelines for Collection Development,* pp. 14–15.

[16]Barbara Golden, "A Method of Quantitatively Evaluating a University Library Collection," *Library Resources and Technical Services,* 18 (Summer 1974), pp. 270–272.

[17]Krueger, 1: p. 19.

[18]Magrill, p. 277.

[19]Hall, p. 20.

[20]Katz, p. 86.

[21]"Standards for Community, Junior, and Technical College Learning Resources Programs," *C&RL News,* 51 (September 1990), pp. 757–767.

[22]Evans, p. 323.

[23]Perkins, p. 16.

[24]Magrill and Corbin, p. 249.

[25]Krueger, Vol. 1.

[26]Krueger, Karen, *Coordinated Cooperative Collection Development for Illinois Libraries, vol. 2, A How-to-Manual for Local Libraries on Client-Centered Analysis and Development* (Springfield: Illinois State Library, June 1983).

[27]Krueger, Vol. 3.

[28]Krueger, 1: p. 20.

[29]Ibid. p. 21.

COLLECTION DEVELOPMENT: LOOK BEFORE YOU LEAP FOR THOSE WHO HESITATE ARE LOST

Karen Fischer

The following is based on the idea that a learning resources center (LRC) is like a closed ecosystem: You cannot change one part without affecting the rest. At the same time, the world of the small community college LRC is changing and is likely to change in ways difficult for us to anticipate 10, 15, or 20 years down the road. The best advice I can offer is to try to keep the global picture in your mind and focus on the future. It's always important to "look before you leap" and not hop on the bandwagon of the latest fad only to see it fizzle. Yet if you hesitate too long, you may miss a golden opportunity to better serve your clientele. And therein lies the conundrum of LRC management.

What follows are not cookbook answers to all your collection development problems, but some questions to provide food for thought interspersed with some personal observations and followed by a bibliography for more detailed information on the topics discussed. I really don't believe that collection development for reference can be separated from looking at the LRC as an organic whole. So let's begin with an overview of collection development before we focus our microscope on reference.

First of all, as in nature, we need background baseline information on the system as a whole as it currently exists before we can decide if change is needed in a particular aspect. For a college LRC this includes an understanding of its place within its parent institution. What is the mission of the LRC? Is there a written mission statement and does it include the clientele the LRC is trying to serve? Is the clientele the students, faculty, and staff of the college? Does the clientele include any other recognized groups, such as all residents of the college district, high-school students, adult literacy students, developmental learning students, or English as a Second Language students? Does the mission statement treat all groups equally, or is there a hierarchy of groups to be served with the resources available? What group takes top priority? Do students' needs always come first? Do faculty needs sometimes take precedence?

It is trite but true that a college LRC serves a support role to the academic teaching departments. Who is involved in the process of developing a written mission statement for the LRC is important. Determining the groups the LRC is to serve and finding out what they perceive their needs to be is basic to planning the future direction of the LRC and where staff and financial resources should be applied.

How you define your collection and what you include within it depend on a number of things: your clientele, your stated mission, your geographic location, and your resources. Most important of all, I would suggest, is knowing whom you are trying to serve. Most community college LRCs are too small to be all things to all people. It seems to me that a LRC director who has presided over a formal process of defining whom the LRC serves and why is in a better position to argue for the funds needed to accomplish the goals necessary to carry out the LRC's mission. Consulting with the clientele as part of a mission and goal-setting process fosters mutual understanding and can garner support among important campus groups for funding your long-range plan, including upgrading the reference collection.

Collection Assessment

Once you know whom you are trying to serve, have a broad mission statement, and have developed a specific set of goals, the next step is to examine your resources. An important resource is the collection you already have. Just as biologists inventory an area to see what plants and animals already exist there before recommending human interventions to correct problems, so too you need to know what you already have in your collection before you decide what changes you want to make in terms of future purchasing and weeding. If, for example, librarian Elsie Dewey has had the responsibility for acquisitions at your institution for a long time, she probably feels pretty confident that she knows what's in the collection and what areas have gotten the lion's share of the book budget in the last few years. Unfortunately, just because she knows where the greatest needs are, it does not follow that she will be able to translate those needs into more dollars from her budget authority.

More than one college president or academic dean has called the college LRC "a bottomless pit" or "a black hole" when it comes to money. The problem for Elsie is to prove to the people who hold the purse strings on campus that she really knows what's needed and that more money *will make a real difference in the LRC's ability to serve its clientele*. If you were a budget authority, which of the following two justifications would impress you more: "I need an additional $10,000 to improve the book collection in the area of environmental studies. The science department has added an environmental component to the biology sequence courses, and we don't have enough books to support student term papers," or "The science department is in the process of revamping its curriculum. Starting next year there will be a continuing emphasis on environmental studies integrated into the biology courses. I have assessed our collection in that area and we are at a 1a level according to the LIRN conspectus. The science department and I agree that we need to bring the collection in environmental studies up to a 1b level to support course-related assignments. The biology faculty and I have identified a core list of titles we need to add over the next three years to reach this level. The total cost to purchase the additional 285 books needed is $10,000." The first argument makes the LRC seem isolated and reactive to curriculum changes on campus. The second argument seems more concrete and directly related to the needs of the LRC's faculty clientele. It also shows communication and agreement on the need between the librarian and the science department.

It is a given that most community college LRCs are small

with a small number of staff. If you are going to survive in this environment, you must recognize that your clientele will expect your LRC to provide all the same type of services that a much larger library would provide. You, personally, cannot do everything that needs doing, and your staff probably cannot do everything either. All you can do is decide what things are most important and concentrate your time and staff resources on those things that will help you accomplish the LRC's stated mission. In fulfilling that part of your mission that asks you to provide appropriate materials in support of instruction, you need to base your decisions on more than gut feelings. Formally assessing your collection would be a worthwhile investment of your time. It is a mistake to see assessment as a luxury to be conducted only by large research libraries.

If you are the Elsie of your LRC, you have a right to groan at this point, because assessing a collection entails extra work. Something else will have to take a backseat so that this can be done. On the other hand, because community college LRC collections tend to be small, a formal assessment does not have to be elaborate and take a year to complete in order to provide valuable information. Even if Elsie does something as simple as having a reliable student worker count shelf list cards by LC or Dewey classification categories, she will have a better sense of where the strength of her collection lies in terms of volumes. If, at the same time, she also notes how many shelf cards there are for items less than five or 10 years old, she can confirm a pattern of where the book budget has been going for the past few years. She can have student workers check standard bibliographies such as *Books for Junior College Libraries* (now somewhat dated), *The Vocational- Technical Core Collection,* and *Books for College Libraries* to see if her collection has important authors and key titles. Professional associations in the fields in which her institution offers degrees and certificates sometimes publish core lists. She can also check annual "best reference books of the year" type lists in *Library Journal* or *American Libraries* to see how her current acquisitions stack up. She has now replaced her gut feelings about her collection with objective data. I would bet that Elsie will find out things about her collection that she didn't know and will end up with data to back up the things she has been saying regarding the state of the collection and its need for improvement. She is then in a better position to argue for needed funds herself, or to provide her LRC budget adminis-trator with convincing arguments to use in the annual campus budget negotiations.

Having been through an assessment using the LIRN Con-spectus worksheets, I can only say to the doubting Elsie that I am convinced that the time it takes to do a formal collection assessment is well spent, especially if the faculty are informed of the results. Some LRCs choose to involve faculty in the assessment process. If your faculty are motivated to help the LRC maintain a quality collection, their subject expertise is invaluable. Whether assessed by librarians alone or with the help of faculty, formal assessment provides a golden opportu-nity to interact with and educate faculty about the LRC. Elsie is much more likely to be seen by the college community as a professional with an area of expertise. In any case, she is in a much better position to answer program or institutional accred-itation questions about the collection, justify budget requests, and demonstrate needs on grant applications.

Collection Policies

It is now time for the equivalent of a forest-management plan: the description of your goals for the collection and their impact on it as it now exists. If you are Elsie, once you have assessed your collection it would be worth your time to write an overall collection development policy or update the current one. Such a document should include general guide-lines about what percentage of your budget goes to buying books to support student study and how much for faculty research; whether you buy paperbacks or hardcover when there is a choice; whether you buy textbooks; and what your policy toward gift books is. It would also be a good idea to put in writing your belief in the Library Bill of Rights and the need to provide information on multiple sides of an issue. You are then ready to consult with the faculty in their various departments and programs and come up with a five-year plan for developing the collection in their areas. From your assessment of the collection you know what areas are strong and which need improvement. You can show your data to the faculty. I have found that they appreciate your efforts to provide objective information about the state of the collection. By having them help determine the acquisitions policy in their areas, they understand better what you are trying to accomplish and have more incentive to recommend good titles. Also, for those few faculty who order inappropriate items, you have a written plan they helped to create. You can ask them how their request fits into the written policy for their area. It helps keep you both focused on what you are trying to accomplish.

Vocational-Technical Materials

A major problem for community college LRCs is the selection of vocational-technical materials. The traditional academic subjects are covered in reviewing journals such as *Choice.* You can get it in card form and send the cards around to faculty. There is no such convenient equivalent journal for vocational-technical materials. On the one hand, you could say that the vocational-technical programs of the campus don't really need the LRC very much. Their students don't come in and do term papers the way the sociology or psychology students do. The vocational faculty often set up their own office libraries with practical reference books the students need to have handy when they are selecting tools or carrying out a process.

On the other hand, the idea that the community college LRC doesn't really have to serve the vocational-technical part of the curriculum is a self-fulfilling prophecy. How inviting a place is the LRC for vocational-technical students and faculty? Vocational students working toward associate of science degrees have to take the first-year English sequence, too. When you do class orientations or offer formal bibliographic instruction classes, do you include examples geared to vocational-technical areas as well as to literature and the social sciences?

As we head into the Nineties vocational-technical programs are under increasing pressure to produce graduates who are not only skilled in a particular trade, but who also are literate and possess interpersonal communications and math skills. By working with the vocational-technical faculty to develop appropriate LRC-related assignments to foster these skills, you help the students have a successful LRC experience. You and your staff are prepared to help them because you know what the assignment is trying to accomplish. Your work with the faculty will help you in deciding how the reference collection can serve the vocational-technical faculty and students.

NonPrint Materials

In some community colleges there is a traditional library and a separate media center, run by separate individuals who are rivals for some of the same budget dollars. In others, whether the physical facilities are housed in the same building or in separate buildings, the administration is under the same person. I prefer the second model if the person in charge is interested in providing information in the most appropriate format and sees the two operations as complementing each other. There are some coordination questions to be asked. How are audiovisual materials accessed in your LRC? Are they included in the same catalog that tells your clientele what books you have? Or must the people you are trying to serve use a printed list or a separate file in a separate location to find out what videos, audiotapes, and motion pictures you have? When you think of collection development, do you think only in terms of books and periodicals? Is there any coordination between purchasing videos and books on the same subject? Do you have a collection development policy that addresses audiovisual materials? Because motion pictures and videos tend to cost more than a book on the same subject, there is often more scrutiny before their purchase. Often audiovisual purchases are based on what faculty intend to show in the classroom and budgets are too limited to buy videos of general interest.

Reference Collection

Many of the issues already discussed in general terms apply to reference as well. Why do you have a reference collection?

We have already addressed the issue of deciding on your clientele. Your reference collection will reflect whom you are trying to serve, your stated mission, whether you are an isolated rural institution or have other larger libraries close by, and your financial and staff resources.

Because most LRCs have limited budgets to spend on expensive reference works, collection development for reference entails making some hard decisions. Rather than make them on a case-by-case basis, it would be better to base them on an underlying philosophy of reference service. It would be worthwhile to involve all who staff the reference desk in deciding what your LRC's reference philosophy is. Is your staff clear on how much and what kind of help students should receive? Should students be treated differently than a member of the general public who asks the same question? (How do you know who is a student and who is not when they ask for help?) How many special privileges do faculty receive?

You will never have the resources of a large research library, but your clientele will expect you to be able to meet their information needs anyway. While the problem in a large research library is knowing the reference collection well enough to find the answer, in a small LRC it is to find the answer when you don't have the appropriate specialized source in your collection. On-line searching, interlibrary loan, and networking with other libraries in the area are some possibilities. Sometimes it's a matter of finding creative ways to cope using what you do have. Someone wants a street map of East Overshoe? A collection of free telephone directories from your local telephone company often provides detailed street maps of small towns in your state that will never have a separate box on the official state highway map. Someone wants the population of a small town that is not listed separately in any source you have except a 15-year-old gazeteer? You could call a library that has access to computerized census data and the staff willing to search it for you. If a ballpark figure would be good enough, you could call the post office in that town and find out how many postal patrons there are. Let your client decide what multiple of that figure might represent a close approximation of the actual population. In fact, the telephone provides access to local government agencies, chambers of commerce, and state agencies for current information that you may not have in printed sources.

How about large expensive reference sets? What is your philosophy regarding reference sets that provide plot summaries of literary classics or literary criticism of important authors? Do you buy pamphlet series that give both pro and con of controversial topics? My personal prejudice is that plot summaries mostly help students who were supposed to read the book and didn't. Something like *Contemporary Literary Criticism (CLC)* or *Contemporary Authors,* on the other hand, provides a good bibliography with each article, giving you and the student you are trying to help other sources to pursue both within and without your building. If you are geographically isolated and need to depend on interlibrary loan to supplement your resources, investing in something like the ongoing *CLC* may be more important than if you are in a major metropolitan area with major research libraries close by. If you can't afford to have books in your collection, having subject bibliographies lets you know what's out there.

As far as what specific reference books your LRC should have, there are a number of standard lists that can help you pick a core collection. Reference books can be expensive, but there are ways to stretch your dollars. How many things need to come every year on standing order? Is there another library in your area that gets some of the same titles you do? Can you cooperate and order some titles every other year, coordinating your purchases with the other library? That way one of you would always have the most recent edition but you would each have to buy it only every two years. You can agree to use telephone/fax to exchange information when only the most recent information is acceptable. Taxpayers supporting both a public library and a community college in the same area might appreciate the wise use of tax dollars. For those reference books that are unique to your LRC that you update often, how about donating the old ones to the public library when your new standing order comes in? Is there something the public library buys that you cannot justify buying new, but could use their newly replaced edition? Perhaps you could work out an exchange of older editions of reference books on a regular basis.

One tricky possibility is to solicit donations of expensive reference works from local businesses. If you could get *Thomas's Register* or *Sweet's Catalog* from a local business when they replaced their copy, your budget could be used for something else. On the other hand, if you depend on donations too much, the administration will never see the real cost of keeping the reference collection current.

Reference collections in community college LRCs these days provide information in more than one format. One of the hardest areas in which to make wise decisions is new technology. What is your philosophy on electronic information sources? What are your resources? How much space can you devote to a reference collection within the building? If you are going to substitute on-line searching with DIALOG or BRS for having the printed index in the building, do you have staff time available for developing the search strategies that are demanded for on-line searching? How will you handle the cost of on-line searching? Will it be self-supporting? Will it be subsidized for everyone? For faculty but not for students? For no one? Will you do it for the general public? If you do it, it would be a good idea to have a liability waiver and an agreement to pay for the printout results, even if they are not exactly what the client thought they would be.

A more recent issue in reference is CD-ROM-based reference sources. There is great pressure to add current technology. Compact disc indexes bring you the advantages of on-line data bases without the telecommunications costs. Yet for the amount of use they may get, the subscription price may be hard to justify. If yours is a small LRC with a small periodical collection, Wilson indexes are a bargain for the information they provide. The cost of *Readers' Guide to Periodical Literature,* for instance, is based on how many of the periodicals to which you subscribe it indexes. I don't see how you can justify the expense of a CD-ROM index based on cost alone. Instead the new technology provides the possibility of more search options than a printed index. There is the convenience of searching once for three or five years' worth of periodical articles. The capacity for Boolean searching makes finding articles far more efficient than manually

searching three separate aspects of a topic in 10 years' worth
of individual printed volumes. You may find, though, that
your clientele will not want to do as much of the searching
themselves as you thought they would. Do you have the staff
available to handle the increased need to consult on search
strategy?

Another dark side of the new technology, besides cost and
staff time, is that students often ignore specialized printed
indexes that may be more relevant to their topic in favor of
the glitzy machine or computer that takes them less time. I
have seen students wait days for the *Magazine Index* machine
to be repaired even though reference librarians had carefully
explained that *Readers' Guide* or another printed index would
provide relevant citations for their topics.

What about videodisc encyclopedias or CD-format encyclopedias or other reference works? An *Encyclopedia Ameri-
cana* in print form can be used by more than one person at a
time. A CD encyclopedia would take a hefty investment in
local area network equipment in order to be accessed by more
than one person at a time. As your clientele visits larger
libraries that have these things, you will be pressured to hop
on the bandwagon, too.

Remember, though, when video equipment first came on
the market? LRCs invested in ¾-inch equipment because it
was industry standard, while Beta and VHS competed for the
home market. How many LRCs use ¾-inch playback equipment now? It is difficult to see into the future and know today
what CD format will become standard in 10 years or what new
technology will replace it. Does this lack of certainty mean
that you should steer clear of CD-ROM products as something only large research libraries with large budgets and
specialized staff should provide? I would suggest that you
need to be as judicious in acquiring this new technology as
you have been in acquiring printed reference works. Invest in
new technology when it allows you to accomplish an important part of your mission better than you can without it.

A major problem is coming up with the money for the new
formats. No doubt you don't have all the printed reference
sources you feel you should have either. Perhaps there is

some way other than your regular reference budget that you can use to finance a demonstration CD product. A friend's organization or college foundation might provide money for something new and exciting. Perhaps you can wrangle a special, one-time budget supplement. Remember, a major expense is the hardware. Once you have the computer monitor with plenty of memory and fast processing speed, CD player, and quiet printer, you can use the same setup for more than one CD product, although not at the same time. If you pick a fairly inexpensive CD product, you and your staff can evaluate the pros and cons before deciding how much of the standing-orders budget, if any, should be converted to CD products over printed indexes.

Conclusion

In the not-too-distant future we will be confronted with the issue of CD products that both index and provide the full text of periodicals. Do we drop periodical subscriptions to adopt the new technology? When reference works are available on personal viewer CDs, will we start checking out reference CDs to faculty and students? The end of the printed book has been predicted several times this century. Microfilm and microfiche were going to replace print after World War II. Then in the audiovisual push of the Sixties, the book was an obsolete way to foster learning. In the Seventies computers were going to replace books. Now books on compact disc are predicted to replace their printed cousins.

Surely the nature of LRCs and reference service will change in response to new technologies. As we try to cope with limited budgets and increased expectations, perhaps we should remember that historically technology is successful when it fulfills a need. Rather than either fear change or embrace it for its own sake, we can be guided by our clearly defined mission. For reference we can strive to provide those resources, in whatever format, that support those services that best allow us to reach our goals. Therefore, look before you leap because one who hesitates is lost.

References

American Libraries, May issue, annual "Outstanding Reference Sources."

Bierbaum, Esther Green. "The Two-Year College LRC: Promise Deferred?" *College & Research Libraries*, Vol. 51, no. 6 (November 1990), pp. 531–538.

Bushing, Mary. *Nonfiction Collection Guidelines for Smaller Libraries: Core Collection Development*. Helena, MT: Montana State Library, 1988.

Cheney, Frances Neel. *Fundamental Reference Sources*. By Frances Neel Cheney and Wiley J. Williams. 2nd ed. Chicago: American Library Association, 1980.

Collection Development Policy of the Oregon State Library, Salem, OR: Oregon State Library, 1989.

Dale, Doris Cruger. "The Learning Resource Center's Role in the Community College System," *College & Research Libraries*, Vol. 49, no. 3 (May 1988), pp. 232–238.

Evans, G. Edward. *Developing Library and Information Center Collections*. Littleton, CO: Libraries Unlimited, 1987.

Guide to Reference Books, Edited by Eugene P. Sheehy. 10th ed. Chicago: American Library Association, 1986.

———. Supplement covering materials from 1985–1990. Edited by Robert Balay. Chicago: American Library Association, 1992.

Guidelines for Collection Development, David L. Perkins, editor. Chicago: American Library Association, 1979.

Haar, John, et. al. "Choosing CD-ROM Products." *College & Research Library News*, Vol. 51, no. 9 (October 1990) pp. 839–841.

Hall, Jack. *The Vocational-Technical Core Collection*. Jack Hall and Victoria Cheponis Lessard. New York: Neal-Schuman Publishers, 1981–1984.

Hisle, W. Lee. "Learning Resource Services in the Community College: On the Road to the Emerald City." *College & Research Libraries*, Vol. 50, no. 6 (November 1989) pp. 613–625.

Katz, William A. *Collection Development: the Selection of Materials for Libraries*. New York: Holt, Rinehart and Winston, 1980.

Library Journal, April 15th issue, annual "Best Reference Books."

Mosley, Madison M., Jr. "Mission Statements for the Community College LRC." *College & Research Library News*, Vol. 49, no. 10 (November 1988) pp. 653–654.

Oberg, Larry R. "Evaluating the Conspectus Approach for Smaller Library Collections." *College & Research Libraries*, Vol. 49, no. 3 (May 1988) pp. 187–196.

Pacific Northwest Collection Assessment Manual. Compiled and edited by Nancy Powell. 3rd ed. Salem, OR: Oregon State Library Foundation, 1990. (Available from Western Library Network, Olympia, WA)

Pirie, James W. *Books for Junior College Libraries: a Selected List of Approximately 19,700 Titles.* Compiled by James W. Pirie. Chicago: American Library Association, 1969.

Recommended Reference Books for Small and Medium-Sized Libraries and Media Centers. Bohdan S. Wynar, editor. Littleton, CO: Libraries Unlimited. (Annual publication)

Reference and Online Services Handbook: Guidelines, Policies, and Procedures for Libraries. Edited by Bill Katz and Anne Clifford. New York: Neal-Schuman Publishers, 1982. 2 Vol.

Schwarzkopf, LeRoy C. *Government Reference Books: a Biennial Guide to U.S. Government Publications.* Compiled by LeRoy C. Schwarzkopf. Littleton, CO: Libraries Unlimited. (biennial publication)

"Standards for Community, Junior and Technical College Learning Resources Programs," *College & Research Libraries News.* Vol. 51, no. 6 (September 1990) pp. 757–767.

Walford, A. J. *Walford's Concise Guide to Reference Materials.* London: The Library Association, 1981.

Walford's Guide to Reference Material. Edited by A. J. Walford. 5th ed. New York: Saur, 1989– . (In progress)

Wortman, William A. *Collection Management: Background and Principles.* Chicago: American Library Association, 1989.

THE PUBLIC SERVICES LIBRARIAN AND COLLECTION DEVELOPMENT

Gloria Terwilliger with Mimi Gronlund and Sylvia Rortvedt

The community college library collection has been characterized as being at the "initial study level" of the continuum of higher education libraries.[1] This characterization is descriptive of the primary mission of the comprehensive community college, which is the support of undergraduate courses and post-secondary occupational and technical education. Although the collections are often relatively small, there is a coherence in their relationship to the curriculum, which is obviously an advantage for students, and for staff, too. The challenge lies in being able to extract enough information from a limited collection to satisfy the general information needs of students and of community patrons.

In most community colleges the librarians play multiple roles rather than specialized ones. The public services librarian provides general reference services, including on-line searching, tours, and bibliographic instruction. He or she may have an occasional shift at the circulation desk and may also be required to perform emergency maintenance on library equipment. As a result of these varied tasks and responsibilities, these librarians develop valuable knowledge about their clientele, their needs, and their habits. The librarians' role in the selection and development of the collection becomes highly personal, as they exercise their intimate awareness of the needs of their community of users.

Further insights into user needs and collection strengths and weaknesses result from the active teaching function of the librarians. Credit courses in library research and course-related bibliographic instruction are developed in consultation with faculty members. Librarians remain abreast of curriculum changes and have firsthand knowledge of specific library research assignments. They have the opportunity to build the collection in areas that support the type of instruction that is being carried out. The peer relationship between faculty and librarians is fostered as they work together to achieve instructional goals and as faculty are further encouraged to provide input into the selection process.

The librarians become familiar with the most popular topics for the freshman research paper. They know the reading level of the various periodicals available at the campus library and can match readers to documents and recommend additional appropriate resources. The librarians know their patrons' habits and of the need for immediate access to source materials. They are aware that most students are rarely deeply committed to a particular topic for a research paper and generally would prefer to change their subject to one for which resources are readily available rather than drive to another library and begin the research process anew.

The awareness of the clients' needs and the familiarity with the college curriculum and mission are the factors that enable the librarians to play a pivotal role in the selection process and to maintain the needed currency in their decision making. The collection-management policy is reviewed regularly. Collection-development objectives are clarified, and procedures are updated on a continuing basis. The policy serves as a planning tool and as a communication device.[2]

Collection Management Policy

This policy is a guide to the planned development of the library collection. It expresses purposes and standards in making the collection effective in serving the needs of the college community, and it provides guidelines for decisions about collection additions or removals.

The library supports the mission and goals of the college by establishing and maintaining a collection of relevant materials, developing services that promote and facilitate library use, assisting users in finding information, instructing students in library research skills including the gathering, evaluating, and utilizing of information, and by offering activities that enhance the intellectual and cultural environment of the campus.

In accordance with the philosophy and objectives of the college and of the American Library Association's Library Bill of Rights and Intellectual Freedom Statement, the library is responsible for 1) making available the widest diversity of views and expressions, including those that are unorthodox or unpopular with the majority; 2) opposing and challenging all attempts to impose censorship on the library; and 3) preserving the constitutional right of freedom of expression.

The library strives to include representative materials related to the needs of cultural or racial minorities, as well as materials reflecting diverse social, religious, political, and moral viewpoints.

All faculty members share with the librarians the responsibility for the selection of materials. Faculty should integrate materials selection with curriculum development and revitalization and should order materials early enough to ensure that students have them when needed. Specialists are urged to use their knowledge for development of the library collections. Recommendations from campus administrative faculty, classified staff, and students are encouraged.

Collection Priorities

It is the policy of the library to select, commensurate with budgetary and space allocations, written, recorded, and other materials that support:

1. The aims and objectives of the college.
2. The curriculum offered at the campus.
3. The teaching needs of faculty.
4. The special needs of the diverse campus population.
5. Professional development reading for faculty and staff.
6. Materials not directly related to campus programs, but of importance for an educated and informed college community.
7. Recreational materials as funds permit.

Criteria for Selection and Removal

Priority is given to the development of a strong working collection, maintained at the highest level of usefulness through careful selection and removal decisions about all kinds of materials. The collection is developed to supplement required classroom materials. It will not include textbooks for courses, consumable publications such as workbooks, or items for in-class use only. Materials purchased through library funds become part of the college inventory of library materials. Teaching faculty recommendations are sought. Circulation statistics and other users records are compiled and consulted to measure the extent to which books, periodicals, and other library materials are being used.

1. **Criteria for Selection**
   a. The materials contribute to the development and maintenance of subject collections, which support the campus curriculum;
   b. A projected demand exists and the collection cannot currently satisfy the demand;
   c. The information is current and authoritative;
   d. The style, treatment, and level of difficulty are in accordance with the mission of the library;
   e. The cost is justified in terms of anticipated use.
2. **Criteria for Removal**
   a. One or more of the above selection criteria fails to be satisfied;
   b. The material is damaged or worn beyond repair. For further clarification of policy, refer to the *Criteria for Weeding the Collection.*

The library director, in consultation with the professional staff, annually allocates the materials budget among books, periodicals, media, and standing orders and reference materials. Consensus among the professional librarians is sought in the purchase of expensive materials and on subscriptions to or cancellations of periodicals and reference book standing orders.

The budget for nonprint media is apportioned among the various types of nonprint items by the library media specialist, with the approval of the director. Formal allocations by subject or budgetary units are avoided, but attention is given to all teaching fields, with documentation of this effort available to the faculty.

Policy by Formats

A. Books

1. *Paperback or Hardbound Editions*
   Hardbound editions are purchased when the material is considered to have long-term value and is expected to receive heavy use. If either of these conditions is not satisfied, a paperback version is purchased, if available. When duplicate copies of a title are required, paperback editions are the preferred format.

2. *Replacement*
   Lost materials are replaced if they meet current criteria for selection and if they are available through the usual book ordering sources.

3. *Foreign Language Materials*
   Foreign language materials that support the college's curricular objectives and that aid in foreign language study are purchased. Dictionaries and a few works of grammar and literature are purchased for many languages.

B. Periodicals

1. *Ongoing Orders*
   Periodical titles are reviewed annually for renewal. Special attention is given to titles that have increased substantially in price since the last subscription period or whose continued cost is unwarranted on the basis of use. Any significant changes in the collection are made in consultation with the faculty.

2. *New Subscriptions*

Budgetary restrictions due to the long-term maintenance costs limit the acquisition of new serial titles.
The library assistant for periodicals annually esti-
mates the amount of money necessary to maintain
existing subscriptions and suggests a figure for new
materials to the director. New subscriptions are
evaluated according to the collection priorities in
Section IV.B.1. of this policy. The following criteria
also apply:
1. Usefulness of subject in relation to campus
    programs;
2. Similar materials already received;
3. Cost of subscriptions in relation to use;
4. Inclusion in periodical indexes;
5. Availability in other area libraries.

3. *Backfiles of Periodicals*
    The purchase of microforms is preferable to paper
    backfiles for the printed volumes of periodicals,
    except for titles or for which usage depends on the
    visual presentation of the topic, (such as Art). In the
    latter instance, paper backfiles are maintained.

C. Media

The library media specialist selects and responds to
requests for nonprint materials. Cost, budget, and
potential use govern acquisitions decisions. Materials
are acquired through purchase, following preview by
faculty, and also through original production. The
Criteria for Selection and Removal of Materials applies to
nonprint items.

D. Pamphlets

An effective and up-to-date pamphlet collection is
maintained as a strong resource. Systematic acquisition of new materials includes subscriptions to pamphlet services and requests for free materials. By
actively soliciting materials from various interest
groups and associations, the library makes timely

information available on a wide range of views and
expressions.

E. Reference Collection

The reference collection consists of materials used
frequently to answer questions, provide bibliographic
access to other materials, and to assist in research
projects. These materials are noncirculating and provide quick access to information in all fields of
knowledge. Included in the collection are periodical
indexes, subject and general bibliographies, and other
standard reference works, both print and on-line.
Reference standing orders are reviewed annually.

Gifts

Gifts are accepted only when they add strength to the
collection and when the donor places no significant limitations on housing, handling, or disposition of duplicate,
damaged, or unwanted items. Storage space and staff time
requirements are considered in accepting gift materials. A
written acknowledgement of the gift is provided for the
donor for tax purposes, but any monetary appraisal is the
responsibility of the donor.

Patron Involvement

The involvement of library patrons has often been overlooked because of the logistics and communication problems
involved in identifying patrons who could provide useful
information. The library has developed an effective dialogue
with its patrons through its highly popular *Suggestion Book.*
For over 15 years students have been expressing their
frustrations, grievances, ideas, and opinions on a wide range
of subjects in the book. Its format hasn't changed since the
first questions were written and answered. A standard three-
ring binder filled with unlined paper[3] is displayed on a stand
near the circulation desk. The use of unlined paper is

apparently less restrictive than lined paper. Students have made creative use of the space, including drawings and running conversations with one another. Questions, comments, criticisms, and occasional profundities are written on the right-hand page. Responses are prepared by the librarians on Mondays and Thursdays and are typed in the corresponding space on the left-hand page.

The following questions, comments, and responses reflect only a fraction of the 2,000-plus questions and answers that have been recorded over the years. The variety of subjects probed by students affords an opportunity to explain library and college policies, to describe procedures, and, in general, to provide in-depth explanations to a broad audience. The *Suggestion Book* has a following among the student body and is read by counselors, by some of the faculty, and regularly by the dean of students. Original spelling and syntax have been retained.

> **Student:** I am very happy to see you have a subscripson [sic] to "Der Spiegel" it's a good magazine but dificult to read eaven for most native germans suggest a nother magazine be added or paper to make easer reading. "Der Stein" "Die Rundshow" (paper)
> **Librarian:** *Der Spiegel* was recommended by one of our German instructors. Although *Der Stein* and *Die Rundshow* are easier and more entertaining, our instructor feels that they are less useful in an academic library. We also take a German newspaper, the *Washington Journal.*

> **Student:** What happened to the current issues of the magazine *Cycle Guide?*
> **Librarian:** *Cycle Guide* is no longer being published. The last issue received in the library was August of 1987. We still subscribe to *Cycle,* which is quite similar in its coverage.

> **Student:** I want to ask you why in this library don't have any magazines about Hotel Mangment. Fore example [sic] Lodging hospitality etc . . .
> **Librarian:** Because NOVA libraries, like all libraries, are limited by space and money, we have to share our resources and rely upon each other for specialized subject matter. Consequently, each campus library collection reflects the instructional programs at that campus. Since the Annandale Campus offers the Hotel/Restaurant Management Program, magazines on hotel management are available at that library.

> **Student:** It would be *wonderful* if your only copy of *USA Today* could be kept at the reserve desk as is one copy of the *Post.* When I come to class in the evening it is always gone. It's nice to read between classes and on

break. Thank you. (I'd buy my own, but the machine out front is always empty by the time I get here.)

Librarian: We're happy when we can grant the wishes of *Suggestion Book* writers. The current issue of *U.S.A. Today* will be kept at the Reserve Desk from now on. Thanks for a helpful suggestion!

Student: Why do we call the place were we park our cars a driveway whereas we call the place where we drive a parkway?

Response: We think you would enjoy the book *Jumbo Shrimp and Other Almost Perfect Oxymorons: Contradictory Expressions That Make Absolute Sense* by Warren S. Blumenfeld. We have just ordered a replacement copy for ourselves, but it is also available at the nearby public library.

Student: I think "The Four Seasons" by Vivaldi is a must for a CD collection.

Librarian: We agree. It was included in a recent order of classical CDs and we hope to have it in the next month or so.

Student: Why don't you subscribe to an African Magazine? We Africans at NOVA feel like *abandoned*. You don't care about our small community. My advise would be to subscribe to *Jeune Afrique* for French speaking Africans, and "Africa" for English speaking Africans. Thank you!

Librarian: Please don't feel abandoned! NOVA cares about all its students and the library tries hard to serve every group within the college community. Currently we are taking one African periodical, *Africa News*, a weekly news magazine that was recommended by one of our faculty members. We did subscribe to *Africa, Thought and Practice*, which temporarily ceased publication a couple of years ago and has never started up again. Although we are not able to add two titles to our collection, we will order a subscription to *Africa* as soon as the new fiscal year begins. We will probably not receive the first issue until September. Thanks for bringing this need to our attention.

The comments and questions occasionally range from the whimsical to the absurd, and tax the librarians' ingenuity in responding, i.e., **Student:** If this book were to end, what would you like the last question to be? **Librarian:** Where shall I leave the million dollars?

> **Student:** All beliefs have sacred sites, shrines, and places of pilgrimage. Believers visit them. To what site do atheists go?
> **Librarian:** Could it be that they're out of sites? We suggest that you browse through the pages of the *Encyclopedia of Unbelief* for a possible answer to this tantalizing question. This two-volume publication may be found in the reference collection—REF/BL 2705.E53 1985.

> **Student:** Has the collection ever been reviewed for coverage of the most important authors and at least minimal coverage of all important topics?

A visiting librarian, who spent considerable time leafing through the book, may have written this question. In keeping with our practice of responding to all questions, the answer provided an opportunity to summarize the collection-development policy for the benefit of students and other readers of the book.

> **Librarian:** Collection evaluation is an ongoing process and a major responsibility of the reference librarians. While we try to have at least minimal coverage of all subject areas, those that support the courses offered at this campus are our top priority. Because of the information explosion, "networking" is a necessity for all libraries. We depend not only upon the collections of the other four campus libraries, but upon those at the public and university libraries in this area.

Evaluation and Weeding

Maintaining the vitality of a relatively small collection is essential. The size of many community college library collec-

<u>I am REAL short!   I can't reach books on the upper shelves so</u>
<u>why not lower them?</u>

Sorry.   There is no place else to put the materials on the
top shelves.   However, scattered around the library are a number
of "kick stools" which folks use to reach the top shelves. The
stools can be moved around on their castors, but will lock in
place when you step on them, so are safe to use in retrieving
material from the top shelves.   If all else fails, ask a
librarian for help.

tions is limited by space considerations. Capital projects that include new library or LRC buildings are infrequent, and more often than not, the space available has a major impact on the kind of criteria used in determining what should remain in the collection and what should be withdrawn.

Weeding is inextricably entwined with evaluation, for each item removed from circulation has to be evaluated for its timeliness, significance, and relevance. The librarians are continually evaluating the collection. When they take students to the shelves to help them locate materials, they make mental notes of the book-stock condition in that particular area, keeping a close watch on the status of resources that support the list of Term Paper Topics, which is also under constant review to provide currency and relevance. Each member of the professional staff participates in shelf reading, with assignments rotated periodically in order to broaden familiarity with the collection. Weeding is automatically related to the shelf-reading process.

The librarians at the Alexandria campus of Northern Virginia Community College have developed a system for weeding over a period of years, which involves the entire professional staff. Consultations with faculty members are used to supplement the collective judgment of the staff when necessary.

The process begins with an assessment of an item and its physical removal of an item from the shelves. The book—or cassette, videotape, recording, or other form of library material—is placed on an appropriately labeled book truck awaiting the review process. Each item marked for withdrawal is reviewed by librarians, by the library supervisor, and finally by the LRC director. The Withdrawal Form is invaluable to the process, as it includes the discriminating judgments of the staff member who initially removed the material.

Occasionally materials earmarked for withdrawal that have an "old" imprint date but that contain significant historical information are returned to circulation. Sometimes a superceded continuation held in the reference collection will be recommended for inclusion in the circulation collection rather than discarded. In most cases, however, the critical thinking required for initial removal of an item is usually upheld through the review process.

The criteria for weeding the collection developed by the librarians at the Alexandria campus of Northern Virginia Community College are reproduced below.

The selection policy reflects a general purpose of maintaining a collection that reflects currency, readability, and vitality. The college selection policy specifies support of:

1. The aims and objectives of the college;
2. Courses offered in the campus curriculum;
3. Teaching methods of the faculty;
4. Special needs of the students, including leisure reading and current-event materials;
5. Professional development reading for faculty and staff.

The process of selecting out materials is essential to the effectiveness of the collection. Weeding is complex, involving a combination of predetermined criteria, general knowledge, and subjective judgment. The use factor is important in determining whether or not material should remain, although noncirculation is not necessarily conclusive, especially in the sphere of the classics. Use factors are available from the annual circulation printouts and from the checkout dates stamped on book pockets.

These criteria are to be used as guidelines for initial culling. Materials recommended for discard are reviewed by the professional staff in the library and by the LRC director, and a collective judgment is reached. Faculty are consulted as necessary.

Appearance: Weed Specific Criteria
1. Books of antiquated appearance, which might discourage use.
2. Badly bound volumes with soft pulpy paper and/or shoddy binding.
3. Badly printed works, including those with small print, dull or faded print, cramped margins, poor illustrations, paper that is translucent so that the print shows through.

```
┌─────────────────────────────────────────────┐
│                                             │
│            WITHDRAWAL  FORM                 │
│                                             │
│                                             │
│   WITHDRAW___ MAKE CIRC.___ BOOKSALE___     │
│                                             │
│         Reason for Withdrawing:             │
│                                             │
│   DATED MATERIAL              _____ │
│                                             │
│   DOESN'T MEET CURRENT                      │
│   SELECTION CRITERIA          _____ │
│                                             │
│   POOR PHYSICAL CONDITION  _____  │
│                                             │
│   UNNEEDED DUPLICATE          _____ │
│                                             │
│   WE HAVE NEWER EDITION      _____ │
│                                             │
│   RARELY/NEVER CIRCULATED _____   │
│                                             │
│   OTHER_____│
│                                             │
│   _____ │
│                                             │
│   INITIALS_____  DATE_____  │
│                                             │
└─────────────────────────────────────────────┘
```

Figure 1. Withdrawal Form.

4. Worn out volumes whose pages are dirty, brittle, or yellow, with missing pages, frayed bindings, broken backs, or dingy or dirty covers.

Superfluous Materials: Weed
1. Unneeded duplicate titles.
2. Previous or older editions.
3. Books that would not meet current selection criteria.

Content: Weed
1. When information is dated.
2. When a book is poorly written.
3. When information is incorrect.
4. When improved editions exist.
5. Earlier titles in repetitious fiction series.

Specific Classes of Works with Specific Age for Weeding: Consider for Weeding

Seminal works in a discipline should be retained, e.g., Whyte's *The Organization Man,* c. 1957, or B. F. Skinner's *Walden Two,* c. 1962.

Consider for Weeding
1. All ordinary textbooks after 10 years.
2. Technologies and medicine (especially health care) between five and 10 years old.
3. Travel books after ten years, except classics.
4. Economics, business, and science when the books are more than 10 years old.
5. Fiction best-sellers of ephemeral value after 10 years.
6. Social science, topical material, after 10 or 15 years.
7. Encyclopedias upon purchase of new editions (preferably every five years) except for editions of recognized scholarly merit.
8. Almanacs, yearbooks and manuals—get the latest editions and keep older editions at least five, preferably 10 years, based on individual merit.
9. Dictionaries—rarely.
10. Biographical sources—rarely.
11. Directories—generally retain only current edition.
12. Inexpensive geographic sources—five to 10 years or

when outdated. Expensive ones, or those of historical value, rarely if ever.

Weeding Criteria for Periodical and Serials: Consider Weeding

1. Periodicals not indexed.
2. Serials that have ceased publication and that have no cumulative index.
3. Incomplete sets.
4. Early volumes of serials, especially longer runs of 50 or 60 volumes.
5. Specialized periodicals for courses/programs no longer offered.
6. Unused or inappropriate periodicals.

Conclusion

Collection development and management are evaluative processes, with implications for planning, goal definition, and goal setting, policy development, and decision-making in general. Elizabeth Futas has made these points in her article "The Role of Public Services" (1985). She speaks about the public services librarians who have developed "unique back-grounds from dealing with both the community of users and the collection."

She further describes the desired qualifications that make public services librarians successful at their jobs and gives them the information that is essential to conducting collection evaluations. "Only public services librarians who are sensitive to users' interests and who see the larger picture of library goals and objectives are capable of extracting qualitative evaluations of the collections from their experiences with the people they serve . . . who make the most of their positions and add the knowledge that libraries so desparately need in order to evaluate their collections, plan for the long-term, and contribute to decision-making as a whole."[3]

The community college librarian has the opportunity, the setting, and the scale to match the collection with the users. The process is slow and fluctuates with funding aberrations, but the relationships exist for the imaginative librarian who can grasp them and mold them into living, effecting working systems.

References

[1]*Guidelines for Collection Development,* American Library Association. Collection Development Committee. (Chicago: American Library Association, 1979,) p.2.

[2]*Guidelines for Collection Development,* op. cit. p. 4.

[3]Elizabeth Futas, "The Role of Public Services in Collection Evaluation," in *Library Trends,* Vol. 22 (3) (Winter 1985), pp. 397–416.

EVALUATING THE PERIODICALS COLLECTION

W. Jeanne Gardner

Periodicals are the backbone of the library collection, providing access to current information. Maintaining an up-to-date journal collection that meets users' needs is a time-consuming challenge every librarian faces if this portion of the collection is to remain a vital, utilized entity. One pores over the selection tools to determine that the collection at least holds the major titles in each area, and then ponders the pros and cons of expense, access (index coverage), and promotion when a faculty member, administrator, or student requests a new title.

Between subscription costs, mailing costs, and international money exchange rates a sizable portion of the library's budget is allocated to the periodicals or journal area. Deborah Selsky reports in "Library Market Outlook" that libraries spent 46 percent of their budget on periodicals in 1989.[1] When 20, 35, or even 46 percent of the budget goes to one line item, the librarian should begin to think about building a justification for this expense that will satisfy the most stringent comptroller, accountant, or administrator who scrutinizes the campus budget looking for "fat".

It has been my experience that administrators react more positively to hard facts, or data, than to the librarian's feeling that something is actively utilized. Also, being more comfortable making a decision or presenting an argument based on facts rather than intuition has led me to utilize existing record keeping to collect data and build a record of use for the periodical collection.

Building the Statistical Base

The college learning resources center (LRC) has in place a mechanism that enables us to determine usage of periodicals. Although we haven't put in place a monitoring device for current display periodical issue usage, the system that measures retrospective periodical title usage provides a good picture of the activity of the collection. This system extends to microfilm back files of periodicals as well as loose and bound titles.

The LRC operates from the objective of providing "access to recorded knowledge and information while introducing users to basic search strategies that may be applied to a class, a job, or ongoing personal development." When LRC staff are invited to give a LRC introduction, faculty are asked to identify the number of students in the class and what library assignment or assignments the students will be given. This enables LRC staff to provide a LRC introduction that is tailored to the assignment.

The students receive a two-pronged introduction. They first view two Wilson VHS tapes[2,3] in the classroom. They are then escorted to the LRC for a physical tour. During the tour the public service aspects of the LRC are explained and/or pointed out: circulation desk, checkout length for books and audiovisual materials, location of periodicals, reference materials, indexes, and the circulating collection, card catalog and on-line catalog, interlibrary loan functions and limitations, and LRC hours. A Tip Sheet outlining the Library of Congress classification system and providing a diagram of the layout of the LRC is handed out, as well as one discussing how to use *The Readers' Guide to Periodical Literature*. The students are then asked to spend the remainder of the class period using the indexes and the on-line catalog to access The Colorado Alliance for Research Libraries Systems, Inc., on-line periodical index, *Uncover*. This enables the library staff to give students individualized assistance, respond to questions, and provide guidance in selecting a topic appropriate to the assignment.

During each tour students are introduced to the journal

request slips, which are located on each index table. The dual purpose of filling out journal request slips is explained. As well as providing statistics (we tell the students utilization is an important criterion when budget cuts have to be imposed), the slip enables staff to locate the desired issue, bound volume, or microfilm for the patron. Due to space limitations, periodicals and microfilm are kept in closed shelving, accessed only by LRC personnel. Once users understand the reasons behind filling out the slips, opposition disappears.

Individuals who come to the LRC to use the indexes and periodical collection are also informed of the functions of the periodical request slips as they receive a mini-introduction to the LRC.

Each user is asked to provide the following information for each article being requested: periodical title, volume number, page number, and date; user identification (student, faculty, other), and the day's date. A return slot is checked or initialed by LRC staff to indicate that the magazine or microfilm was returned to the circulation desk. This last item is a remnant of those days not too long ago when we did not have an automated circulation system. Periodicals will be added to the serials automated data base in 1991, and this procedure will be reviewed and revised as needed.

After the users turn the slips in to the staff, they are collected at the circulation desk and tallied at the end of each month. The monthly statistics are cumulated into semester and annual statistics as well. Although these statistics have been maintained for a number of years, it was not until 1988–1989 that formal evaluation and reporting of these figures in a periodical usage report was begun.

When a faculty member or administrator joins the college, he or she is alerted to the LRC routing service. With the exception of popular titles (*Time, Newsweek, People Magazine, Life,* and so on), faculty members and administrators may identify periodical titles they wish to view on a regular basis. The faculty member's or administrator's name is placed on the routing slips for the titles selected, and issues of the periodical are routinely sent to these people. This practice accounts for most of the administrative utilization of periodicals and a large portion of the faculty utilization.

Reporting

The periodical usage report includes the title of each periodical in the collection, its status, cost, and if indexed in a LRC index, what index. The status may be current, complimentary, discontinued (the LRC subscription has been canceled), no longer published (the publisher stopped publishing the title), a gift, or a suspended title (publisher is not currently publishing issues but has not officially ceased publication of the title).

A comparison of the periodicals collection for the two-year period 1988–1989 and 1989–1990 is shown in Table 1.

A majority of the titles in the periodical collection support curricular, teaching, and administrative functions. A reliance

TABLE 1
PERIODICAL COLLECTION CATEGORIES

	1988/89	1989/90
subscriptions	156	169
complimentary titles	20	20
gift titles	44	41
discontinued titles	27[1]	31
no longer published titles	n/a	8
suspended titles	0	1
unknown	7	0
TOTAL	254	270

[1]In 1988/89 the discontinued and no longer published titles were reported together.

on user statistics alone to determine whether or not to keep the collection holdings that support the curriculum would place the burden totally on the departments. Instead, a model that takes into consideration utilization and promotion of the periodical collection is applied to determine the disposition of a periodical title that shows little or no utilization over a period of time.

During LRC tours students are shown how to use the commercial indexes to retrieve journal information. The LRC also produces a periodicals list at the beginning of each semester to assist students in using the periodicals collection. This is an alphabetical list of the journal titles available in the LRC, the exact holdings, and if indexed, in which LRC indexes. If the periodical titles are not indexed but the table of contents for each issue of the title is maintained in a three-ring binder, this is noted in the index column of the periodicals list. When available, a Tip Sheet is provided to guide students through the LRC materials related to that curricular or subject area.

Tip Sheets have been developed for several, but not all programs. The Tip Sheet is a one- to two-sided handout that identifies the periodicals relevant to a program, the LRC indexes that are most appropriate to use to locate these periodical materials, and other LRC resources related to the program.

Students may take these free Tip Sheets and use them for future reference. A Tip Sheet identifying periodical titles of general interest is duplicated and placed at the circulation desk at the beginning of each semester to encourage students to begin using and become comfortable with the periodicals collection.

Should a title be identified at risk due to low use statistics, the library director discusses the title with the department chairperson, and/or faculty members. Together a decision is made regarding the title. Such points as if the title is relevant to the curriculum, if the title is being underutilized because it needs promoting, or if it is difficult to use because it is not indexed are considered.

Immediate action to discontinue a title is not necessarily

taken. Some low utilization titles are important collection holdings. Faculty may wish to reevaluate their lectures and library assignments rather than immediately "ax" a title with a poor utilization record, or LRC staff may develop a plan to promote the title with a reevaluation at the end of the semester or academic term.

After the 1988–1989 journal usage statistics were evaluated on a title-by-title basis, titles were identified that were not indexed but that the faculty felt were important resources. The tables of contents of these periodicals were photocopied, placed in three-ring binders, and put on the index tables.

Periodical Use

When the first study of periodical activity was done in 1989, a thesis of the study was that periodical usage would be higher for those periodical titles that were indexed. For the most part this was found to be true. A comparison of 1988–1989 and 1989–1990 use by indexed and nonindexed titles is shown in Table 2.

The LRC offers users access to 184 current periodical titles. These include subscriptions, gifts, and complimentary titles. Of these titles, 113 are indexed, and 71 are not indexed. These 184 titles were utilized by students 816 times. The 113 indexed titles were utilized by students 734 times.

The 1989–1990 use statistics suggest that the table-of-contents approach to nonindexed periodical titles is effective. The 71 nonindexed titles were utilized 82 times, an increase of 67 times, or 447 percent, over the previous year.

Faculty used the collection to a lesser degree than did students, using selected titles 70 times for a 67 percent utilization increase over the previous year. Five periodical titles were circulated to faculty offices, reaching 46 faculty members.

Routing accounts for a large portion of the administrative circulation. Fourteen titles were circulated to 365 administrators, while nine nonrouted LRC titles were utilized by 10 administrators.

TABLE 2
TWO-YEAR COMPARISON OF FACULTY AND
STUDENT UTILIZATION OF INDEXED AND NON-
INDEXED PERIODICALS

	1988/89	1989/90
Indexed titles		
Students	591	734
Faculty	28	40
Non-indexed titles		
Students	15	82
Faculty	18	30
TOTAL	254	270

Eighty-four periodicals in the collection are not indexed. This figure includes 51 subscriptions. Fifteen titles were used by students 82 times. Ten titles were used by faculty 30 times. Six additional titles were routed to faculty 164 times. Thirteen titles were circulated to administrators and support staff 1,878 times.

Whisler indicates "that 20 percent of a collection accounts for 80 percent of its use."[4] An analysis of the 270 titles in the periodicals collection shows that students and faculty utilized 117 of the 270 titles. Put another way, 43 percent of the collection accounted for 100 percent of the use. Using Whisler's formula, 34 percent of the collection accounted for 80 percent of its use.

Within the indexed versus not indexed segments of the collection, 88 of the 184 indexed titles, or 48 percent of the indexed titles, accounted for 100 percent of the usage, and 29 of the 85 nonindexed titles, or 34 percent, accounted for all nonindexed activity.

Conclusion

It is no longer possible to hope that the library or any of its collections will stand on their own merit. An ever more expensive item, the periodicals collection continues to justify itself because of its timely access to current and scholarly articles on topics that may never be published in book format. Yet the time is past when a few words can be used to justify a major portion of the learning materials budget. Instead, the librarian would do well to know who uses the collection, what they are using, and to keep this information readily available so that when the annual budget-planning sessions occur, the librarian is ready and fully prepared to document the importance of the periodicals collection.

References

[1]Deborah Selsky, "Library Market Outlook," *Library Journal,* (August 1990), p. 32.

[2]*How to use the Readers' Guide,* (New York: The Wilson Video Resource Collection, 1987), VHS.

[3]*How to use the Library,* (New York: The Wilson Video Resource Collection, 1989), VHS.

[4]John A. Whisler, "Periodicals Circulation Statistics at a Mid-Sized Academic Library: Implications for Collection Management," *Resource Sharing & Information Networks,* 5, No. 1/2 (1989), p. 361.

NOTES ON CONTRIBUTORS

Dr. Alira is Assistant Director for Instruction and Research Services Division, University of Colorado at Denver, 6801 E. Eagle Place, Highlands Ranch, Colorado 80126.

Dr. Susan Anderson is Director of Libraries, St. Petersburg Junior College, P.O. Box 13489, St. Petersburg, Florida 33733; while **Dr. Susanne E. Fischer,** at the same college, is Director of Institutional Research, Institutional Program Planning.

Jennie S. Boyarski is Director of Library Services at Paducah Community College, P.O. Box 7380, 255 Charlotte Anne Drive, Paducah, Kentucky 42002-7380.

Al Carlson is Director of the Learning Resource Center at Patrick Henry Community College, P.O. Box 5311, Martinsville, Virginia 24115-5311.

L. Gene Elliott is Director of Library Services at Greenville Technical College, P.O. Box 5539, Greenville, South Carolina 29606.

Karen Fischer is at the Central Oregon Community College Library, 2600 N.W. College Way, Bend, Oregon 97701.

W. Jeanne Gardner is Director, Learning Resources Center at Pueblo Community College, 900 West Orman Avenue, Pueblo, Colorado 81004.

Diane Grund is Associate Dean/Learning Resources, Manager/Business-Oriented Search Service (BOSS), at Moraine Valley Community College, 10900 S. 88th Avenue, Palos Hills, Illinois 60465.

V. Sue Hatfield is Director for Library Services, DeKalb College, 555 North Indian Creek Drive, Clarkston, Georgia 30021.

Dr. Mark Y. Herring is Dean and Director of the Library Services, Mabee Learning Center, Oklahoma Baptist University, P.O. Box 61310, Shawnee, Oklahoma 74801.

Kate Donnelly Hickey is Director of the College Library at Pennsylvania College of Technology, One College Avenue, Williamsport, Pennsylvania 17701.

Tisa M. Houck is Library Assistant at Chattanooga State Technical Community College, 4501 Amnicola Hwy., Chattanooga, Tennessee 37406.

Wanda K. Johnston is formerly Director of Library Services at St. Louis Community College at Florissant Valley and is currently Director of Learning Resources, Broome Community College, Box 1017, Binghamton, New York 13902. While **Joan S. Clarke,** formerly a reference librarian at St. Louis Community College at Florissant Valley, is Director of Instructional Resources at St. Charles County Community College, 4601 Mid Rivers Mall Drive, St. Peters, Missouri 63376.

Marilyn Searson Lary is the Director of Library Resource Center at Dalton College, 213 N. College Drive, Dalton, Georgia 30720.

Douglas K. Lehman is Director, Library Technical Services at Miami-Dade Community College, 11380 NW 27th Avenue, Miami, Florida 33167.

Mary Adams Loomba is Associate Professor at Library and Learning Resource Center, Westchester Community College, 75 Grassland Roads, Valhalla, New York 10595.

Dale Luchsinger is Director Emeritus of Library and Media Services, Athens Area Technical Institute, U.S. Highway 29, North Athens, Georgia 30610.

Pamela A. Price is Director of Library Services at Mercer County Community College, 1200 Old Trenton Road, Trenton, New Jersey 08690.

Donald Ray is Head of Public Services/Collection Development at Mercy College Library, 555 Broadway, Dobbs Ferry, New York 10522.

Dr. Derrie B. Roark is Associate Vice President of Learning Resources Services at Hillsborough Community College, P.O. Box 5096, Tampa, Florida 33675-5096.

Stanley N. Ruckman is Library Director at New Mexico State University at Alamogordo, 2400 North Scenic Drive, Alamogordo, New Mexico 88311.

Richard N. Shaw is Director, Learning Resources Center at Technical College of the Lowcountry, 100 South Ribaut Road, P.O. Box 1288, Beaufort, South Carolina 29901-1288.

Gloria Terwilliger is Director Emeritus of Learning Resources, Alexandria Campus, Northern Virginia Community College, 3001 North Beauregard St., Alexandria, Virginia 22311. She wishes to acknowledge the assistance of **Mimi Gronlund,** Head Librarian, and **Sylvia Rortvedt,** Instructional Services Librarian at Northern Virginia Community College.

Patricia Twilde is Reference Librarian at Northern Virginia Community College, Annandale Campus Library, 8333 Little River Turnpike, Annandale, Virginia 22003.

ABOUT THE EDITOR

BILL KATZ (Ph.D., Chicago), is Professor, School of Information Science and Policy, at the State University of New York in Albany. He is the author of the standard text on reference services, *Introduction to Reference Services,* now in its sixth edition. Currently he edits *The Reference Librarian* and *The Acquisitions Librarian* and is a former editor of *RQ* and the *Journal of Education for Librarianship.* For Scarecrow Press, he has edited *Reference and Information Services: A Reader for Today* (1982); *Reference and Information Services: A New Reader* (1986), a *Reference and Information Services: A Reader for the Nineties* (1991); and from 1971 to 1988, the annual *Library Lit.—the Best of . . .* covering the years 1970 to 1987.